Managerial Paper P4

ORGANISATIONAL MANAGEMENT AND INFORMATION SYSTEMS

For exams in 2007

Practice & Revision Kit

In this January 2007 new edition

- We discuss the **best strategies** for revising and taking your CIMA exams

- We show you how to be well prepared for the **2007 exams**

- We give you **lots of great guidance** on tackling questions

- We include **genuine student answers** with BPP commentary

- We show you how you can **build your own exams**

- We provide you with **three** mock exams including the **November 2006 exam**

BPP's **i-Pass** product also supports this paper.

BPP
LEARNING MEDIA

First edition January 2005 (revised June 2005)
Third edition January 2007

ISBN 9780 7517 4194 0 (previous ISBN 0 7517 2520 X)

British Library Cataloguing-in-Publication Data
A catalogue record for this book is available from the
British Library

Published by

BPP Learning Media Ltd
BPP House, Aldine Place
London W12 8AA

www.bpp.com/learningmedia

Printed in Great Britain by
W M Print
45-47 Frederick Street
Walsall, West Midlands
WS2 9NE

Your learning materials, published by BPP Learning
Media Ltd, are printed on paper sourced from
sustainable, managed forests.

We are grateful to the Chartered Institute of Management
Accountants and the Association of Chartered Certified
Accountants for permission to reproduce past
examination questions and some answers. The answers
to past examination questions have been prepared by
BPP Learning Media Ltd, unless where otherwise stated.

BPP)))
LEARNING MEDIA

Contents

Question index

The headings in this checklist/index indicate the main topics of questions, but questions often cover several different topics.

Important

The exam format for paper P4 will change from the May 2007 sitting onwards. Section A will be worth a total of 40 marks, and Section C questions will be worth 30 marks each. Further guidance is given on page 26.

Because of this change we have included the original version of questions set in the CIMA exams for 2005 and May 2006, together with amended versions that reflect the change in mark allocation from May 2007. You have the option of attempting either version of each question.

	Marks	Time allocation Mins	Page number Question	Answer

Part C: Managing human capital

	Marks	Time allocation Mins	Question	Answer
19 Multiple choice questions: Managing human capital 1	20	36	58	126
20 Multiple choice questions: Managing human capital 2	20	36	60	126
21 Multiple choice questions: Managing human capital 3	20	36	61	127
22 Multiple choice questions: Managing human capital 4	20	36	63	127
23 Objective test questions: Managing human capital 1	20	36	65	128
24 Objective test questions: Managing human capital 2	20	36	65	128
25 Maslow	30	54	66	129
26 HR division and strategy (11/05 – original)	20	36	66	131
27 HR division and strategy (11/05 – amended)	30	54	67	133
28 Question with answer plan: Human resource plan and activities (Pilot paper – original)	20	36	68	135
29 Question with answer plan: Human resource plan and activities (Pilot paper – amended)	30	54	68	137
30 HR plan and workforce flexibility (5/05 – original)	20	36	69	140
31 HR plan and workforce flexibility (5/05 – amended)	30	54	70	142
32 Motivation and reward (5/06 – original)	20	36	71	144
33 Motivation and reward (5/06 – amended)	30	54	72	146

Part D: Marketing

	Marks	Time allocation Mins	Question	Answer
34 Multiple choice questions: Marketing 1	20	36	73	148
35 Multiple choice questions: Marketing 2	20	36	74	149
36 Multiple choice questions: Marketing 3	20	36	76	149
37 Objective test questions: Marketing 1	20	36	78	150
38 Objective test questions: Marketing 2	20	36	78	150
39 Marketing action plan (11/05 – original)	20	36	79	151
40 Marketing action plan (11/05 – amended)	30	54	80	153
41 Question with analysis: Consumer buying decision making process	30	54	81	155
42 Marketing and information technology	30	54	83	158
43 Environmental change and marketing (5/06 – original)	20	36	83	160
44 Environmental change and marketing (5/06 – amended)	30	54	84	161

Part E: Managing change

	Marks	Time allocation Mins	Question	Answer
45 Multiple choice questions: Managing change 1	20	36	85	163
46 Multiple choice questions: Managing change 2	20	36	86	164
47 Objective test questions: Managing change	20	36	88	164
48 Question with analysis: Introducing change	30	54	89	165
49 Question with helping hand: Implementing change: types of change (Pilot Paper – original)	20	36	91	167
50 Question with helping hand: Implementing change: types of change (Pilot Paper – amended)	30	54	92	169
51 Job reductions: resistance to change (5/05 – original)	20	36	93	171
52 Job reductions: resistance to change (5/05 – amended)	30	54	93	173

	Marks	Time allocation Mins	Page number Question	Answer
Part F: Section B 30 mark questions (covering all syllabus)				
53 Total learning experience	30	54	94	175
54 S&C software project (05/06)	30	54	96	177
55 Tracey plc	30	54	97	180
56 Question with answer plan: Zircon company	30	54	98	181
57 Zodiac plc	30	54	99	184
58 Services marketing	30	54	100	186
59 Questions with helping hand: Hubbles (Pilot paper)	30	54	100	187
60 Round the table (11/05)	30	54	101	189
61 V (5/05)	30	54	102	191

Mock exam 1

Questions 62 to 65

Mock exam 2

Questions 66 to 69

Mock exam 3 (November 2006 – amended)

Questions 70 to 73

Planning your question practice

Our guidance from page 35 shows you how to organise your question practice, either by attempting questions from each syllabus area or by **building your own exams** – tackling questions as a series of practice exams.

BPP
LEARNING MEDIA

Topic index

Listed below are the key Paper P4 syllabus topics and the numbers of the questions in this Kit covering those topics.

If you need to concentrate your practice and revision on certain topics or if you want to attempt all available questions that refer to a particular subject, you will find this index useful.

Note that **MCQ and objective test questions** are not included in this index.

Syllabus topic	Question numbers
Appraisal	25, 33, 52, 57
Architectures	53
Benchmarking	18, Mock 3 Q2
Buying behaviour	41
Capacity and demand	17, 60
Change management	8, 26, 27, 43, 44, 48, 49, 50, 51, 52, Mock 2 Q2, Mock 3 Q2
Changeover	54, 55, Mock 1 Q3
Consumer behaviour	41
Critical periods	26, 27, 51, 52, 55, Mock 2 Q2
Databases	53, 55, Mock 2 Q2, Mock 3 Q3
Data flow diagram (DFD)	7
Decision table	7, 8
Direct marketing	61
Employment practices	51, 52
Entity life history (ELH)	6, 7
Entity relationship model (ERM)	6, 7
Ethics	44, 61, Mock 1 Q4, Mock 3 Q4
Flexibility	30, 31, 60
General systems theory	7, Mock 1 Q2
Hardware	53
High performance work arrangements	26, 27, 30, 31
Human resource management	25-33, 59, 61, Mock 1 Q4, Mock 3 Q2, Q3
Implementation	54, Mock 1 Q3
Internet	15, 42, 60, 61, Mock 3 Q3
Inventory management	16, 57
Job design	39, 40, Mock 2 Q2
Job description	39, 40, 55, Mock 2 Q2
Lean principles	17, 60
Market research	42
Marketing communications	42, 61
Marketing concept	39 – 44, Mock 3 Q4
Marketing mix	55, 58, 59, 60, 61
Marketing plan	39, 40, 59, Mock 2 Q4, Mock 3, Q4
Marketing services	60
Marketing and technology	42, 55, 61, Mock 3 Q3
'M' marketing	61
Motivation	25, 32, 33, 50, 56
Negotiation	51, 52, Mock 2 Q2
Operations management	15, 16, 55, 57, 59
Outsourcing	57, Mock 3 Q2

Syllabus topic	Question numbers
Organisational development	50, 51, 52, 55, Mock 1 Q2, Mock 3 Q2
Post-implementation	54, Mock 2 Q3
Pricing	56, Mock 2 Q2
Purchasing	15, 18
Quality management	16, 17, 18, 57, Mock 2 Q2
Recruitment	26, 27, 29
Redundancy	51, 52
Reward systems	25, 32, 33, 50
Selection	29, Mock 3 Q3
Segmentation	57, Mock 1 Q2, Mock 2 Q2, Q4, Mock 3 Q4
Services	49, 50, 58
Six sigma	17
Social responsibility	44, 61, Mock 3 Q4
Software	53, 60, Mock 1 Q3
Supply chain/networks	15, 16
System architectures	53
System changeover	55
System design and implementation	7, 8, 9, 53, 55
System development cycle	9, 55
Systems theory	7, Mock 1 Q2
Testing	8, 9, Mock 2 Q2
Training	54, Mock 2 Q3
Workforce flexibility	30, 31, 60

Using your BPP Practice and Revision Kit

Tackling revision and the exam

You can significantly improve your chances of passing by tackling revision and the exam in the right ways. Our advice is based on recent feedback from CIMA examiners.

- We look at the dos and don'ts of revising for, and taking, CIMA exams

- We focus on Paper P4: we discuss revising the syllabus, what to do (and what not to do) in the exam, how to approach different types of question and ways of obtaining easy marks

Selecting questions

We provide signposts to help you plan your revision.

- A full **question index**

- A **topic index** listing all the questions that cover key topics, so that you can locate the questions that provide practice on these topics, and see the different ways in which they might be examined

- A **BPP question plan** highlighting the most important questions and explaining why you should attempt them

- **Build your own exams**, showing you how you can practise questions in a series of exams

Making the most of question practice

At BPP we realise that you need more than just questions and model answers to get the most from your question practice.

- Our **Top tips** provide essential advice on tackling questions, presenting answers and the key points that answers need to include

- We show you how you can pick up **Easy marks** on questions, as we know that picking up all readily available marks often can make the difference between passing and failing

- We summarise **Examiner's comments** to show you how students who sat the exam coped with the questions

- A number of questions include **Analysis** and **Helping hands** attached to show you how to approach them if you are struggling

- We include an **annotated student answer** to highlight how these questions can be tackled and ways answers can be improved.

Attempting mock exams

There are three mock exams that provide practice at coping with the pressures of the exam day. We strongly recommend that you attempt them under exam conditions. **Mock exams 1 and 2** reflect the question styles and syllabus coverage of the exam: **Mock exam 3** is the actual November 2006 exam amended to reflect the changes to exam format from May 2007 onwards. To help you get the most out of doing these exams, we not only provide help with each answer, but also guidance on how you should have approached the whole exam.

Passing CIMA exams

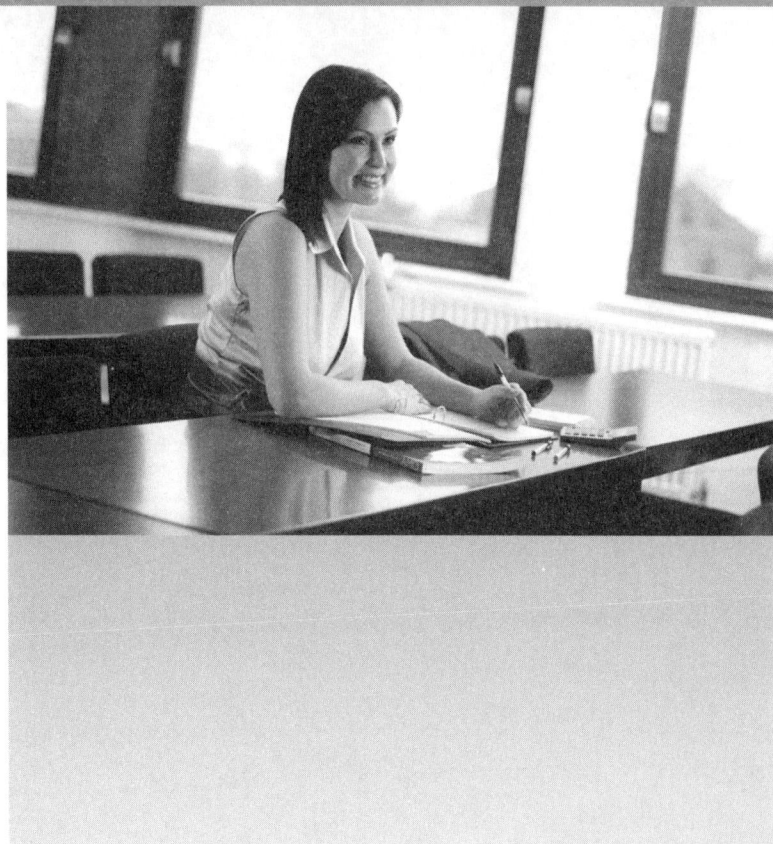

Revising and taking CIMA exams

To maximise your chances of passing your CIMA exams, you must make best use of your time, both before the exam during your revision, and when you are actually doing the exam.

- Making the most of your revision time can make a big, big difference to how well-prepared you are for the exam

- Time management is a core skill in the exam hall; all the work you've done can be wasted if you don't make the most of the three hours you have to attempt the exam

In this section we simply show you what to do and what not to do during your revision, and how to increase and decrease your prospects of passing your exams when you take them. Our advice is grounded in feedback we've had from CIMA examiners. You may be surprised to know that much examiner advice is the same whatever the exam, and the reasons why many students fail don't vary much between subjects and exam levels. So if you follow the advice we give you over the next few pages, you will **significantly** enhance your chances of passing **all** your CIMA exams.

How to revise

☑ Plan your revision

At the start of your revision period, you should draw up a **timetable** to plan how long you will spend on each subject and how you will revise each area. You need to consider the total time you have available and also the time that will be required to revise for other exams you're taking.

☑ Practise Practise Practise

The **more exam-standard questions** you do, the **more likely you are to pass** the exam. Practising full questions will mean that you'll get used to the time pressure of the exam. When the time is up, you should note where you've got to and then try to complete the question, giving yourself practice everything that the question tests.

☑ Revise enough

Make sure that your revision covers the breadth of the syllabus, as in most papers most topics could be examined in a compulsory question. However it is true that some topics are **key** – they often appear in compulsory questions or are a particular interest of the examiner – and you need to spend sufficient time revising these. Make sure you know the basics – the fundamental ideas, theories, models and techniques.

☑ Deal with your difficulties

Difficult areas are topics you find dull and pointless, or subjects that you found problematic when you were studying them. You mustn't become negative about these topics; instead you should build up your knowledge by reading the **Passcards** and using the **Quick quiz** questions in the Study Text to test yourself. When practising questions in the Kit, go back to the Text if you're struggling.

☑ Learn from your mistakes

Having completed a question you must try to look at your answer critically. Always read the **Top tips** guidance in the answers; it's there to help you. Look at **Easy marks** to see how you could have quickly gained credit on the questions that you've done. As you go through the Kit, it's worth noting any traps you've fallen into, and key points in the **Top tips** or **Examiner's comments** sections, and referring to these notes in the days before the exam. Aim to learn at least one new point from each question you attempt, a technical point perhaps or a point on style or approach.

☑ Read the examiners' guidance

We refer throughout this Kit to **Examiner's comments**; these are available on CIMA's website. As well as highlighting weaknesses, examiners' reports often provide clues to future questions, as many examiners will quickly test again areas where problems have arisen. CIMA's website also contains articles that are relevant to this paper, which you should read.

☑ Complete all three mock exams

You should attempt the **Mock exams** at the end of the Kit under **strict exam conditions** to gain experience of selecting questions, managing your time and producing answers.

BPP LEARNING MEDIA

How NOT to revise

☒ Revise selectively

Examiners are well aware that some students try to forecast the contents of exams, and only revise those areas that they think will be examined. Examiners try to prevent this by doing the unexpected, for example setting the same topic in successive sittings or setting topics in compulsory questions that have previously only been examined in optional questions.

☒ Spend all the revision period reading

You cannot pass the exam just by learning the contents of Passcards, Course Notes or Study Texts. You have to develop your **application skills** by practising questions.

☒ Audit the answers

This means reading the answers and guidance without having attempted the questions. Auditing the answers gives you **false reassurance** that you would have tackled the questions in the best way and made the points that our answers do. The feedback we give in our answers will mean more to you if you've attempted the questions and thought through the issues.

☒ Practise some types of question, but not others

Although you may find the theoretical parts of certain papers challenging, you shouldn't just practise repeating textbook theory. These papers will also contain elements that require application, and you therefore need to spend time practising these question parts as well.

☒ Get bogged down

Don't spend a lot of time worrying about all the minute detail of certain topic areas, and leave yourself insufficient time to cover the rest of the syllabus. Remember that a key skill in the exam is the ability to **concentrate on what's important** and this applies to your revision as well.

☒ Overdo studying

Studying for too long without interruption will mean your studying becomes less effective. A five minute break each hour will help. You should also make sure that you are leading a **healthy lifestyle** (proper meals, good sleep and some times when you're not studying).

How to PASS your exams

☑ Prepare for the day

Make sure you set at least one alarm (or get an alarm call), and allow plenty of time to get to the exam hall. You should have your route planned in advance and should listen on the radio for potential travel problems. You should check the night before to see that you have pens, pencils, erasers, watch, calculator with spare batteries, also exam documentation and evidence of identity.

☑ Select the right questions

You should select the optional questions you feel you can answer **best**, basing your selection on the topics covered, the requirements of the question, how easy it will be to apply the requirements and the availability of easy marks.

☑ Plan your three hours

You need to make sure that you will be answering the correct number of questions, and that you spend the right length of time on each question – this will be determined by the number of marks available. Each mark carries with it a **time allocation** of **1.8 minutes**. A 30 mark question therefore should be selected, completed and checked in 54 minutes. With some papers, it's better to do certain types of question first or last.

☑ Read the questions carefully

To score well, you must follow the requirements of the question, understanding what aspects of the subject area are being covered, and the tasks you will have to carry out. The requirements will also determine what information and examples you should provide. Reading the question scenarios carefully will help you decide what **issues** to discuss, what **techniques** to use, **information** and **examples** to include and how to **organise** your answer.

☑ Plan your answers

Five minutes of planning plus twenty-five minutes of writing is certain to earn you more marks than thirty minutes of writing. Consider when you're planning how your answer should be **structured**, what the **format** should be and **how long** each part should take.

Confirm before you start writing that your plan makes **sense**, covers **all relevant points** and does not include **irrelevant material.**

☑ Show evidence of judgement

Remember that examiners aren't just looking for a display of knowledge; they want to see how well you can **apply** the knowledge you have. Evidence of application and judgement will include writing answers that only contain **relevant** material, using the material in scenarios to **support** what you say, **criticising** the **limitations** and **assumptions** of the techniques you've used and making **reasonable recommendations** that follow from your discussion.

☑ Stay until the end of the exam

Use any spare time to **check and recheck** your script. This includes checking you have filled out the candidate details correctly, you have labelled question parts and workings clearly, you have used headers and underlining effectively and spelling, grammar and any arithmetic are correct.

How to FAIL your exams

⊠ Don't do enough questions

If you don't attempt sufficient questions on the paper, you are making it harder for yourself to pass the questions that you do attempt. If for example you don't do a 30 mark question, then you will have to score 50 marks out of 70 marks on the rest of the paper, and therefore have to obtain 71% of the marks on the questions you do attempt. Failing to attempt all of the paper is symptomatic of poor time management or poor question selection.

⊠ Include irrelevant material

Markers are given detailed mark guides and will not give credit for irrelevant content. Therefore you should **NOT** braindump into your answer all you know about a broad subject area; the markers will only give credit for what is **relevant**, and you will also be showing that you lack the ability to **judge what's important.** Similarly forcing irrelevant theory into every answer won't gain you marks, nor will providing uncalled for features such as situation analyses, executive summaries and background information.

⊠ Fail to use the details in the scenario

General answers or reproductions of old answers that don't refer to what is in the scenario in **this** question won't score enough marks to pass.

⊠ Copy out the scenario details

Examiners see **selective** use of the right information as a key skill. If you copy out chunks of the scenario that aren't relevant to the question, or don't use the information to support your own judgements, you won't achieve good marks.

⊠ Don't do what the question asks

Failing to provide all the examiner asks for will limit the marks you score. You will also decrease your chances by not providing an answer with enough **depth** – producing a single line bullet point list when the examiner asks for a discussion.

⊠ Present your work poorly

Markers will only be able to give you credit if they can read your writing. There are also plenty of other things as well that will make it more difficult for markers to reward you. Examples include:

- Not using black or blue ink
- Not showing clearly which question you're attempting
- Scattering question parts from the same question throughout your answer booklet
- Not showing clearly workings or the results of your calculations

Paragraphs that are too long or which lack headers also won't help markers and hence won't help you.

Using your BPP products

This Kit gives you the question practice and guidance you need in the exam. Our other products can also help you pass:

- **Learning to Learn Accountancy** gives further valuable advice on revision

- **Passcards** provide you with clear topic summaries and exam tips

- **Success CDs** help you revise on the move

- **i-Pass CDs** offer tests of knowledge against the clock

- **Learn Online** is an e-learning resource delivered via the Internet, offering comprehensive tutor support and featuring areas such as study, practice, email service, revision and useful resources

You can purchase these products by visiting www.bpp.com/mybpp.

Visit our website www.bpp.com/cima/learnonline to sample aspects of Learn Online free of charge.

Passing P4

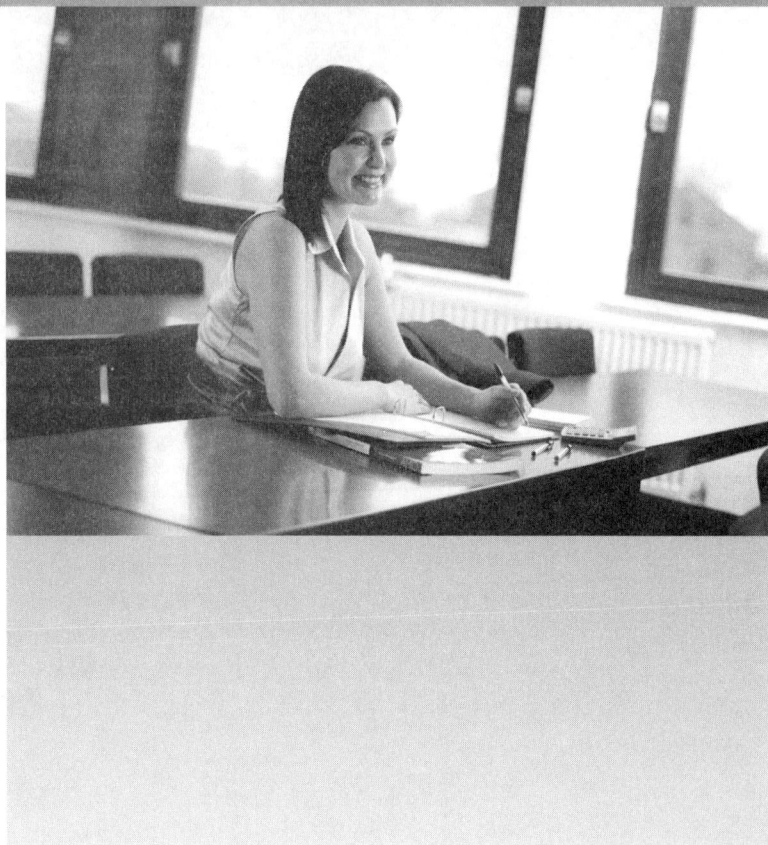

Revising P4

Organisational management and information systems

Organisational management and information systems are of course central to this paper and hence should be central to your revision.

On **organisation management** you need to know:

- How organisations develop
- How and why resistance to change occurs and what can be done to overcome it
- What problems are associated with quality issues
- How to design and implement quality programmes
- How organisations can manage relationships with suppliers
- The marketing process
- How marketing principles are applied
- How to produce a strategic marketing plan
- How the human resources management functions
- How to produce a human resources plan and manage supporting activities
- How evaluation, appraisal, reward and motivation schemes for employees work

The **information systems** element requires you to:

- Explain the features of information systems hardware and software
- Identify opportunities within organisations and situations to implement information technology
- Explain how information technology projects are developed and implemented
- Recommend strategies for changeover between systems

Regard this as a checklist to give you ideas but don't expect to use them all in the exam.

Question practice

You should use the Passcards and any brief notes you have to revise these topics, but you mustn't spend all your revision time passively reading. Question practice is vital; doing as many questions as you can in full will help develop your ability to analyse scenarios and produce relevant discussion and recommendations. The revision plan on page 35 tells you what questions cover so that you can choose questions covering a variety of organisational situations and issues.

You should make sure you leave yourself enough time during your revision to practise the Section A multiple choice and objective questions as you cannot avoid them. These questions offer you an opportunity to test your breadth of knowledge in a time-effective manner. Do not overlook them. You should ensure your answers to the OT questions fall within the word limit – time management on shorter questions is equally as important as with longer ones.

Passing the P4 exam

Displaying the right qualities

The examiners will expect you to display the following qualities.

Qualities required	
A good understanding	Questions will often test your grasp of **generally accepted** management thinking in the main syllabus areas, there will often be some **flexibility** allowed, there may be **no** single right answer.
Business awareness	You will be tested in different questions on your ability to **identify** and **understand** the **management implications** of the problems you are faced with.
Evaluation and recommendation	You must be able to **analyse** a situation, **generate** and **evaluate** a range of **options** and be ready to **recommend** a **reasonable** course of action.

Avoiding weaknesses

Although there have only been three sittings of P4, the examiners have already identified weaknesses that occur in many students' answers at every sitting. You will enhance your chances significantly if you ensure you avoid these mistakes:

- Failing to read requirements or misreading a question
- Failing to pick up prompts in the scenario – scenarios are full of clues and prompts
- Failing to apply knowledge to the given scenario/context
- Twisting the questions into what you think they should be
- Time management – Questions 3 and 4 are often left till last and are rushed
- Exceeding 50 word/one page limits
- Repeating the same material in different parts of a question
- Brain dumping everything you know about the topic area being tested – seeing a familiar word in a question and going off on a tangent
- Misreading question requirements

Using the reading time and tackling the paper

Before the three hours exam time starts, you are allowed 20 minutes to read through the paper. Use this time wisely – in effect it gives you an extra 20 minutes to gain the marks you need to pass.

What should you do in this 20 minutes? You could read through the two questions in Section C – and decide which one of these you will answer. However, this could remove your focus from the Section A questions and clutter your mind with extra information.

We recommend you use the 20 minutes to simply start working through the Section A questions – by writing your answers on the question paper. These answers can then be transferred very carefully to your answer booklet when the exam starts. Remember though, you must not write in your answer booklet during the reading time.

Using the time in this way should mean that later in the exam, when you reach Section C, you have sufficient time to read both questions carefully and make the best decision as to which one you will attempt.

Once the exam starts, we recommend you finish off the Section A questions first, then tackle the six sub–questions in Section B, before moving on and choosing and then answering one question from Section C.

Tackling multiple choice questions

Of the total marks available for Paper P4, multiple choice questions (MCQs) comprise 20 per cent (10 × 2 marks).

The MCQs in your exam will contain four possible answers. You have to **choose the option that best answers the question**. The incorrect options are called distracters. There is a skill in answering MCQs quickly and correctly. By practising MCQs you can develop this skill, giving yourself a better chance of passing the exam.

You may wish to follow the approach outlined below, or you may prefer to adapt it.

Step 1   Skim read all the MCQs and identify which appear to be the easier questions.

Step 2   Work out **how long** you should allocate to each MCQ bearing in mind the number of marks available and any guidance the examiner has given about how long they should take in total. Also remember that the examiner will not expect you to spend an equal amount of time on each MCQ; some can be answered instantly but others will take time to work out.

Step 3   Attempt each question – **starting with the easier questions** identified in Step 1. Read the question thoroughly. You may prefer to work out the answer before looking at the options, or you may prefer to look at the options at the beginning. Adopt the method that works best for you.

You may find that you recognise a question when you sit the exam. Be aware that the detail and/or requirement may be different. If the question seems familiar, read the requirement and options carefully – do not assume that it is identical.

Step 4   Read the options and see if one matches your own answer.

Step 5   You may find that none of the options matches your answer.

- Re-read the question to ensure that you understand it and are answering the requirement

- Eliminate any obviously wrong answers

- Consider which of the remaining answers is the most likely to be correct and select that option

Step 6   If you are still unsure, make a note and continue to the next question. Likewise if you are nowhere near working out which option is correct, leave the question and come back to it later.

Step 7   Revisit unanswered questions. When you come back to a question after a break, you often find you can answer it correctly straightaway. If you are still unsure, have a guess. You are not penalised for incorrect answers, so **never leave a question unanswered!**

Tackling objective test questions

What is an objective test question?

In Paper P4, objective test questions take the form of **word-limited answers**. You are asked to state or explain things in no **more than 50 words**.

Dealing with OT questions

Again you may wish to follow **the approach we suggest below**, or you may be prepared to adapt it.

Step 1   Work out **how long** you should allocate to each OT. For each 4 mark OT, allocate approximately 7.2 minutes.

Step 2   **Attempt each question**. Read the question thoroughly, and think about how you can answer it within the **word restriction** placed on it (for example 50 words).

Step 3   You may find that you recognise a question when you sit the exam. Be aware that the detail and/or requirement may be different. If the question seems familiar read the requirement and options carefully – do not assume that it is identical. Have you followed the requirement exactly?

Step 4   You may find that you are unsure of the answer. Re-read the question to ensure that you understand it and are answering the requirement.

Step 5   If you are still unsure, **continue to the next question**.

Step 6   Revisit questions you are uncertain about. When you come back to a question after a break you often find you are able to answer it correctly straight away. If you are still unsure have a guess. You are not penalised for incorrect answers, so **never leave a question unanswered!**

Step 7   Rule off answers to each OTQ in the answer booklet.

Tackling longer written questions

You'll improve your chances by following a step–by–step approach to Section C questions along the following lines.

Step 1   **Read the requirement**

You need to identify the knowledge areas being tested and what information will therefore be significant.

Step 2   **Identify the action verbs**

These convey the level of skill you need to exhibit. See the list on page 30.

Step 3   **Identify what each part of the question requires**

When planning, you will need to make sure that you aren't reproducing the same material in more than one part of the question.

Step 4   **Check the mark allocation to each part**

This shows you the depth anticipated and helps allocate time.

Step 5   **Read the scenario carefully**

Put points under headings related to requirements (e.g. by marginal notes). Consider the techniques you'll need to use.

Step 6   **Consider the consequences of the points you've identified**

If you are required to provide recommendations based on the information you've been given, consider the limitations of any analysis you undertake or other factors that may impact upon your recommendations.

Step 7   **Write a plan**

You may be able to do this on the question paper as often there will be at least one blank page in the question booklet. However any plan you make should be reproduced in the answer booklet when writing time begins.

Step 8   **Write the answer**

Make every effort to present your answer clearly.

Remember that **depth of discussion** is also important. Discussions will often consist of paragraphs containing 2–3 sentences. Each paragraph should:

- **Make a point**
- **Explain the point** (you must demonstrate **why** the point is important)
- **Illustrate the point** (with material or analysis from the scenario, perhaps an example from real–life)

Keep your answer **to the point**, avoid wasting time 'waffling' as you will not earn good marks and you risk running out of time in later questions

Gaining the easy marks

Many longer questions will allocate some 'easy' marks for reproducing 'book knowledge' – then the remainder of the marks are available for applying this knowledge.

Recent exams

Change in exam format

The format for the P4 exam from May 2007 has been changed to the format as shown below. Papers up to November 2006 split the marks 50:30:20. CIMA has said that the change will make no difference to the style of exam questions set.

Format of the paper

		Number of marks
Section A:	10 multiple choice questions worth 2 marks each and 5 objective test questions, worth 4 marks each	40
Section B:	1 compulsory question with six short sub–parts worth 5 marks each	30
Section C:	1 out of 2 questions, worth 30 marks each	30
		100

Time allowed: 3 hours

Question weighting will reflect syllabus weighting.

Section A will always contain 10 multiple choice questions and 5 short written objective test questions.

Further guidance on multiple choice questions and objective test questions is included on pages (23) and (24).

Section B will contain 1 question with a number of sub–parts. This section will require breadth of syllabus knowledge and good time management skills.

Section C questions may include issues from a number of areas of the syllabus. Careful planning of answers is essential.

November 2006

Section A (answer all questions) Fifteen questions worth 2 marks, five worth 4 marks. 50 marks

1   Twenty questions drawn from all syllabus areas

Section B (answer all questions) One scenario question with six sub–parts worth 5 marks each. 30 marks

2   (a)   Change failure
      (b)   HR role in change
      (c)   Outsourcing
      (d)   Benchmarking
      (e)   Establishing a new culture
      (f)   Performance measurement

Section C (answer one from two scenario questions) 20 marks

3   (a)   Opportunity evaluation (12 marks)
      (b)   Selection process guidelines (8 marks)

4   (a)   Situation analysis of marketing and ethical issues (10 marks)
      (b)   Strategic marketing plan development (10 marks)

Examiner's comments. Not available at time of going to press.

This paper is Mock exam 3 in this Kit. Sections (a) and (c) of this mock exam have been amended to reflect the changes to exam format from May 2007 onwards.

May 2006

Section A (answer all questions) Fifteen questions worth 2 marks, five worth 4 marks. 50 marks

1   Twenty questions drawn from all syllabus areas

Section B (answer all questions) One scenario question with six sub–parts worth 5 marks each. 30 marks

2   (a)   Business processes and software fit
      (b)   Changeover – phased approach versus a 'big bang' approach
      (c)   Important individuals and groups during implementation
      (d)   User involvement in implementation
      (e)   Training requirements of different users
      (f)   Post–implementation review

Section C (answer one from two scenario questions) 20 marks

3   (a)   Responding to environmental change – dangers of not responding (8 marks)
      (b)   Responding to environmental change – types of change that could be made (12 marks)

4   (a)   Application of Herzberg's motivation–hygiene theory (10 marks)
      (b)   Redesigning remuneration and reward packages (10 marks)

Examiner's comments. The examiner's general comments were:

Most candidates handled Question 1 (Section A) with ease and a substantial number also produced confident answers to Question 2 (Section B).

There was a more even take up of Question 3 or Question 4 as part of the elective choice under Section C of the paper. Section C of the paper produced the most disappointing results, indicating that candidates have some difficulty in relating their knowledge to the context of a scenario.

November 2005

Section A (answer all questions) Fifteen questions worth 2 marks, five worth 4 marks. 50 marks.

1   Twenty questions drawn from all syllabus areas.

Section B (answer all questions) One scenario question with six sub–parts worth 5 marks each. 30 marks.

2   (a)   Level capacity strategy and JIT.
      (b)   Demand strategies and marketing.

      (c)   Chase strategies and the flexible organisation.

      (d)   Capacity management (service and manufacturing).

      (e)   Software for inbound logistics.

      (f)   Computerised assistance to improve demand.

Section C (answer one from two scenario questions). 20 marks

3   (a)   The role of the HR division. (10 marks)
      (b)   HR strategy changes. (10 marks)

4   (a)   Marketing action plan issues for product, place and promotion. (10 marks)
      (b)   Produce a draft job description. (10 marks)

Examiner's comments. The examiner's general comments were:

Most candidates appeared to have coped with the requirements of the paper. Overwhelmingly, candidates scored heavily on Question 1 with a mixed performance in the remainder of the paper. In terms of Part C (the elective section) Question 4 proved to be the more popular choice.

May 2005

Section A (answer all questions.) Fifteen questions worth 2 marks, five worth 4 marks. 50 marks.

1   Twenty questions drawn from all syllabus areas.

Section B (answer all questions) One scenario question with six sub–parts worth 5 marks each. 30 marks.

2   (a)   Marketing mix
      (b)   Human resource implications of direct selling
      (c)   Direct marketing
      (d)   Advantages of the Internet as a marketing channel
      (e)   Using Internet and mobile phone technology for marketing
      (f)   Ethical issues

Section C (answer one from two scenario questions). 20 marks

3   (a)   Developing a human resource plan (12 marks)
      (b)   Achieving workforce flexibility (8 marks)

4   (a)   Managing redundancies (10 marks)
      (b)   Overcoming resistance to change (10 marks)

Examiner's comments. The examiner's general comments were:

Generally candidates appeared to cope well with this new examination paper. Most candidates handled question 1 with ease and a substantial number also produced fine answers to question 2. In terms of the elective questions in Section C, question 4 proved to be the more popular choice.

Pilot paper

Section A (answer all questions.) Fifteen questions worth 2 marks, five worth 4 marks. 50 marks.

1   Twenty questions drawn from all syllabus areas.

Section B (answer all questions) One scenario question with six sub–parts worth 5 marks each. 30 marks.

2   (a)   Selling approach v marketing approach
        (b)   Customer needs
        (c)   Marketing mix
        (d)   Competitive position
        (e)   Human resources and purchasing
        (f)   Efficient purchasing and organisational performance

Section C (answer one from two scenario questions). 20 marks

3   (a)   Human resource plan (8 marks)
        (b)   Human resource activities (12 marks)

4   (a)   Change theory (Lewin) (10 marks)
        (b)   Incremental v transformational change (10 marks)

What the examiner means

The table below has been prepared by CIMA to help you interpret exam questions.

Learning objective	Verbs used	Definition	Examples in the Kit
1 Knowledge What you are expected to know	• List • State • Define	• Make a list of • Express, fully or clearly, the details of/facts of • Give the exact meaning of	6, 15, 27, 29
2 Comprehension What you are expected to understand	• Describe • Distinguish • Explain • Identify • Illustrate	• Communicate the key features of • Highlight the differences between • Make clear or intelligible/state the meaning of • Recognise, establish or select after consideration • Use an example to describe or explain something	6, 7, 8, 9, 15, 16, 17, 18, 25, 27, 30, 31, 32, 33, 39, 40, 41, 42, 48, 49, 50, 52, 53, 54, 55, 56, 57, 58, 59, 60, 61
3 Application How you are expected to apply your knowledge	• Apply • Calculate/compute • Demonstrate • Prepare • Reconcile • Solve • Tabulate	• To put to practical use • To ascertain or reckon mathematically • To prove the certainty or to exhibit by practical means • To make or get ready for use • To make or prove consistent/ compatible • Find an answer to • Arrange in a table	6, 8, 18, 26, 27, 28, 29, 39, 40
4 Analysis How you are expected to analyse the detail of what you have learned	• Analyse • Categorise • Compare and contrast • Construct • Discuss • Interpret • Produce	• Examine in detail the structure of • Place into a defined class or division • Show the similarities and/or differences between • To build up or complete • To examine in detail by argument • To translate into intelligible or familiar terms • To create or bring into existence	25, 28, 29, 30, 31, 32, 33, 43, 44, 51, 52, 54, 55, 56, 58, 60
5 Evaluation How you are expected to use your learning to evaluate, make decisions or recommendations	• Advise • Evaluate • Recommend	• To counsel, inform or notify • To appraise or assess the value of • To advise on a course of action	16, 42, 48, 53, 55, 57

Exam update

Examiners occasionally base exam questions on articles from *Financial Management (CIMA's magazine)*. Students should check recent editions for relevant articles.

A recent relevant article was 'Organisation management and information systems', Bob Scarlett, Financial Management, November 2006.

Useful websites

The websites below provide additional sources of information of relevance to your studies for *Organisational Management and Information Systems.*

- BPP   www.bpp.com

  For details of other BPP material for your CIMA studies

- CIMA   www.cimaglobal.com

  The official CIMA website

- *Financial Times*   www.ft.com

- *The Economist*   www.economist.com

- *Wall Street Journal*   www.wsj.com

- IT terminology   www.pcwebopaedia.com

  An online dictionary and search engine for computer and Internet terminology

- General accounting and business   www.accountingweb.com

Planning your question practice

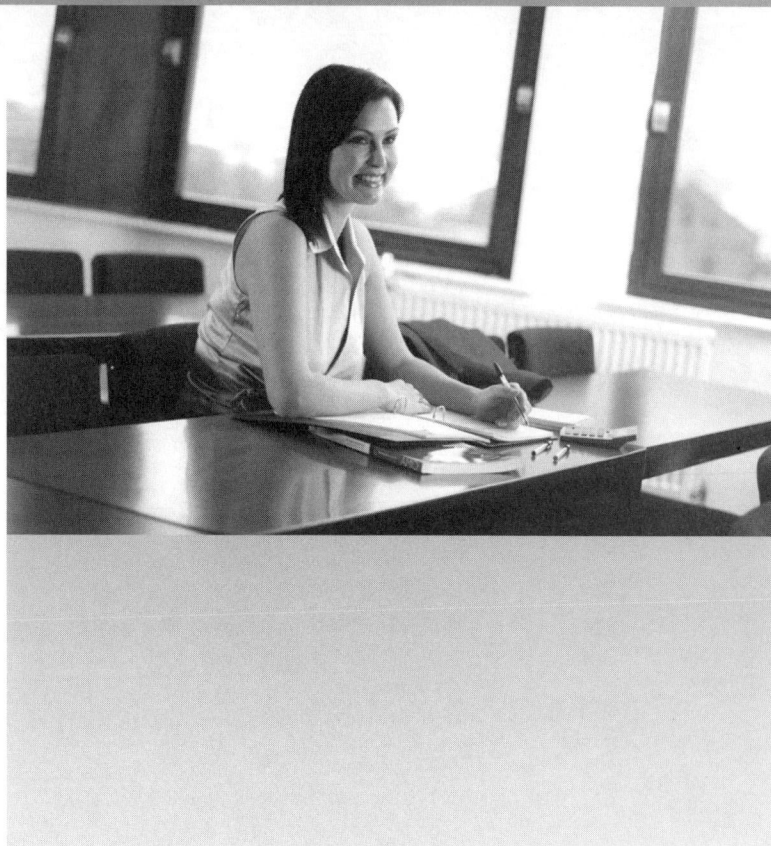

Planning your question practice

We have already stressed that question practice should be right at the centre of your revision. Whilst you will spend some time looking at your notes and the Paper P4 Passcards, you should spend the majority of your revision time practising questions.

We recommend two ways in which you can practise questions.

*   Use **BPP's question plan** to work systematically through the syllabus and attempt key and other questions on a section-by-section basis

*   **Build your own exams** – attempt the questions as a series of practice exams

These ways are suggestions and simply following them is no guarantee of success. You or your college may prefer an alternative but equally valid approach.

BPP's question plan

The plan below requires you to devote a **minimum of 40 hours** to revision of Paper P4. Any time you can spend over and above this should only increase your chances of success.

Step 1   **Review your notes** and the chapter summaries in the Paper P4 **Passcards** for each section of the syllabus.

Step 2   **Answer the key questions** for that section. These questions have boxes round the question number in the table below and you should answer them in full. Even if you are short of time you must attempt these questions if you want to pass the exam. You should complete your answers without referring to our solutions.

Step 3   **Attempt the other questions** in that section. If you are short on time we suggest that you prepare **answer plans** rather than full solutions. Planning an answer means that you should spend about 40% of the time allowance for the questions brainstorming the question and drawing up a list of points to be included in the answer.

Step 4   **Attempt Mock exams 1, 2 and 3** under strict exam conditions.

Syllabus section	2007 Passcards chapters	Questions in this Kit	Comments	Done ☑
Information systems	1 – 3	1, 2 & 3	Answer at least one bank of these MCQs – they provide excellent practice for the exam.	☐
		4 & 5	Answer at least one bank of these short written response questions – these provide excellent practice for the exam.	☐
		7	The question revises all the major system design tools and techniques.	☐
		9	The system development lifecycle is a key model, you should be able to describe all the stages.	☐
Operations management	4 – 6	10, 11 & 12	Attempt at least one bank of the MCQs as they provide excellent practice for the exam.	☐
		13 & 14	Attempt at least one bank of the OT questions as they provide excellent practice for the exam.	☐
		16	This is a good example of a Section C exam question. It covers a range of operational issues and ensures you have practised assimilating and using a large amount of information.	☐
		17	Balancing capacity and demand is key to successful operations management. This question tests your understanding of it. The 'lean' concept and Six Sigma are modern ideas and topical. These are both areas easily neglected by students, do not fall into this trap.	☐
Managing human capital	7 – 9	19, 20, 21 & 22	Answer at least two banks of the MCQs as they provide excellent practice for the exam.	☐
		23 & 24	Answer at least one bank of the OT questions as they provide excellent practice for the exam.	☐
		25	This question is good revision of Maslow and appraisal systems. Such systems can easily feature in exam questions.	☐
		29	HR plans and recruitment and selection polices are an important part of the syllabus. Students often need practice in putting an HR plan together as it can be tricky if you are uncertain what is required. Answering this question will prepare you well if it comes up on the exam.	☐
		33	Answer this question as it is a recent example of the examiner's exam style. It also covers employee motivation and indicates how you should apply academic theories.	☐

Syllabus section	2007 Passcards chapters	Questions in this Kit	Comments	Done ☑
Marketing	10 – 12	34, 35 & 36	Answer at least one bank of these MCQs – they provide excellent practice for the exam.	☐
		37 & 38	Answer at least one bank of the objective test questions – they provide excellent practice for the exam.	☐
		40	Attempt this as it is an example of questions that require you to appreciate the commercial situation facing an organisation and to consider a suitable response.	
		42	A short question, but one that requires you to consider the effect of the internet and how technology can be used for marketing purposes. This can be tricky as you will have to structure your answer carefully to maximise your marks. Not all questions have an obvious structure to follow so this is good practice for this eventuality.	☐
Managing change	13 – 14	45 & 46	Answer at least one bank of these MCQs – they provide excellent practice for the exam.	☐
		47	Answer all of the objective test questions – they provide excellent practice for the exam.	☐
		50	This question is a good test of change theory, something students tend to need practice on.	☐
		52	Some questions, such as this, cover more than one syllabus area and it is important that you practice switching between different topics. This question also covers the whole area of overcoming resistance to change.	☐
30 mark questions – all of syllabus	All	53 to 61	You should attempt all of the questions 53 to 61. Many students spend too long on them in the exam, risking failure on later questions due to time running out. Use these to practise your time management skills, they also allow you to cover the whole syllabus very quickly. Remember to keep your answers to the point, waffle costs time and does not earn you any marks. Write enough to earn the marks and then move on!	☐

Build your own exams

Having revised your notes and the BPP Passcards, you can attempt the questions in the Kit as a series of practice exams. You can organise the questions in the following ways:

- Either you can attempt complete old papers; recent papers are listed below.

	P4			
	Pilot paper	May'05	Nov'05	May'06
Section A				
1 MCQs	3.1, 3.2, 3.3, 3.4, 3.5, 3.6, 11.10, 12.10, 21.1, 21.2, 21.3, 21.4, 21.5, 21.6, 21.7	3.7, 3.8, 12.1, 12.2, 12.3, 12.4, 12.5, 12.6, 12.7, 12.8, 19.6, 20.2, 21.8, 21.9, 21.10,	10.1, 19.1, 19.4, 19.5, 22.7, 22.8, 22.9, 22.10, 34.1, 34.3, 34.4, 34.6, 34.7, 46.7, 46.8,	10.3, 10.6, 10.9, 22.1, 22.2, 22.3, 22.4, 22.5, 22.6, 34.2, 34.5, 34.10, 45.2, 45.4, 45.8,
Short-response	5.1, 14.1, 14.2, 14.3, 47.4	5.2, 5.3, 5.4, 5.5, 14.4	4.1, 4.4, 13.1, 38.3, 47.5	13.2, 13.3, 13.4, 24.5, 37.1
Section B				
2	59	61	60	54
Section C				
3	28/29	30/31	26/27	32/33
4	49/50	51/52	39/40	43/44

Note. By attempting all the MCQs plus the first option for each Section C question you will have completed the original exam as it appeared under the old exam format.

If you wish to attempt an amended version that reflects the new format from May 2007, you should select **any** ten MCQs and the second option for the Section C questions.

- Or you can make up practice exams, either yourself or using the mock exams that we have listed below.

	Practice exams					
	1	2	3	4	5	6
Section A						
1	3 & 24	35 & 13	20 & 38	10 & 47	46 & 5	12 & 23
Section B						
2	57	54	58	61	56	55
Section C						
3	41	7	15	6	18	8
4	50	17	48	31	33	44

- Whichever practice exams you use, you must attempt **Mock exams 1, 2 and 3** at the end of your revision.

Questions

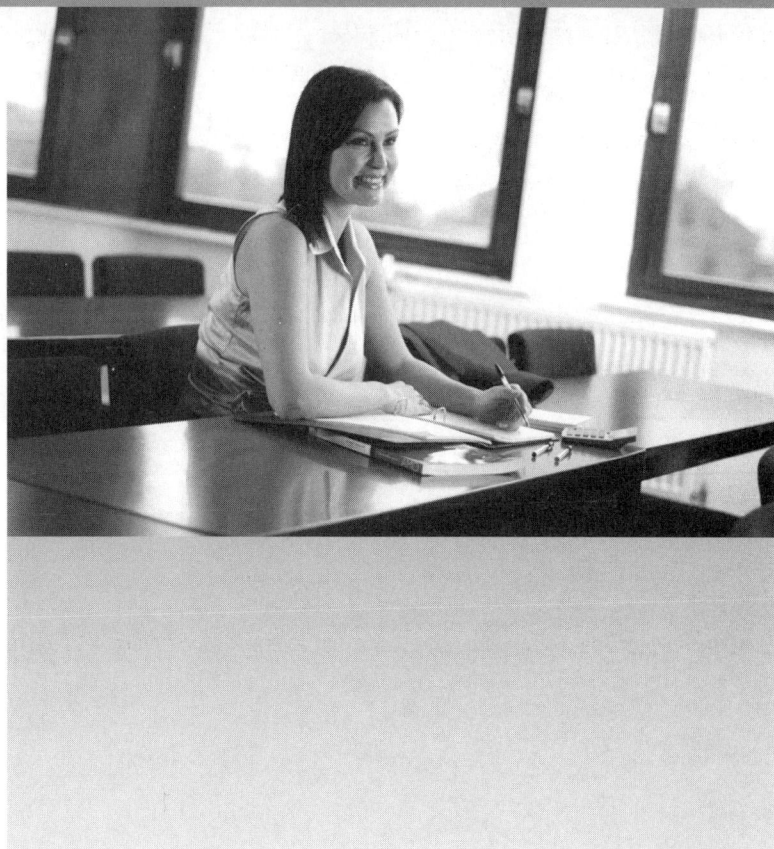

INFORMATION SYSTEMS

Questions 1 to 9 cover Information Systems, the subject of Part A of the BPP Study Text for Paper P4.

1 Multiple choice questions: Information systems 1   36 mins

1.1   Which one of the following is the main limitation of RAM?

    A   It can only be read from, not written to

    B   Only one program can be stored in RAM at any one time

    C   Data is lost if the power supply is lost

    D   Transferring data to RAM from hard disk takes a long time   **(2 marks)**

1.2   Within a database, what is data redundancy?

    A   Deletion of data that is no longer used

    B   Data becoming out of date due to changes in file formats

    C   The existence of the same data in more than one place

    D   Storing old data in a data warehouse   **(2 marks)**

1.3   The abbreviation ROM stands for which one of the following?

    A   Random Online Memory

    B   Read Only Memory

    C   Recognition by Optional Mark

    D   Readable Optical Memory   **(2 marks)**

1.4   Which one of the following is an advantage of centralised processing?

    A   Processing activities can be shared between computers

    B   Economies of scale for large transaction processing systems

    C   Greater sense of personal ownership

    D   Allows greater independence for users   **(2 marks)**

1.5   All the following statements refer to electronic point of sale (EPOS) technology used by many retailers.

    (i)   EPOS technology enables a business to assess which items of stock are selling quickly.

    (ii)   EPOS technology can be used only by businesses selling durable goods as it is less suited to perishable products.

    (iii)   EPOS technology can facilitate electronic data interchange links between a retail business and its suppliers.

    (iv)   EPOS technology can facilitate the just-in-time (JIT) organisation of production.

    Which of the above are correct?

    A   (i), (ii) and (iv) only

    B   (i) and (iv) only

    C   (i), (iii) and (iv) only

    D   (ii) and (iii) only   **(2 marks)**

1.6   What does the phrase 'a system's environment' refer to?

    A   External elements that have direct or indirect influence on the process and elements of a system

    B   Humidity and temperature monitoring

    C   The hardware and software used in the system

    D   Adding value to an input to produce the output   **(2 marks)**

1.7 Many modern Automated Teller Machines (ATMs) allow choices to be made using which one of the following input methods?

    A   Touch screen
    B   Voice recognition
    C   MICR
    D   Optical character recognition   **(2 marks)**

1.8 Which one of the following is true under 'client/server computing'?

    A   Individual users can access shared printers
    B   All data must be stored on file servers
    C   Individual workstations do not run any application software
    D   All data is backed up centrally   **(2 marks)**

1.9 What does the system boundary separate?

    A   Individual sub-systems within a system
    B   Input and output devices from the central processor
    C   The system and its components from its environment
    D   The components of a system, allowing them to work independently   **(2 marks)**

1.10 In a control system, what is the purpose of a comparator?

    A   Measurement of actual results against planned results
    B   Take remedial action where necessary
    C   Set realistic targets compared to benchmarking with third parties
    D   Collection of information on current production   **(2 marks)**

                                                                                          (Total = 20 marks)

2 Multiple choice questions: Information systems 2   36 mins

2.1 A system might be described as either open or closed. When a system is closed, it is:

    A   Isolated from its environment
    B   Shut down
    C   Protected from unauthorised access
    D   Unable to accept further input but is still capable of functioning   **(2 marks)**

2.2 Which of the following statements describes the law of requisite variety?

    A   The variety within a system should be at least as great as the variety in the environment in which the system is trying to regulate itself
    B   A system must be capable of changing and adapting to meet the requirements of changing objectives
    C   A system should be capable of performing a sufficient variety of tasks to justify its costs
    D   Operators of a system need a sufficient variety of tasks to sustain their motivation and efficiency
                                                                                                    (2 marks)

2.3 A system will tend to fall into disorder and inefficiency unless it receives new inputs from its environment. In the terminology of general systems theory, new inputs from the environment provide:

    A   Requisite variety
    B   Entropy
    C   Feedback
    D   Negative entropy   **(2 marks)**

2.4 A public relations agency employs a team of people to scan press, television and other media for information that may be relevant to a particular client. When an item is identified, the media scanner refers the item to a supervisor. The supervisor then decides whether to inform the agency's customer liaison officer for that particular client. The customer liaison officer decides whether to pass the information to the client.

This process for dealing with information is an example of:

A   Decoupling
B   Filtering
C   Feedback
D   Entropy   **(2 marks)**

2.5 What term is used to describe the system that controls how data is held and accessed in a database?

A   Data dictionary
B   Data warehouse
C   Database administrator
D   Data mine   **(2 marks)**

2.6 Which one of the following may be used to interrogate a database?

A   A scanner
B   Structured walkthrough
C   A query language
D   A scanner   **(2 marks)**

2.7 In a data flow diagram (DFD), which one of the following represents a source and/or destination of data?

A   A root node
B   An entity
C   A data process
D   A data flow   **(2 marks)**

2.8 A data flow diagram includes the following box.

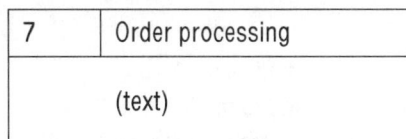

7	Order processing
(text)	

Which of the following statements about this box is correct?

A   This is an example of a flow and is the seventh such item in this DFD diagram
B   This is an example of an entity and is the seventh such item in this diagram
C   This is an example of a data store and is the seventh such item in this diagram
D   This is an example of a data process and is the seventh such item in this DFD diagram   **(2 marks)**

2.9 A decision table shows four elements relevant to a decision – each in their own quadrant of the table.

Which one of the following options shows the correct four quadrants?

A   Condition stub, condition entry, action stub, action entry
B   IF stub, IF entry, THEN stub, THEN entry
C   Factor stub, factor entry, action stub, action entry
D   Condition question, condition answer, action question, action answer   **(2 marks)**

2.10 What systems design aid is used to construct the logical data requirements for the system, independently of the organisation and processes of the system?

    A   Data flow diagram
    B   Entity life history
    C   Flowchart
    D   Entity relationship model   **(2 marks)**

(Total = 20 marks)

3 Multiple choice questions: Information systems 3   36 mins

3.1 Bar code readers, scanners and keyboards are examples of

    A   Hardware input devices
    B   Software input devices
    C   Systems processing devices
    D   Hardware processing devices   **(2 marks)**
    Pilot paper

3.2 Local area networking is used for

    A   Communication between computers within a limited geographical area

    B   Structuring an organisation within a division or business unit

    C   Exchange of information through a trade association or region

    D   Managing a complex operational issue by global interface with trade associations and professional bodies   **(2 marks)**
    Pilot paper

3.3 Entropy is a term used to describe

    A   The tendency of a system to break down due to randomness
    B   The tendency of a system to develop over time leading to randomness
    C   A means of testing candidates in an interview to overcome randomness
    D   A means of developing open learning using computers   **(2 marks)**
    Pilot paper

3.4 Many large organisations have established a computer intranet for the purpose of

    A   Providing quick, effective and improved communication amongst staff using chat rooms
    B   Providing quick, effective and improved communication to staff
    C   Providing quick, effective and improved communication to customers
    D   Providing quick, effective and improved ordering procedures in real time   **(2 marks)**
    Pilot paper

3.5   The main advantages of a database management system include

A   The development of separate data sources
B   Unlimited access and open communications
C   End user flexibility and a devolution of responsibility
D   Data integrity and elimination of duplication

(2 marks)
Pilot paper

3.6   An expert system describes

A   A database built upon past knowledge and experience
B   A powerful off the shelf software solution
C   An on-line library of operating advice and handy hints
D   An electronic version of working papers assembled by the Research and Development department

(2 marks)
Pilot paper

3.7   The operating system

A   Forms part of a system's software
B   Forms part of a system's hardware
C   Is another term for a system's hardware
D   Is a standalone end-user (operator) system solution

(2 marks)
5/05

3.8   The five elements of a computer system are

A   Data, communication, flexibility, hardware and data integrity
B   Installation, hardware, maintenance, audit and compliance
C   Hardware, software, procedures, data and people
D   Input, processing, monitoring, control and reporting

(2 marks)
5/05

3.9   Three common network topologies are

A   Star, ring, diamond
B   Star, round, tree
C   Star, ring, tree
D   Square, ring, tree

(2 marks)

3.10   Which approach to system changeover has the highest risk?

A   Parallel
B   Direct
C   Pilot
D   Phased

(2 marks)

(Total = 20 marks)

4 Objective test questions: Information systems 1   36 mins

Required

Each of the sub-questions numbered **4.1** to **4.5** below require a brief written response. Each sub-question is worth 4 marks. The response should be in note form and should not exceed 50 words.

4.1   Explain the relationship between 'data independence' and a database approach to flexible data management.

(4 marks)

`11/05`

4.2   Explain the difference between centralised and distributed processing.   **(4 marks)**

4.3   Identify four methods of gathering information in the systems analysis process and briefly explain the merits of each method.   **(4 marks)**

4.4   Briefly explain the main factors management should take into account when choosing computer hardware.

(4 marks)

`11/05`

4.5   Identify and explain three types of system maintenance.   **(4 marks)**

(Total for these sub-questions = 20 marks)

5 Objective test questions: Information systems 2   36 mins

Required

Each of the sub-questions numbered **5.1** to **5.5** below require a brief written response. Each sub-question is worth 4 marks. The response should be in note form and should not exceed 50 words.

5.1   Describe the main benefits of in-house developed information systems.   **(4 marks)**

`Pilot paper`

5.2   Describe the main advantages of an organisation developing and using an 'extranet'.   **(4 marks)**

`5/05`

5.3   Explain the relationship between open systems and adaptive maintenance.   **(4 marks)**

`5/05`

5.4   Parallel running and pilot schemes are methods of systems changeover. Explain the reasons why an organisation might instead choose a direct approach to a system changeover.   **(4 marks)**

`5/05`

5.5   Explain the reasons why a department of an organisation might be continuing to use manual records rather than using a new, recently installed and fully operational computer system.   **(4 marks)**

`5/05`

(Total for these sub-questions = 20 marks)

If you struggled with the MCQ and OT questions in Q1-Q5, go back to your BPP Study Text for Paper P4 and revise Chapters 1, 2 and 3 before you tackle the longer questions on Information Systems.

6 Entity relationship model

54 mins

An entity-relationship model (ERM) is structured around three concepts; **entities**, **attributes** relating to entities and the **relationships** between entities.

Required

(a) Explain each of the three concepts identified above and describe the notation used to portray these in an ERM (do not draw diagrams at this stage). **(9 marks)**

(b) List four attributes likely to be recorded for the entity 'Student'. **(4 marks)**

(c) You have been provided with the following information regarding B limited.

- B Limited consists of five departments
- Each department has a number of employees
- Departments are headed by one Departmental Manager
- The Departmental Managers together form the Managerial Board
- These five managers are paid by monthly salary. They are on the monthly payroll
- Some of the other employees are also salaried and are paid on the monthly payroll
- The remaining employees receive weekly wages and are paid on the weekly payroll

What type of relationship exists between the following entities?

(i) B Limited and Department
(ii) Department and Employee
(iii) Department and Departmental Manager
(iv) Managerial Board and Departmental Manager
(v) Employee and Weekly payroll **(5 marks)**

(d) Describe the purpose and notation of an Entity Life History (ELH) model. **(4 marks)**

(e) Produce an ELH model to show the following situation related to students studying at a community college. Your model should show the information provided in the text below.

Entity name, Student

Three processes: Enrol; Study; Leave

Students study one or more Courses

Courses are classified as either Vocational or Qualification

Each Qualification course has an Assessment

Assessment results are either 'Pass' or 'Fail' **(8 marks)**

(Total = 30 marks)

7 Data flow diagram errors

54 mins

Four systems design tools/techniques are listed below.

- Data Flow Diagram
- Entity Relationship Models
- Entity Life Histories
- Decision Tables

Required

(a)   Explain both the purpose of each technique and how each of the techniques assist the systems analyst in the system design process.   **(20 marks)**

An analyst has recorded the following information at an interview and documented this information in the following data flow diagram.

> Orders are received directly from customers. The order details are checked to ensure that the product and payment-type are valid values. Rejected orders are sent back to the customer. Accepted order details are stored on an order file. At the end of the day, despatch notes are raised for all orders received that day. A copy of the despatch note is sent to the customer and a second copy is sent to the warehouse. The despatch-date is noted on the order file. At the end of the week an invoice is raised and sent to the customer. The invoice-date is noted on the order file.

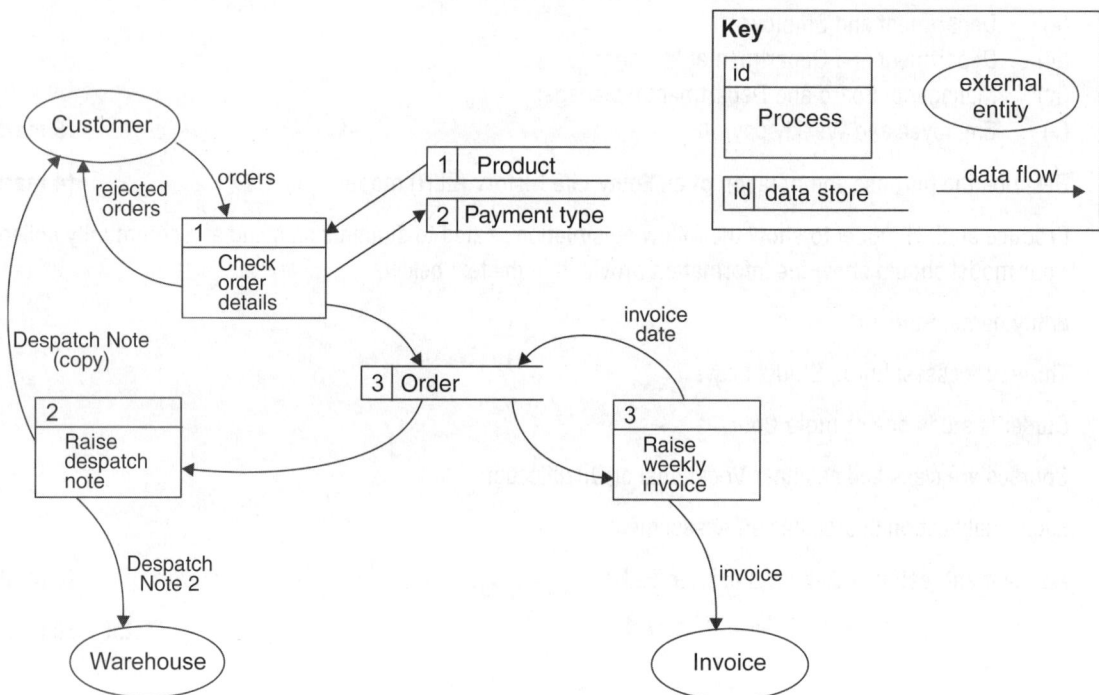

(b)   Analyse the diagram above to identify *three* errors in the diagram and explain how each error should be corrected.   **(9 marks)**

(c)   At which stage of systems development would a data flow diagram be used?   **(1 mark)**

(Total = 30 marks)

8 Decision table and software testing   **54 mins**

The following business rules are to be introduced by car insurance.com limited.

'The standard quote value is given if the car is garaged and the insured is willing to pay a £250 excess on the policy. An excess, in this instance, means that the insured has to bear the first £250 of the claim. The insured can also ask for the removal of the £250 excess condition. This leads to their standard quote value being increased by 5%. If the car is not garaged, then a further £100 is added to the standard quote value '.

Required

(a)   Construct a decision table for an insurance quotation using the above business rules.   **(9 marks)**

(b)   Briefly explain how this decision table will contribute to testing the software that automates these business rules.   **(3 marks)**

Two important aspects of testing are volume (performance) testing and usability testing.

(c)   Briefly describe the role and conduct of volume (performance) testing.   **(3 marks)**

(d)   Briefly describe the role and conduct of user acceptance testing.   **(3 marks)**

The new rules introduced by car insurance.com represent a radical change in company policy.

(e)   Identify six techniques the company could use to overcome any user resistance to the change in policy and list two examples for each technique of how the company could implement them.   **(12 marks)**

(Total = 30 marks)

9 Question with student answer: System development   **36 mins**

Five stages associated with a computerised information system development process are listed below.

Identify and explain the main activities carried out during each of these stages.

• Planning and feasibility	**(4 marks)**
• Analysis	**(4 marks)**
• Design	**(4 marks)**
• Development	**(2 marks)**
• Implementation	**(6 marks)**

(Total = 20 marks)

This question and answer was produced prior to the recent changes in exam format. It is included here as it is a good example of an actual student answer.

10 Multiple choice questions: Operations management 1 36 mins

10.1   International standard ISO 14001 'Environmental Management Systems' encourages processes for controlling and improving an organisation's

     A   performance on 'green' issues

     B   performance on quality issues as they relate to the competitive environment

     C   performance on scanning an industry environment

     D   performance on its internal investment in people   **(2 marks)**

11/05

10.2   What is 'Theory Z'?

     A   An addition to McGregor's motivation theory

     B   The application of Japanese managerial practices into Western culture

     C   An explanation of how the attainment of career paths by individuals results in lack of association with a specific company

     D   The last theory produced by Maslow, relating to the application of hygiene factors to the Japanese model of lean production   **(2 marks)**

10.3   The 5-S model refers to

     A   internal analysis involving structure, sub-structure, systems, sub-systems and strategy.

     B   internal analysis involving style, shared values, skills, staffing and "soft" information.

     C   operations management practices of structurise, systematise, sanitise, standardise and self-discipline.

     D   the Japanese six-sigma model adapted to Western practice.   **(2 marks)**

5/06

10.4   Which one of the following best describes the ABC inventory management system?

     A   Monitors inventory levels, so when these drop below a critical level, more inventory is ordered

     B   Requires that inventory is counted on a regular basis (perhaps every week) and re-ordered as necessary

     C   Focuses inventory management on the 20% of items (representing 80% of inventory expenditure) which need careful monitoring

     D   Identifies the amount of buffer stock required to ensure that stockouts are kept to a minimum   **(2 marks)**

10.5   What type of benchmarking involves a direct comparison with a competitor, with a view to make substantial organisational changes?

     A   Competitive benchmarking

     B   Functional benchmarking

     C   Operational benchmarking

     D   Strategic benchmarking   **(2 marks)**

10.6 Gaining International Standards (ISO) in quality is mainly dependent upon

A effective processes for documentation and control.
B a shared quality philosophy.
C commitment from middle managers.
D benchmarking customer related performance against competitors.

(2 marks)
5/06

10.7 Which one of the following statements is incorrect?

A A key concept in the total quality management (TQM) philosophy is consistency
B An important aspect of TQM is achieving customer satisfaction
C An aspect of TQM is kaizen, or continuous improvement
D An objective of TQM is to identify all defective output

(2 marks)

10.8 The 5S philosophy of quality management is based on five Japanese words beginning with the letter S and translated into an English equivalent word, also beginning with an S. If four of the S words are structurise, systemise, self-discipline and standardise, which of the following is the fifth?

A Seek
B Strive
C Succeed
D Sanitise

(2 marks)

10.9 Kaizen is a quality improvement technique that involves

A continuous improvement by small incremental steps.
B a complete revision of all organisational processes and structures.
C immediate, often radical "right first time" changes to practice.
D a problem solving fishbone technique to identify cause and effect.

(2 marks)
5/06

10.10 Which one of the following statements represents the ultimate aim of Total Quality Management (TQM)?

A Eliminate the costs of poor quality
B Eliminate all quality-related costs
C Reduce costs of poor quality
D Reduce the workforce

(2 marks)

(Total = 20 marks)

11 Multiple choice questions: Operations management 2   36 mins

11.1 Which one of the following statements relating to Statistical Process Control (SPC) is true?

A SPC eliminates poor quality
B SPC measures product specifications
C SPC requires 24 hour supervision
D SPC measures process variability

(2 marks)

11.2 Which one of the following statements relating to Quality Management is true?

A Internal failure due to poor quality has no effect on delivery time
B Reducing internal failure reduces losses of capacity
C As the quality level of a process increases, appraisal costs will go up due to increased testing effort
D The cheapest way to improve quality is to increase post-production inspection

(2 marks)

11.3 Which one of the following is a likely result of introducing Total Quality Management (TQM)?

    A   Reduced trade union activity
    B   Shorter working day
    C   Tighter control over employees
    D   Decreased output inspection   **(2 marks)**

11.4 Which of the following is sometimes used to refer to the process of 'continuous improvement'?

    A   Kaizen
    B   Six Sigma
    C   Lean principles
    D   Kanban   **(2 marks)**

11.5 Lean production (or lean manufacturing) is a system originally developed for which organisation?

    A   IBM
    B   General Electric
    C   Toyota
    D   Weight watchers   **(2 marks)**

11.6 Which one of the following is shown in the centre or 'hub' of the strategic supply wheel model developed by *Cousins*?

    A   Corporate and supply strategy
    B   Portfolio of relationships
    C   Cost/benefit analysis
    D   Skills and competencies   **(2 marks)**

11.7 Which one of the following options represents possible supply sourcing strategies?

    A   Internal, external and combined
    B   Local, regional, national and international
    C   On-line, off-line, domestic and overseas
    D   Single, multi, parallel and delegated   **(2 marks)**

11.8 Which one of the following describes a level capacity plan?

    A   Activity and demand are always both stable
    B   Activity is maintained at maximum levels
    C   Activity is maintained at minimum levels
    D   Activity is maintained at a constant level regardless of demand   **(2 marks)**

11.9 Which one of the following describes a chase demand plan?

    A   Activity is adjusted depending upon demand
    B   Activity is maintained at maximum levels
    C   Activity is maintained at minimum levels
    D   Activity is maintained at a constant level regardless of demand   **(2 marks)**

11.10 The five S (5-S) practice is a technique aimed at achieving

    A   Effective investment of resources in training and recruitment
    B   Standardised procedures to improve the physical and thinking organisational environments
    C   Excellence in strategy, style, skills, staff and structure
    D   Diversity of activity and independence of thought in order to achieve closeness to the customer

    (2 marks)
    Pilot paper

    (Total = 20 marks)

12 Multiple choice questions: Operations management 3 36 mins

12.1 Core features of world-class manufacturing involve

    A   Competitor benchmarking and an investment in training and development
    B   An investment in IT and technical skills
    C   Global sourcing networks and an awareness of competitor strategies
    D   A strong customer focus and flexibility to meet customer requirements   **(2 marks)**

5/05

12.2 An ABC system refers to

    A   A Japanese style problem solving device that is particularly helpful in inventory management
    B   An inventory management method that concentrates effort on the most important items
    C   Accuracy, brevity and clarity in the quality of system reporting
    D   A mainframe solution to managing inventory   **(2 marks)**

5/05

12.3 Corrective work, the cost of scrap and materials lost are

    A   Examples of internal failure costs
    B   Examples of external failure costs
    C   Examples of appraisal costs
    D   Examples of preventative costs   **(2 marks)**

5/05

12.4 Economies of scope refers to

    A   The economic viability of making alterations to systems
    B   An organisation becoming economically viable through a process of 'rightsizing'
    C   Mass production assembly lines achieving economies through volume of output
    D   Economically producing small batches of a variety of products with the same machines   **(2 marks)**

5/05

12.5 *Reck* and *Long*'s strategic positioning tool identifies an organisation's

    A   Purchasing approach
    B   Sales approach
    C   Manufacturing approach
    D   Warehousing approach   **(2 marks)**

5/05

12.6 Inbound logistics is

    A   A secondary activity that refers to price negotiation of incoming raw materials
    B   A secondary activity that refers to receipt, storage and inward distribution of raw materials
    C   A primary activity that refers to inbound enquiries and customer complaints
    D   A primary activity that refers to receipt, storage and inward distribution of raw materials   **(2 marks)**

5/05

12.7 Supply chain partnerships grow out of

    A   Quality accreditation
    B   Recognising the supply chain and linkages in a value system
    C   An expansion of trade
    D   Adopting a marketing philosophy   **(2 marks)**

5/05

12.8 Training workers in methods of statistical process control and work analysis

    A   Overcomes a crisis of control in an organisation's life cycle
    B   Is part of a succession planning approach to Human Resources
    C   Is part of a quality management approach
    D   Is part of a scientific management approach   **(2 marks)**

5/05

12.9 Which of the following statements is true in relation to JIT?

    A   JIT means more funds tied up in stock than with traditional production
    B   JIT is not compatible with TQM
    C   Stock-outs are more likely with JIT than with traditional production
    D   Buffer stocks are common under JIT   **(2 marks)**

12.10 Quality management thinker J.M. Juran has suggested that 85% of an organisations quality problems are

    A   A result of ineffective control by supervisors and mangers
    B   A result of ineffective systems
    C   A result of ineffective workers
    D   A result of ineffective bonus schemes   **(2 marks)**

Pilot paper

(Total = 20 marks)

13 Objective test questions: Operations management 1 36 mins

Required

Each of the sub-questions numbered **19.1** to **19.5** below require a brief written response. Each sub-question is worth 4 marks. The response should be in note form and should not exceed 50 words.

13.1 Distinguish Quality Assurance (QA) systems from quality control systems.   **(4 marks)**

11/05

13.2 Describe the relationship between operations management and (using Mintzberg's terminology) the organisational technostructure.   **(4 marks)**

5/06

13.3 Explain how continuous inventory systems might work against an organisation's Just-in- Time (JIT) philosophy.   **(4 marks)**

5/06

13.4   Identify examples of external failure costs, and explain their significance for an organisation with a
        reputation for quality.   **(4 marks)**

        `5/06`

13.5   Distinguish between business automation, business rationalisation and business process re-engineering.
                                                                                             (4 marks)

                                                    (Total for these sub-questions = 20 marks)

14 Objective test questions: Operations management 2 36 mins

Required

Each of the sub-questions numbered **21.1** to **21.5** below require a brief written response. Each sub-question is
worth 4 marks. The response should be in note form and should not exceed 50 words.

14.1   Explain the relationship between a (Just in Time) JIT system and cash flow management.   **(4 marks)**

        `Pilot paper`

14.2   Explain how computer software can assist in achieving quality in a manufacturing organisation.   **(4 marks)**

        `Pilot paper`

14.3   Distinguish quality control from quality circles.   **(4 marks)**

        `Pilot paper`

14.4   Describe the ways in which Total Productive Maintenance might contribute towards a manufacturing
        organisation's quality programme.   **(4 marks)**

        `5/05`

14.5   Explain the philosophy of TQM.   **(4 marks)**

                                                    (Total for these sub-questions = 20 marks)

If you struggled with the MCQ and OT questions in Q10-Q14, go back to your BPP Study Text for Paper P4 and
revise Chapters 4, 5 and 6 before you tackle the longer questions on Operations Management.

15 Virtual Companies and purchasing

54 mins

'In today's dynamic global business environment, forming a virtual company can be one of the most important strategic uses of information technology.' *O'Brien 2000*

Required

(a)   Define the term 'virtual company'.   **(2 marks)**

(b)   Explain how technological advances have enabled the widespread formation of virtual companies and supply chains.   **(8 marks)**

(c)   It is now widely recognised that an efficient purchasing department can add significantly to the competitive advantage of an organisation.

      Required

      Describe the function and operation of the purchasing department/function and explain how a well-managed purchasing department/function can contribute to effective organisational performance.   **(20 marks)**

(Total = 30 marks)

16 TQM and sourcing

54 mins

PicAPie Ltd employs a total quality management program and manufactures 12 different types of pie from chicken and leek to vegetarian. The directors of PicAPie are proud of their products, and always attempt to maintain a high quality of input at a reasonable price.

Each pie has four main elements:

*   Aluminium foil case
*   Pastry shell made mainly from flour and water
*   Meat and/or vegetable filling
*   Thin plastic wrapping

The products are obtained as follows:

*   The aluminium is obtained from a single supplier of metal related products. There are few suppliers in the industry resulting from fall in demand for aluminium related products following increased use of plastics.

*   The flour for the pastry shell is sourced from flour millers in four different countries – one source of supply is not feasible because harvests occur at different times and PicAPie cannot store sufficient flour from one harvest for a year's production.

*   Obtaining meat and vegetables is difficult due to the large number of suppliers located in many different countries. Recently, PicAPie obtained significant cost savings by delegating sourcing of these items to a specialist third party.

*   Plastic wrapping is obtained either directly from the manufacturer or via an Internet site specialising in selling surplus wrapping from government and other sources.

Required

(a)   Explain the main characteristics of a Total Quality Management (TQM) programme.   **(10 marks)**

(b)   Identify the sourcing strategies adopted by PicAPie and evaluate the effectiveness of those strategies for maintaining a constant and high quality supply of inputs. Your answer should also include recommendations for changes you consider necessary.   **(20 marks)**

(Total = 30 marks)

BPP
LEARNING MEDIA

17 Operations Management

54 mins

One important operations management task is balancing the amount an organisation is able to produce (capacity) with the amount they are able to sell (demand).

Required

(a)   Explain how the following planning and control activities help with balancing capacity and demand.

   (i)   Loading   **(6 marks)**
   (ii)   Sequencing and scheduling   **(8 marks)**
   (iii) Monitoring and controlling   **(6 marks)**

(b)   The 'Lean concept' and Six Sigma are popular contemporary theories with implications for operations management.

   (i)   Explain what the 'Lean concept' is and briefly explain one management tool or technique used under the Lean principles.   **(4 marks)**

   (ii)   Explain what Six Sigma is and identify a management tool or technique used in conjunction with Six Sigma.   **(6 marks)**

(Total = 30 marks)

18 Benchmarking and quality cost

54 mins

(a)   Within a diversified group, one division, which operates many similar branches in a service industry, has used internal benchmarking and regards it as very useful. Group central management is now considering the wider use of benchmarking.

   Required

   Explain the aims, operation, and limitations of internal benchmarking, and explain how external benchmarking differs in these respects.   **(20 marks)**

(b)   Another division within the group is involved in the manufacture of electrical appliances. This division recently implemented a general 'quality' initiative. Group central management have asked for general information relating to categories of quality costs.

   Required

   Prepare a briefing note that identifies and briefly explains four categories of quality costs – with a brief example for each category that is relevant to an electrical goods manufacturer.   **(10 marks)**

(Total = 30 marks)

MANAGING HUMAN CAPITAL

Questions 19 to 33 cover Managing Human Capital, the subject of Part C of the BPP Study Text for Paper P4.

19 Multiple choice questions: Managing human capital 1   36 mins

19.1   F W Taylor's thinking on motivation in the workplace involved a belief that

     A   social groups and individuals as part of a culture should be key considerations
     B   reward for effort and workplace efficiency should be key considerations
     C   managers had two different sets of assumptions about their subordinates
     D   'motivators' and 'hygiene factors' should be key considerations   **(2 marks)**

     11/05

19.2   *Maslow*'s hierarchy of needs is an example of which kind of theory of motivation?

     A   Expectancy theory
     B   Process theory
     C   Equity theory
     D   Content theory   **(2 marks)**

19.3   Which one of the following options shows *Maslow*'s hierarchy of needs from bottom to top?

     A   Physiological, safety, love/social, esteem, self-actualisation
     B   Physical/safety, social/family, self-esteem, fulfilment
     C   Physical/safety, love/social, belonging, esteem, self-actualisation
     D   Physiological/safety, family, social, esteem, self-actualisation   **(2 marks)**

19.4   360 degree feedback is part of a system that encourages

     A   organisational appraisal based on feedback from customers and suppliers

     B   organisational appraisal based on relative industry and competitor performance

     C   performance appraisal based on feedback from peers, subordinates, line managers and even external parties

     D   personal appraisal based on line manager feedback and self-appraisal documentation   **(2 marks)**

     11/05

19.5   In terms of employment CIMA's ethical guidelines require members to

     A   act responsibly in the way that all other professionals do
     B   act responsibly but in a way that satisfies organisational demands and pressures
     C   act responsibly but in a way that satisfies the individual's own ethical code
     D   act responsibly, honour any legal contract of employment and conform to employment legislation   **(2 marks)**

     11/05

19.6 An assessment centre

    A   Helps selection by assessing job candidates by using a comprehensive and interrelated series of techniques

    B   Is the training headquarters where job interviews take place

    C   Is a desk based process of reviewing job application forms for suitability

    D   Is the place where job applicants are subjected to psychological testing   **(2 marks)**

5/05

19.7 Which one of the following is true?

    A   Managers aren't required to comply with organisational policies and procedures
    B   Employee compliance is typically based on the threat of disciplinary action
    C   Employee compliance relies on a strong organisation culture
    D   Employee compliance is typically based on tight formal controls   **(2 marks)**

19.8 There are three observable and measurable types of target that can be derived from training objectives. Which of the following is not one of them?

    A   Behaviour – what the trainee should be able to do
    B   Standard – to what level of performance
    C   Commitment – with what degree of motivation
    D   Environment – under what conditions   **(2 marks)**

19.9 Which one of the following shows the four learning styles identified by *Honey and Mumford*?

    A   Activist, reflector, conceptualist, theorist
    B   Pragmatist, reflector, activist, theorist
    C   Theorist, experimenter, reflector, pragmatist
    D   Processor, reflector, theorist, activator   **(2 marks)**

19.10 Which one of the following is a feature of human resource management as distinct from personnel management?

    A   Industrial relations research
    B   Development of incentive and reward programmes
    C   Training activities
    D   Setting policy for employment relationships   **(2 marks)**

(Total = 20 marks)

20 Multiple choice questions: Managing human capital 2

36 mins

20.1 Which one of the following is unlikely to be a feature of a successful incentive scheme?

A   Profit sharing

B   A clear link between performance and reward

C   Significant influence by uncontrollable factors

D   Key results are identified and specified in detail   **(2 marks)**

20.2 The use of standard questions in job interviews help ensure

A   Fairness

B   Validity

C   Reliability

D   Completeness   **(2 marks)**

5/05

20.3 A climate of learning or a learning climate is a feature of a learning organisation. Which one of the following would not help create such a climate?

A   A remuneration scheme that rewards successful innovation and penalises failed experiment

B   A culture of continuous improvement

C   A senior management lead in questioning their own assumptions

D   Creation of processes to move knowledge around   **(2 marks)**

20.4 Occupational (or work-based) competences relate to the outputs and standards required in specific workplace roles. Which one of the following is not a specific occupational competence for a payroll clerk?

A   An awareness of income tax rates

B   The ability to communicate clearly in writing

C   An awareness of relevant overtime agreements

D   The ability to prepare monthly summary payroll cost report   **(2 marks)**

20.5 Which one of the following is the factor that *Taylor* believed would be most effective in motivating workers?

A   Remuneration levels

B   Job security

C   Good working conditions

D   Minimal supervision   **(2 marks)**

20.6 An employee who exposes the ethical misconduct of others in an organisation is known as a(n):

A   Ombudsman

B   Whistleblower

C   Auditor

D   None of the above   **(2 marks)**

20.7 Consider this statement. 'Just as many young people starting work in developed countries today will spend their entire career within a single organisations as was the case thirty years ago'. Which one of the following options is the most suitable response to this statement?

A   The statement is true

B   Without detailed statistics we can't judge the statement

C   The statement is false

D   This situation reflects a lack of 'backbone' in young people today   **(2 marks)**

20.8 One possible problem with interviews as a recruitment selection tool is 'the halo effect'. What is the halo effect?

A The interviewer might make a general judgement about the interviewee on the basis of a single attribute or characteristic

B The interviewer might make an incorrect assessment of the qualities of the interviewee

C The interviewer might stereotype the interviewee on the basis of appearance or spoken accent

D The interviewee may attempt to respond to questions in a way that he or she thinks the interviewer wants to hear

(2 marks)

20.9 Ensuring diversity within an organisation is likely to lead to:

A An increased number of potential candidates for each job
B Wider points of view within the organisation
C A more representative workforce
D All of the other options **(2 marks)**

20.10 Which one of the follwing statements best represents the principle of 'integrity' as explained in CIMA's Ehical Guidelines?

A Professional accountants must not tell lies
B Professional accountants must not be party to anything which is deceptive or misleading
C Professional accountants can not be expected to resign over a matter of principle
D Integrity is almost as important as technical competence **(2 marks)**

(Total = 20 marks)

21 Multiple choice questions: Managing human capital 3

36 mins

21.1 When someone commences a new job, the process of familiarisation is known as

A Probationary period
B Recruitment
C Appraisal
D Induction **(2 marks)**
Pilot paper

21.2 An effective appraisal system involves

A Assessing the personality of the appraisee
B A process initiated by the manager who needs an update from the appraisee
C Advising on the faults of the appraisee
D A participative, problem-solving process between the manager and appraisee **(2 marks)**
Pilot paper

21.3 The motivating potential score, developed by *Hackman* and *Oldham*, is calculated to assess

    A   The knowledge of an individual
    B   The satisfaction with work
    C   The content of the job
    D   The quality of work performed

(2 marks)

Pilot paper

21.4 Job rotation involves

    A   A redesign of a person's post based upon job analysis
    B   The movement of an individual to another post in order to gain experience
    C   The expansion and enrichment of a person's job content
    D   The relocation of a post holder in order to benefit from the experience of a number of potential mentors

(2 marks)

Pilot paper

21.5 A grievance procedure is established by an organisation in order that

    A   There is a standing process to deal with the arbitration of disputes
    B   The organisation can fairly discipline members of the workforce for wrongdoing
    C   The workforce might formally raise issues where ill treatment has occurred
    D   Collective bargaining between the employer's side and the workforce might proceed smoothly

(2 marks)

Pilot paper

21.6 An 'assessment centre' approach is used

    A   As part of an appraisal process
    B   As part of a process of training and development
    C   As part of a selection process
    D   As part of an exit interview process

(2 marks)

Pilot paper

21.7 Selection tests that fail to produce similar results over time when taken by the same candidate are

    A   Contradictory
    B   Unreliable
    C   Too general
    D   Unstable

(2 marks)

Pilot paper

21.8 The so-called 'psychological contract' is a notion that is based on

    A   Segmenting then accessing a market
    B   The buyer/supplier relationship
    C   A distinctive style of testing used in selection procedures
    D   The expectations the organisation and employee have of one another

(2 marks)

5/05

21.9 According to *Douglas McGregor*

A 'Theory X' people dislike work, need direction and avoid responsibility
B 'Theory Y' people dislike work, need direction and avoid responsibility
C Self actualising people dislike work, need direction and avoid responsibility
D Hygiene factors determine whether people like work, need direction or take responsibility **(2 marks)**

5/05

21.10 The purpose of a person specification is to provide details of

A Organisational size and diversity of activity
B The types of responsibilities and duties to be undertaken by the post holder
C Personal characteristics, experience and qualifications expected of a candidate
D Individual terms of engagement and period of contract **(2 marks)**

5/05

(Total = 20 marks)

22 Multiple choice questions: Managing human capital 4

36 mins

22.1 Charles Handy's vision of a 'shamrock' organisation suggests a workforce that comprises three different type of worker, namely

A strategic, operational and support.
B qualified, trainee and unskilled.
C 'white collar', 'blue collar' and e-worker.
D core, contractual and flexible labour. **(2 marks)**

5/06

22.2 Job family structures are examples of

A motivational tools.
B similar levels of responsibility reflected across several distinct functions or disciplines.
C Japanese employment practice.
D pay structures for jobs within distinct functions or disciplines. **(2 marks)**

5/06

22.3 Abraham Maslow's theory of motivation is often represented as

A a hierarchy of needs.
B individual behaviour labelled X or Y.
C a scientific relationship between work and reward.
D a series of negative and a series of positive factors. **(2 marks)**

5/06

22.4 The set of activities designed to familiarise a new employee with an organisation is called

A job analysis.
B induction.
C selection.
D manipulation and co-optation. **(2 marks)**

5/06

22.5 Recruitment involves

    A   advertising a vacancy and interviewing.
    B   conducting interviews and tests.
    C   advertising a vacancy and initial screening of candidates.
    D   ensuring that contract negotiation complies with organisational policy.

(2 marks)

`5/06`

22.6 Three hundred and sixty (360) degree feedback is normally associated with

    A   exit interviews.
    B   quality circle activity.
    C   appraisal processes.
    D   reflection as part of a cycle of learning.

(2 marks)

`5/06`

22.7 The processes of job analysis and individual performance appraisal are related in the sense that

    A   they are different terms for the same process
    B   performance appraisal is based on job analysis
    C   both form part of the selection process
    D   job analysis is based on performance appraisal

(2 marks)

`11/05`

22.8 Content theories of motivation tend to focus mainly on

    A   the needs of the group
    B   feelings of complacency or dissatisfaction
    C   the needs of individuals
    D   the use of 'carrots' and 'sticks' as devices

(2 marks)

`11/05`

22.9 Third party consultants, therapy groups and confrontation are normally all associated with

    A   industrial disputes over terms and conditions
    B   the process of job evaluation
    C   a firm experiencing severe trading difficulties
    D   organisational development (OD)

(2 marks)

`11/05`

22.10 It is the role of 'outplacement consultants' to

    A   provide help to redundant employees including training and finding jobs
    B   provide help to employees wishing to gain experience in other roles
    C   arrange for placing products in an untested market place
    D   arrange for placing under-used assets at the disposal of start up businesses

(2 marks)

`11/05`

(Total = 20 marks)

23 Objective test questions: Managing human capital 1

36 mins

Required

Each of the sub-questions numbered **21.1** to **21.5** below require a brief written response. Each sub-question is worth 4 marks. The response should be in note form and should not exceed 50 words.

23.1	Briefly explain Schein's categories of worker.	(4 marks)
23.2	Briefly state the two advantages and two disadvantages of in-house training.	(4 marks)
23.3	List four questions that could determine whether a Profit Related Pay scheme would be effective.	(4 marks)
23.4	Explain the four main elements of the human resource cycle.	(4 marks)
23.5	Explain three general purposes of appraisal.	(4 marks)

(Total for these sub-questions = 20 marks)

24 Objective test questions: Managing human capital 2

36 mins

Required

Each of the sub-questions numbered **22.1** to **22.5** below require a brief written response. Each sub-question is worth 4 marks. The response should be in note form and should not exceed 50 words.

24.1	Outline *Lawrence and Lorsch's* contingency theory.	(4 marks)
24.2	Distinguish between recruitment and selection.	(4 marks)
24.3	Explain what a 'hygiene factor' is in relation to employment and provide an example.	(4 marks)
24.4	Identify and explain the potential benefits of flexible working to the employer and to the employee.	(4 marks)
24.5	Identify the main stages involved in developing human resource plans and programmes following the production of a corporate plan.	(4 marks)

5/06

(Total for these sub-questions = 20 marks)

If you struggled with the MCQ and OT questions in Q19-Q24, go back to your BPP Study Text for Paper P4 and revise Chapters 7, 8 and 9 before you tackle the longer questions on Managing Human Capital.

25 Maslow

54 mins

Employees in the Marina Manufacturing Company (MMC) have been complaining recently about their basic salary. They have two main areas of complaint:

- Firstly, the overall wage rates are slightly above the industry average although significant amounts of overtime are worked, and

- Secondly, there is no incentive to work any faster; they are paid an hourly wage regardless of the number of items produced on the production lines each day.

The Human Resources Director has promised to implement some revised remuneration system in the near future which will hopefully address the employees' concerns. At a board meeting to discuss the new remuneration system, the personnel director made the following suggestions:

- All salaries to be increased by 20% pa

- A Performance Related Pay scheme to be introduced applying to total factory production. Performance bonus to be paid when production exceeds the factory average production for the last four weeks.

- Annual review of salaries and PRP starting in 18 months time.

The board were generally in favour of the changes, although concern was expressed that funding a 20% wage increase would require redundancies.

Required

(a)   Explain Maslow's hierarchy of needs, briefly identifying any problems with the theory.   **(8 marks)**

(a)   Describe the general purpose of, and common objectives of, a performance appraisal system.   **(10 marks)**

(c)   With reference to Maslow's theory, discuss the weaknesses in the PRP scheme suggested by the Human Resources Director and suggest methods of overcoming those weaknesses.   **(12 marks)**

(Total = 30 marks)

26 HR division and Strategy (11/05 – original)

36 mins

NS is a large insurance company. The company is structured into four Divisions and supported by a small headquarters that includes the personnel function (recently renamed the Human Resources (HR) Division). The post of Head of HR is vacant following the retirement of the long serving post holder, and the HR strategy is in urgent need of review and revision.

NS has recently announced a new corporate initiative of continuous improvement through the empowerment of its workforce. The Chief Executive explained: 'we value our people as our most prized asset. We will encourage them to think, challenge and innovate. Only through empowering them in this way can we achieve continuous improvement. Staff will no longer be expected just to obey orders, from now on they will make and implement decisions to being about continuous improvement. We want to develop clear performance objectives and be more customer focused.'

Your line manager is one of the four Divisional directors and will soon form part of a panel that will interview candidates for the vacant role of HR director. She is particularly keen to ensure that the successful candidate would be able to shape the HR Division to the needs of the organisation. She is aware of your CIMA studies and has asked for your help in preparing for the interview.

Required

Produce outline notes for your Divisional director which discuss the main points you would expect candidates to highlight in response to the following two areas she intends to explore with candidates at the interview, specifically:

(a)   The likely role that the HR Division will perform in the light of the changing nature of the organisation; and

(10 marks)

(b)   The aspects of the HR strategy that will change significantly, given the nature of recent developments within NS.   **(10 marks)**

(Total = 20 marks)

27 HR division and Strategy (11/05 – amended)   54 mins

NS is a large insurance company. The company is structured into four Divisions and supported by a small headquarters that includes the personnel function (recently renamed the Human Resources (HR) Division).

(a)   (i)   State two objectives of human resource management (HRM)   **(2 marks)**

(ii)   Explain why HRM is important to organisations such as NS insurance.   **(8 marks)**

The post of Head of HR is vacant following the retirement of the long serving post holder, and the HR strategy is in urgent need of review and revision.

NS has recently announced a new corporate initiative of continuous improvement through the empowerment of its workforce. The Chief Executive explained: 'we value our people as our most prized asset. We will encourage them to think, challenge and innovate. Only through empowering them in this way can we achieve continuous improvement. Staff will no longer be expected just to obey orders, from now on they will make and implement decisions to being about continuous improvement. We want to develop clear performance objectives and be more customer focused.'

Your line manager is one of the four Divisional directors and will soon form part of a panel that will interview candidates for the vacant role of HR director. She is particularly keen to ensure that the successful candidate would be able to shape the HR Division to the needs of the organisation. She is aware of your CIMA studies and has asked for your help in preparing for the interview.

Required

Produce outline notes for your Divisional director which discuss the main points you would expect candidates to highlight in response to the following two areas she intends to explore with candidates at the interview, specifically:

(b)   The likely role that the HR Division will perform in the light of the changing nature of the organisation; and

(10 marks)

(c)   The aspects of the HR strategy that will change significantly, given the nature of recent developments within NS.   **(10 marks)**

(Total = 30 marks)

28 Question with answer plan: Human resource plan and activities (Pilot paper – original)

36 mins

A year ago, the owner-manager of a taxi service also moved into a new business area of fitting tyres. This came about as a result of the experience of using unbranded tyres on the fleet of ten taxis. Based on several years of use, the owner-manager found that the unbranded tyres lasted almost as long as the branded tyres, but had the advantage of being obtainable at half the price. The set-up costs of the tyre-fitting business were relatively modest and the owner-manager initially fitted the tyres himself. Demand picked up quickly, however, and he was forced to employ an experienced fitter. A few months later, demand accelerated again and he has just advertised for another fitted but, unfortunately, without success.

The tyre-fitting business has produced additional challenges and the owner-manager is finding it increasingly difficult to manage both the taxi service and the new business where he seems to be spending more and more of his time. He already employs one receptionist/taxi controller, but has realised that he now needs another.

As if this were not enough, he is in the middle of extending his operations still further. Customers who buy tyres frequently request that he check the wheel alignment on their car following the fitting of new tyres. He has started to provide this service, but when done manually it is a slow process, so he has invested heavily in a new piece of electronic equipment. This new technology will speed the alignment operation considerably, but neither he nor his tyre-fitter can operate the equipment. The owner feels that tyre fitters should be able to operate the equipment, and an additional member of staff is not required just to operate it.

To add to all these problems, two of his taxi drivers have resigned unexpectedly. Past patterns suggests that of the ten drivers, normally one or two leave each year, generally in the summer months, though now it is winter.

Given all these staffing difficulties, the owner-manager has made use of a relative who happens to have some HR expertise. She has advised the owner-manager on recruitment and selection, training and development. The relative also suggests that the business needs a well thought out human resource plan.

Required

(a)   Prepare an outline human resource plan for the business and explain each aspect of your plan.   **(12 marks)**

(b)   Discuss the important human resource activities to which attention should be paid in order to obtain the maximum contribution from the workforce.   **(8 marks)**

(Total = 20 marks)

Important. For requirement (b), exclude those areas upon which the relative has already provided advice to the owner-manager (recruitment and selection, training and development).

---

29 Question with answer plan: Human resource plan and activities (Pilot paper – amended)

54 mins

Much has been written about the need to treat candidates fairly and equally when recruiting or selecting.

Required

(a)   Explain the difference between recruitment and selection.   **(4 marks)**
(b)   Discuss how organisations can review and improve their recruitment policy and practice.   **(14 marks)**

A year ago, the owner-manager of a taxi service also moved into a new business area of fitting tyres. This came about as a result of the experience of using unbranded tyres on the fleet of ten taxis. Based on several years of use, the owner-manager found that the unbranded tyres lasted almost as long as the branded tyres, but had the advantage of being obtainable at half the price. The set-up costs of the tyre-fitting business were relatively modest

BPP
LEARNING MEDIA

and the owner-manager initially fitted the tyres himself. Demand picked up quickly, however, and he was forced to employ an experienced fitter. A few months later, demand accelerated again and he has just advertised for another fitter but, unfortunately, without success.

The tyre-fitting business has produced additional challenges and the owner-manager is finding it increasingly difficult to manage both the taxi service and the new business where he seems to be spending more and more of his time. He already employs one receptionist/taxi controller, but has realised that he now needs another.

As if this were not enough, he is in the middle of extending his operations still further. Customers who buy tyres frequently request that he check the wheel alignment on their car following the fitting of new tyres. He has started to provide this service, but when done manually it is a slow process, so he has invested heavily in a new piece of electronic equipment. This new technology will speed the alignment operation considerably, but neither he nor his tyre-fitter can operate the equipment. The owner feels that tyre fitters should be able to operate the equipment, and an additional member of staff is not required just to operate it.

To add to all these problems, two of his taxi drivers have resigned unexpectedly. Past patterns suggests that of the ten drivers, normally one or two leave each year, generally in the summer months, though now it is winter.

Given all these staffing difficulties, the owner-manager has made use of a relative who happens to have some HR expertise. She has advised the owner-manager on recruitment and selection, training and development. The relative also suggests that the business needs a well thought out human resource plan.

Required

(c)   Prepare an outline human resource plan for the business and explain each aspect of your plan.   **(12 marks)**

(Total = 30 marks)

Important. For requirement (c), exclude those areas upon which the relative has already provided advice to the owner-manager (recruitment and selection, training and development).

---

30 HR plan and workforce flexibility (5/05 – original)   36 mins

The country Mythland contains several areas of high unemployment, one such area is where CX Beers were produced until recently. CX was an old, family-owned brewery that supplied licensed outlets, including local restaurants, with its beer. CX represented one of the last local brewers of any size, despite retaining many working practices that evolved at least a century ago. Situated on a (now) underused dockside site, the company had, over the years, invested little in plant and machinery and someone jokingly once suggested that much of the brewing equipment should rightfully be in a museum! The company was forced to cease trading last month, despite having an enthusiastic, long-serving, highly skilled workforce and a national reputation for the beer 'CX Winter Warmer' (thanks to winning several national awards). The workforce, many of whom have only ever worked for CX Beers are now facing up to the difficulty of finding alternative employment.

In a press statement the owners said that the brewery's closure was sad for the area, the local workforce and traditionally brewed beer in general. The owners blamed the situation on inefficient and expensive brewing methods, fierce competition from large rival brewers and limited geographical sales. They also mentioned a dependence on seasonal sales that made cash flow difficult (35% over the Christmas period). They concluded that they would like the CX tradition to continue by selling the company as a going concern, however unlikely this was.

It is speculated that property developers may be interested in the site as the dockland area is showing signs of regeneration as a leisure and tourism attraction (thanks to the efforts of the Mythland government). However, two of CX's managers would like to save the business and are drawing up a business plan for a management buy-out. They have three main initiatives that they feel could, in combination, save the enterprise:

- Use the site as a basis for a 'living' museum of traditionally brewed beer (with out of date brewing equipment and methods of working as an attraction)

- Produce bottled beer for sales in supermarkets

- Employ a more flexible but suitably experienced workforce

One of the managers (your former boss) has asked for your help in advising him how to draft a detailed human resource (HR) plan to inform the business plan.

Required

(a) Describe the main issues and stages involved in developing a human resource (HR) plan for the CX buy-out idea. **(12 marks)**

(b) Discuss how the buy-out team can achieve workforce flexibility. **(8 marks)**

(Total = 20 marks)

31 HR plan and workforce flexibility (5/05 – amended) 54 mins

The country Mythland contains several areas of high unemployment, one such area is where CX Beers were produced until recently. CX was an old, family-owned brewery that supplied licensed outlets, including local restaurants, with its beer. CX represented one of the last local brewers of any size, despite retaining many working practices that evolved at least a century ago. Situated on a (now) underused dockside site, the company had, over the years, invested little in plant and machinery and someone jokingly once suggested that much of the brewing equipment should rightfully be in a museum! The company was forced to cease trading last month, despite having an enthusiastic, long-serving, highly skilled workforce and a national reputation for the beer 'CX Winter Warmer' (thanks to winning several national awards). The workforce, many of whom have only ever worked for CX Beers are now facing up to the difficulty of finding alternative employment.

In a press statement the owners said that the brewery's closure was sad for the area, the local workforce and traditionally brewed beer in general. The owners blamed the situation on inefficient and expensive brewing methods, fierce competition from large rival brewers and limited geographical sales. They also mentioned a dependence on seasonal sales that made cash flow difficult (35% over the Christmas period). They concluded that they would like the CX tradition to continue by selling the company as a going concern, however unlikely this was.

It is speculated that property developers may be interested in the site as the dockland area is showing signs of regeneration as a leisure and tourism attraction (thanks to the efforts of the Mythland government). However, two of CX's managers would like to save the business and are drawing up a business plan for a management buy-out. They have three main initiatives that they feel could, in combination, save the enterprise:

- Use the site as a basis for a 'living' museum of traditionally brewed beer (with out of date brewing equipment and methods of working as an attraction)

- Produce bottled beer for sales in supermarkets

- Employ a more flexible but suitably experienced workforce

One of the managers (your former boss) has asked for your help in advising him how to draft a detailed human resource (HR) plan to inform the business plan.

Required

(a) Describe the main issues and stages involved in developing a human resource (HR) plan for the CX buy-out idea. **(12 marks)**

(b) Discuss how the buy-out team can achieve workforce flexibility. **(8 marks)**

(c) Describe five benefits to the new organisation and local community of re-employing previous employees. **(10 marks)**

(Total = 30 marks)

32 Motivation and reward (05/06 – original)   36 mins

CQ4 is a leading European industrial gas production company. CQ4's directors are each responsible for a geographical region containing several small strategic business units (SBUs). SBU managers report in monthly review meetings in great detail to their directors. CQ4 is showing signs of declining profitability and a new chief executive has been appointed and wishes to address the situation. She has complete freedom to identify organisational problems, solutions and strategies.

At their annual conference she tells SBU managers that they hold the key to improved company performance. She has a vision of CQ4 achieving longer-term strategic goals of increases in profitability, risk taking and innovation. Under the slogan 'support not report' directors will in future support and provide assistance to their managers to a greater degree, and the frequency and detail of reporting by managers will be reduced.

She announces two new initiatives 'to address the lost years when managers were prevented from delivering truly excellent CQ4 performance':

- Revision of the existing performance appraisal system. Bonuses paid on turnover will be replaced by performance related pay for achievement of individual 'performance target contracts'. Individual SBU managers will sign contracts to deliver these targets. Performance will now be reviewed at yearly rather than monthly meetings with directors. The remuneration and reward package will be adjusted appropriately with the current emphasis on increasing turnover shifting to profitability and innovation.

- A structural review to focus resources and efforts of SBUs on improving net profit. Part of the restructuring will involve SBUs no longer providing their own 'enabling' services such as finance, information technology, and health and safety. These 'distractions from doing the real job' will in future be organised centrally. SBUs will be given far greater responsibility, autonomy and influence over their own profitability.

She tells managers that she is stripping away the things that stop them doing their job properly. In return they must manage their SBU in the way they see most appropriate. They will be better rewarded and 'star achievers' will be fast tracked to senior positions. SBU managers are informed that the HR department has already been tasked with redesigning the remuneration and reward package.

Informal discussions amongst managers afterwards confirm that the new chief executive's message has been well received. Comments such as 'work might be more enjoyable without central interference' and 'for the first time I can do my job properly' were overheard.

Required

(a) Explain the thinking behind the two initiatives announced by the new chief executive using Herzberg's motivation-hygiene (dual factor) theory as a framework.   **(10 marks)**

(b) Discuss the factors that should be taken into account by the HR department when redesigning the remuneration and reward package for SBU managers.   **(10 marks)**

    (Total = 20 marks)

33 Motivation and reward (05/06 – amended)   54 mins

CQ4 is a leading European industrial gas production company. CQ4's directors are each responsible for a geographical region containing several small strategic business units (SBUs). SBU managers report in monthly review meetings in great detail to their directors. CQ4 is showing signs of declining profitability and a new chief executive has been appointed and wishes to address the situation. She has complete freedom to identify organisational problems, solutions and strategies.

At their annual conference she tells SBU managers that they hold the key to improved company performance. She has a vision of CQ4 achieving longer-term strategic goals of increases in profitability, risk taking and innovation.

Under the slogan 'support not report' directors will in future support and provide assistance to their managers to a greater degree, and the frequency and detail of reporting by managers will be reduced.

She announces two new initiatives 'to address the lost years when managers were prevented from delivering truly excellent CQ4 performance':

- Revision of the existing performance appraisal system. Bonuses paid on turnover will be replaced by performance related pay for achievement of individual 'performance target contracts'. Individual SBU managers will sign contracts to deliver these targets. Performance will now be reviewed at yearly rather than monthly meetings with directors. The remuneration and reward package will be adjusted appropriately with the current emphasis on increasing turnover shifting to profitability and innovation.

- A structural review to focus resources and efforts of SBUs on improving net profit. Part of the restructuring will involve SBUs no longer providing their own 'enabling' services such as finance, information technology, and health and safety. These 'distractions from doing the real job' will in future be organised centrally. SBUs will be given far greater responsibility, autonomy and influence over their own profitability.

She tells managers that she is stripping away the things that stop them doing their job properly. In return they must manage their SBU in the way they see most appropriate. They will be better rewarded and 'star achievers' will be fast tracked to senior positions. SBU managers are informed that the HR department has already been tasked with redesigning the remuneration and reward package.

Informal discussions amongst managers afterwards confirm that the new chief executive's message has been well received. Comments such as 'work might be more enjoyable without central interference' and 'for the first time I can do my job properly' were overheard.

Required

(a)   Explain in general terms how performance appraisal systems may be ineffective. Also, identify ways the appraisal system at CQ4 could be improved (other than those identified by the new chief executive)

(10 marks)

(b)   Explain the thinking behind the two initiatives announced by the new chief executive using Herzberg's motivation-hygiene (dual factor) theory as a framework.   **(10 marks)**

(c)   Discuss the factors that should be taken into account by the HR department when redesigning the remuneration and reward package for SBU managers.   **(10 marks)**

(Total = 30 marks)

MARKETING

Questions 34 to 44 cover Marketing, the subject of Part D of the BPP Study Text for Paper P4.

34 Multiple choice questions: Marketing 1   36 mins

34.1 'Market shakeout' involves the weakest producers exiting a particular market and occurs in a period between

    A   growth through creativity and growth through direction
    B   introduction and market growth
    C   market growth and market maturity
    D   market maturity and decline   **(2 marks)**
11/05

34.2 Distribution channels, transport, warehouse and sales outlet locations are all examples of

    A   "place", one component of the marketing mix.
    B   "promotion", one component of the marketing mix.
    C   "physical evidence", one component of the marketing mix.
    D   the management of operations for a service organisation.   **(2 marks)**
5/06

34.3 The choice to buy a fast-moving consumer good (FMCG) is normally

    A   a personal choice involving relatively low financial outlays
    B   a personal choice involving relatively high financial outlays
    C   a choice made on behalf of an organisation involving moderate outlays
    D   a personal choice influenced by new features, fashions and old product wearout   **(2 marks)**
11/05

34.4 Analysing a market into sub-groups of potential customers with common needs and behaviours in order to target them through marketing techniques is called

    A   market research
    B   market development
    C   segmentation
    D   product adaptation   **(2 marks)**
11/05

34.5 Conventional marketing wisdom suggests that for successful segmentation of markets, segments must be

    A   relatively unsophisticated in their needs.
    B   economic, efficient and effective.
    C   measurable, accessible and substantial.
    D   currently lacking in providers.   **(2 marks)**
5/06

34.6 A main aim of electronic data interchange (EDI) is

A   to improve communication exchanges within an organisation
B   to replace conventional documentation with structured electronically transmitted data
C   to allow employees to work at home
D   to create a shared data resource within an organisation

(2 marks)

11/05

34.7 Separate people or groups such as initiators, influencers, buyers and users are all involved in a buying decision in the context of

A   fast moving consumer goods marketing
B   business-to-business marketing
C   business-to-consumer marketing
D   services marketing

(2 marks)

11/05

34.8 A marketing strategy will normally:

A   Provide priorities for the overall corporate strategy
B   Drive the productive capacity of the company
C   Meet the objectives of the company in terms of price and product features
D   Be consistent with other organisational business planning processes

(2 marks)

34.9 Which one of the following statements best represents 'a marketing orientation'?

A   Support for the marketing department from top management
B   A large marketing budget
C   High profile advertising campaigns
D   A focus on customer needs

(2 marks)

34.10 Effective product promotion is centred on

A   production processes.
B   customers and communication.
C   bonuses for sales staff and product quality.
D   effective systems of monitoring and control.

(2 marks)

5/06

(Total = 20 marks)

35 Multiple choice questions: Marketing 2   36 mins

35.1 Why do marketers often segment a market?

A   To allow marketing staff to allocate their workload fairly
B   Because most markets are too large to sell to everyone
C   Because it is well-established best practice
D   Because customers that share certain characteristics are likely to exhibit similar buying behaviour

(2 marks)

35.2 Which one of the following options shows the three main influences on an organisation's price setting strategy?

A   Income, inflation and exchange rates
B   Costs, marketing and ethics
C   Competitors, customers and communication
D   Costs, competition and demand   (2 marks)

35.3 What does the abbreviation B2B mean in a marketing context?

A   Buyer to business
B   Bulk to break-up
C   Boom to bust
D   Business to business   (2 marks)

35.4 Why is the characteristic of a service knows as 'perishability' significant in a marketing context?

A   Because perishability makes it likely that refrigerated facilities will be required
B   Because perishability increases ethical concerns
C   Because perishability makes anticipating and responding to levels of demand crucial
D   Because perishability means demand fluctuates wildly   (2 marks)

35.5 CRM software may be used by marketers. What does the abbreviation CRM stand for?

A   Customer Relationship Management
B   Customer Relationship Marketing
C   Customer Retail Management
D   Client Relationship Management   (2 marks)

35.6 What is a 'cookie'?

A   A type of virus introduced by the infamous 'biscuit gang' of hackers
B   A type of anti-virus software
C   An informal term used to describe a round mouse mat
D   A small file used to identify a user/computer   (2 marks)

35.7 'It is essential that efficient back-office procedures and operations are in place that allow the fulfilment of orders placed via a website.' What does this statement mean?

A   Websites must be hosted on a stable mainframe computer to ensure sufficient capacity

B   Orders received on-line should be printed out in case of system failure

C   Internet server computers should be situated at the back of the office

D   Accepting orders on-line is only the first step – the challenge then is to deliver the product or service ordered   (2 marks)

35.8 Which one of the following statements relating to marketing research is correct?

A   Primary data is collected specifically for the purpose of the research in question. Secondary data is data not collected specifically for one research project

B   Secondary data is collected specifically for the purpose of the research in question. Primary data is data not collected specifically for one research project

C   Qualitative data is collected specifically for the purpose of the research in question. Qualitative data is data not collected specifically for one research project

D   Quantitative data is collected specifically for the purpose of the research in question. Secondary data is not collected specifically for one research project

(2 marks)

35.9 Which one of the following statements relating to marketing research is correct?

A   Quantitative data is collected specifically for the purpose of the research in question. Qualitative data is data not collected specifically for one research project

B   Qualitative data is collected specifically for the purpose of the research in question. Quantitative data is data not collected specifically for one research project

C   Qualitative data is easily measurable using numbers. Quantitative data relates more to feelings and opinions

D   Quantitative data is easily measurable using numbers. Qualitative data relates more to feelings and opinions

(2 marks)

35.10 Which method of sampling involves selecting 'every nth item after a random start'?

A   Stratified sampling
B   Systematic sampling
C   Multistage sampling
D   All of the above   **(2 marks)**

(Total = 20 marks)

36 Multiple choice questions: Marketing 3   36 mins

36.1 Which one of the following statements describes differentiated marketing?

A   Offering different products to different segments of the market
B   Offering one product to the whole market
C   Offering one product to one segment of the market
D   Offering the same range of products to all segments of the market   **(2 marks)**

36.2 What is M-marketing?

A   Marketing to traditional alpha male individuals
B   Launching a product in multiple markets simultaneously
C   Marketing using mobile phones
D   Targeting all major market segments   **(2 marks)**

36.3   Which one of the following shows the correct stages and sequence of the product life cycle?

A   Product, price, promotion, place
B   Introduction, growth, maturity, decline
C   Introduction, growth, middle-age, maturity, decline
D   Product, price, promotion, place, people   (2 marks)

36.4   Direct marketing is sometimes referred to as

A   A one level channel
B   B2B
C   B2C
D   A zero level channel   (2 marks)

36.5   Market segmentation is a technique based on the belief that

A   Every market consists of potential buyers with different needs
B   The needs of Internet customers are different to those dealt with face-to-face
C   Selling one product to all potential customers is often the best strategy
D   Niche marketing is most profitable of all   (2 marks)

36.6   Which of the following are typical bases for segmentation?

A   Lifestyle
B   Gender
C   Age
D   All of the above   (2 marks)

36.7   What does FMCG stand for?

A   Flexibly marketed consumer good
B   Fast moving convenience good
C   Fast moving consumer good
D   Financial marketing consumer group   (2 marks)

36.8   Which of the following are relevant to the concept of marketing?

A   Advertising
B   Packaging
C   A only
D   Both A and B   (2 marks)

36.9   Organisations that focus primarily on product features are said to be

A   Sales oriented
B   Product orientated
C   Market orientated
D   Production orientated   (2 marks)

36.10 A pricing policy designed to establish or increase market share is referred to as

    A   Penetration pricing
    B   Skim pricing
    C   Cost-plus pricing
    D   Market leader pricing   **(2 marks)**

(Total = 20 marks)

37 Objective test questions: Marketing 1   36 mins

Required

Each of the sub-questions numbered **35.1** to **35.5** below require a brief written response. Each sub-question is worth 4 marks. The response should be in note form and should not exceed 50 words.

37.1   Distinguish between push and pull marketing policies and their impact on the promotion of goods.**(4 marks)**

`5/06`

37.2   Briefly explain the main sections of the product life cycle.   **(4 marks)**

37.3   In the context of market positioning, explain the terms undifferentiated, differentiated and concentrated.

    (4 marks)

37.4   Explain the term 'sales potential' and briefly explain three factors that may influence it.   **(4 marks)**

37.5   Explain what the term 'PESTEL factors' means and why these factors are of interest to marketers.

    (4 marks)

(Total for these sub-questions = 20 marks)

38 Objective test questions: Marketing 2   36 mins

Required

Each of the sub-questions numbered **36.1** to **36.5** below require a brief written response. Each sub-question is worth 4 marks. The response should be in note form and should not exceed 50 words.

38.1   Distinguish between strategic and tactical marketing, and provide an example.   **(4 marks)**

38.2   In the context of e-commerce, explain the meaning and importance of 'fulfilment'.   **(4 marks)**

38.3   Compare and contrast product orientated organisations and production orientated organisations. **(4 marks)**

`11/05`

38.4   Define demography and explain how demography can influence marketing activity.   **(4 marks)**

38.5   Identify and explain *Ansoff*'s possible strategies for products and markets as shown in his matrix. **(4 marks)**

(Total for these sub-questions = 20 marks)

If you struggled with the MCQ and OT questions in Q34-Q38, go back to your BPP Study Text for Paper P4 and revise Chapters 10, 11 and 12 before you tackle the longer questions on Marketing.

39 Marketing action plan (11/05 – original)   36 mins

SX is a growing company that has successfully used local radio advertising for the past few years to raise awareness of its products. It supplies fresh 'quality' sandwiches, home baked snacks, the finest coffees and freshly squeezed fruit juices for sale at premium prices in petrol filling stations. Products are produced by traditional methods from very early morning by a team of employees at a central depot and are delivered throughout the day by a few casual workers in a fleet of vehicles.

SX has for the first time undertaken a full strategic marketing planning process. One weakness identified was that the number of deliveries required was increasing, while some of the drivers were becoming increasingly unreliable. The owner is worried that this may create an unfavourable image with customers and lead to delays in delivery.

In terms of opportunities, the owner of SX is now aware that by using technology to a greater degree and identifying customer needs more fully, the firm can grow at an even greater rate. To this end it is proposed that time saving food preparation and packaging equipment be purchased. This will mean considerably fewer people involved in food preparation but the owner feels that some employees could be redeployed as drivers on a permanent basis. The role of driver would be redefined, and in addition to making deliveries, he or she would be expected to:

- Get direct feedback from customers

- Persuade petrol stations to take new product lines

- Provide intelligence on competitor's products and likely future demand

- Hopefully persuade other petrol stations and outlets (such as railway stations and newspaper shops) to stock SX products

The owner is keen to progress change, consequently:

- The Head of delivery and customer relationships has been tasked with developing new job and person details for the driver posts. These will then be discussed with existing food preparation staff.

- A marketing action plan will soon be prepared based on the strategic marketing plan, which will contain immediate marketing issues and actions required. Some detail is already available on people and price so the main areas to consider are product, place and promotion.

Required

(a) Based on your understanding of the changes proposed by SX, identify the main issues that will be included in the marketing action plan and discuss the implications of these. Your response should consider issues of product, place and promotion only. **(10 marks)**

(b) Based upon the information given to you concerning SX, and your own study and experience, produce a draft job description for the redefined post of driver. **(10 marks)**

(Total = 20 marks)

40 Marketing action plan (11/05 – amended)   54 mins

SX is a growing company that has successfully used local radio advertising for the past few years to raise awareness of its products. It supplies fresh 'quality' sandwiches, home baked snacks, the finest coffees and freshly squeezed fruit juices for sale at premium prices in petrol filling stations. Products are produced by traditional methods from very early morning by a team of employees at a central depot and are delivered throughout the day by a few casual workers in a fleet of vehicles.

SX has for the first time undertaken a full strategic marketing planning process. One weakness identified was that the number of deliveries required was increasing, while some of the drivers were becoming increasingly unreliable. The owner is worried that this may create an unfavourable image with customers and lead to delays in delivery.

In terms of opportunities, the owner of SX is now aware that by using technology to a greater degree and identifying customer needs more fully, the firm can grow at an even greater rate. To this end it is proposed that time saving food preparation and packaging equipment be purchased. This will mean considerably fewer people involved in food preparation but the owner feels that some employees could be redeployed as drivers on a permanent basis. The role of drive would be redefined, and in addition to making deliveries, he or she would be expected to:

- Get direct feedback from customers

- Persuade petrol stations to take new product lines

- Provide intelligence on competitor's products and likely future demand

- Hopefully persuade other petrol stations and outlets (such as railway stations and newspaper shops) to stock SX products

The owner is keen to progress change, consequently:

- The Head of delivery and customer relationships has been tasked with developing new job and person details for the driver posts. These will then be discussed with existing food preparation staff.

- A marketing action plan will soon be prepared based on the strategic marketing plan, which will contain immediate marketing issues and actions required. Some detail is already available on people and price so the main areas to consider are product, place and promotion.

Required

(a)   Based on your understanding of the changes proposed by SX, identify the main issues that will be included in the marketing action plan and discuss the implications of these. Your response should consider issues of product, place and promotion only.   **(10 marks)**

(b)   Based upon the information given to you concerning SX, and your own study and experience, produce a draft job description for the redefined post of driver.   **(10 marks)**

The marketing action plan provided the following information relevant to pricing:

- Unit costs fall with increased output
- The local market is price sensitive.
- SX is concerned that a competitor may enter the local market in the near future.

(c)   Explain any four price setting strategies and recommend one to the owner in light of the information available.   **(10 marks)**

(Total = 30 marks)

41 Question with analysis: Consumer buying decision making process

54 mins

The PCW Company sells motor cars from 5 different shops located in one country. Prospective purchasers visit a dealership where cars being sold can be viewed. Test drives, that is taking a car out on the road to see if the purchaser likes the car, are available from dealerships.

Mr P is **considering purchasing** a different, and possibly larger, motor car. The purchase decision has occurred because of the need to transport his children and their musical instruments to school and the need to take more luggage on family holidays. Mr P is the **director of a successful engineering company** located three kilometres from his house. He plays **golf with his colleagues** every Saturday although his golf clubs are normally stored at the place where he plays golf because they will not fit in his existing car.

Mr P is interested in purchasing a Yotoda car, although his children prefer Sissan. Mr P is also concerned that arriving at the golf club in a Sissan would not be 'the done thing'. He also wants to ensure that **environmental damage** is limited as far as possible by his transport choices.

Required

(a) Explain and illustrate with examples, the decision making process Mr P will go through regarding the purchase of a motor car. **(10 marks)**

(b) Identify and explain the social and other factors that will influence Mr P in making the purchase decision. **(10 marks)**

(c) Explain and illustrate with examples the benefits that marketing can provide to business organisations, consumers and society. **(10 marks)**

(Total = 30 marks)

41 Question with analysis: Consumer buying decision making process

54 mins

Seeing cars 'in the flesh' is important to purchasers.	The PCW Company sells motor cars from 5 different shops located in one country. Prospective purchasers visit a dealership where cars being sold can be viewed. Test drives, that is taking a car out on the road to see if the purchaser likes the car, are available from dealerships.
A number of factors will influence the decision.	Mr P is **considering purchasing** a different, and possibly larger, motor car. The purchase decision has occurred because of the need to transport his children and their musical instruments to school and the need to take more luggage on family holidays. Mr P is the **director of a successful engineering company** located three kilometres from his house. He plays **golf with his colleagues** every Saturday although his golf clubs are normally stored at the place where he plays golf because they will not fit in his existing car.
Social and environmental factors are also relevant.	Mr P is interested in purchasing a Yotoda car, although his children prefer Sissan. Mr P is also concerned that arriving at the golf club in a Sissan would not be 'the done thing'. He also wants to ensure that **environmental damage** is limited as far as possible by his transport choices.

Required

You must provide examples!	(a) **Explain and illustrate with examples**, the **decision making process** Mr P will go through regarding the purchase of a motor car. **(10 marks)**
Not only social factors – answer breadth is important	(b) **Identify** and **explain** the **social and other factors** that will **influence** Mr P in making the purchase decision. **(10 marks)**
Wider reading would help you answer this question!	(c) Explain and illustrate with examples the **benefits that marketing can provide** to **business organisations, consumers and society.** **(10 marks)**

(Total = 30 marks)

BPP
LEARNING MEDIA

42 Marketing and information technology   54 mins

(a)   Evaluate the ways in which the Internet has changed the way businesses communicate with their customers, suppliers and within their own organisations.   **(20 marks)**

(b)   Identify how the use of information technology could assist in the marketing research process for a product, service or organisation of your choice.   **(10 marks)**

(Total = 30 marks)

43 Environmental change and marketing (05/06 – original)
36 mins

Banking services within the country of Everland are provided exclusively by a few well established banks, all offering broadly similar 'traditional' banking services. Overall, the industry performance is viewed from within as satisfactory and historically all banks have maintained stable profits and employment levels. Marketeers would describe the industry as being classically 'product oriented'. The profile of senior Everland bank officials and managers is of well qualified professionals, possessing long banking industry experience and considerable financial skills. Within the combined workforce other business skills (in, for instance, HR or marketing) are noticeably lacking.

In the external environment, the government will soon pass new legislation that will effectively break the oligopoly-type position of banks and open the market up to other providers. Senior bank officials, however, are unconcerned, feeling that banks are in 'reasonable shape' to face any new challenge.

You work for the Everland Banking Advisory Group (EBAG), an independent body, and have been asked to analyse the banking industry in the country of Utopia to identify lessons that might be learnt. Your investigation reveals that since the sector opened up to more competition, a much wider range of financial institutions offer banking services. Despite this, banks in Utopia have all prospered over the past few years. This is thanks to wide-ranging changes in how they operate, the products and services they offer and their organisational structures. You identify some significant trends within the banking industry of Utopia, including:

*   The use of marketing techniques
*   A clearer focus on customers (who have become increasingly more demanding)
*   A new generation of bank employees, many with commercial backgrounds
*   Banks now exhibiting a strong sense of ethical and social responsibilities towards customers

Required

(a)   Discuss the dangers to Everland banks if they do not change.   **(8 marks)**

(b)   Discuss the types of change that Everland banks could be making in order to survive and prosper.

(12 marks)

(Total = 20 marks)

44 Environmental change and marketing (05/06 – amended)

54 mins

Banking services within the country of Everland are provided exclusively by a few well established banks, all offering broadly similar 'traditional' banking services. Overall, the industry performance is viewed from within as satisfactory and historically all banks have maintained stable profits and employment levels. Marketeers would describe the industry as being classically 'product oriented'. The profile of senior Everland bank officials and managers is of well qualified professionals, possessing long banking industry experience and considerable financial skills. Within the combined workforce other business skills (in, for instance, HR or marketing) are noticeably lacking.

In the external environment, the government will soon pass new legislation that will effectively break the oligopoly-type position of banks and open the market up to other providers. Senior bank officials, however, are unconcerned, feeling that banks are in 'reasonable shape' to face any new challenge.

You work for the Everland Banking Advisory Group (EBAG), an independent body, and have been asked to analyse the banking industry in the country of Utopia to identify lessons that might be learnt. Your investigation reveals that since the sector opened up to more competition, a much wider range of financial institutions offer banking services. Despite this, banks in Utopia have all prospered over the past few years. This is thanks to wide-ranging changes in how they operate, the products and services they offer and their organisational structures. You identify some significant trends within the banking industry of Utopia, including:

- The use of marketing techniques;
- A clearer focus on customers (who have become increasingly more demanding);
- A new generation of bank employees, many with commercial backgrounds;
- Banks now exhibiting a strong sense of ethical and social responsibilities towards customers.

Required

(a) Discuss the dangers to Everland banks if they do not change. **(8 marks)**

(b) Discuss the types of change that Everland banks could be making in order to survive and prosper.

(12 marks)

The importance of ethics and social responsibility in all areas of business has attracted increased attention in recent years.

(c) Discuss (with examples) the main ethical and social responsibility issues that face modern marketers. (Your answer to this part of the question does not need to relate to the Everland scenario) **(10 Marks)**

(Total = 30 marks)

MANAGING CHANGE

Questions 45 to 52 cover Managing Change, the subject of Part E of the BPP Study Text for Paper P4.

45 Multiple choice questions: Managing change 1   36 mins

45.1 Which of the following is the correct sequence of crises in *Greiner's* growth model?

A   Leadership, autonomy, control, red tape
B   Control, autonomy, leadership, red tape
C   Autonomy, direction, delegation, red tape
D   Creativity, autonomy, delegation, control   **(2 marks)**

45.2 Activities associated with Organisational Development

A   require universal agreement that change must take place.
B   require 'interventions' into the social processes of an organisation.
C   naturally occur through a shared sense of purpose and a strong organisational culture.
D   result from the effect of Greiner's life cycle model.   **(2 marks)**
    5/06

45.3 What name is given to the theory that organisations will tend to pass through four stages: establishment, growth, maturity and decline?

A   The organisation life cycle ('S' curve)
B   *Maslow's* hierarchy
C   The learning organisation
D   A marketing orientation   **(2 marks)**

45.4 The technique of force field analysis depicts

A   change as occurring through a series of restraining and driving forces.
B   growth of organisations through evolution and revolution.
C   an organisation's environment as a series of opportunistic and threatening factors.
D   aggressive management styles used to drive change.   **(2 marks)**
    5/06

45.5 Which of the following approaches to rapid change is most likely to promote an immediate willingness to embrace change, perhaps associated with panic?

A   Coercive change (in the absence of an external shock)
B   Crisis management (in response to an external shock)
C   Neither A nor B
D   Both A and B   **(2 marks)**

45.6 Planned organisational change is most commonly triggered by the need to respond to new threats or opportunities presented by:

A   The organisation's culture
B   Developments in the external environment
C   The internal environment
D   Action by the organisation's management   **(2 marks)**

45.7 One possible response to change is regressive or non-learning behaviour, which is also termed:

A   Passive resistance
B   Passive resignation
C   Active resistance
D   Active resignation   **(2 marks)**

45.8 According to Kurt Lewin, the final stage of his three stage model of change is called

A   Unfreezing
B   Refreezing
C   Unbundling
D   Support and facilitation   **(2 marks)**

`5/06`

45.9 Key competencies for a change agent include:

A   Ability to work alone and communicate primarily by email
B   Obtaining motivation from others and accepting delegated tasks
C   Team building and influencing skills
D   Setting detailed budgets   **(2 marks)**

45.10 Growth can be carried out by acquisition. One of the main reasons for acquisitions is:

A   Increased risk of takeover
B   Enhanced internal growth opportunities
C   Amalgamation of management accounting systems
D   Access to new markets   **(2 marks)**

(Total = 20 marks)

46 Multiple choice questions: Managing change 2   36 mins

46.1 Three important aspects to the way in which change is undertaken and managed are included in the list below. Which one of the of the following is **not** one of them?

A   Scope
B   Manner
C   Culture
D   Pace   **(2 marks)**

46.2 *Greiner* (1972) identified five stages in the life cycle of an organisation. Each stage ends in a particular type of crisis. Which phase of *Greiner's* organisational growth model ends in a crisis of red tape?

A   Growth through creativity phase
B   Growth through direction phase
C   Growth through delegation phase
D   Growth through co-ordination phase   **(2 marks)**

46.3 Which one of the following is consistent with *Kanter's* prescriptions for encouraging organisational creativity?

A   Strict policies and procedures
B   A clear management hierarchy
C   Tolerate failure
D   Employ artistic people   **(2 marks)**

46.4 Which of the following is not part of the 'unfreeze' stage of the *Lewin/Schein* change model?

    A   Providing motivation for change

    B   Investigating ways of making the change

    C   Adopting a new culture

    D   Becoming aware of a trigger for change   **(2 marks)**

46.5 When an organisation experiences sustained growth, management often try to ensure co-ordination and control through:

    A   Less structural rigidity

    B   A decrease in formal controls

    C   Empowerment

    D   An increase in formal rules and procedures   **(2 marks)**

46.6 'Step change' means

    A   organisational change is matched with changes in the external environment – as the environment changes so the organisation follows

    B   the change trend line suddenly jumps upwards or downwards rather than being smooth

    C   change involving a process of moving from one fixed state to another

    D   change that is radical and outside of the normal paradigm of the organisation   **(2 marks)**

46.7 The most radical form of organisational change includes a cultural shift and is described as

    A   emergent change

    B   transformational change

    C   step change

    D   incremental change   **(2 marks)**

    11/05

46.8 Establishing a staff helpline when attempting to cope with resistance to change is an example of

    A   facilitation

    B   manipulation

    C   coercion

    D   co-optation   **(2 marks)**

    11/05

46.9 Management of an organisation have identified a crisis on the horizon. Which of the following is not a valid option for them to take?

    A   Convince others of the crisis and prepare preventative measures

    B   Wait until the crisis arrives so not to damage staff morale

    C   Accept the change will happen anyway and let events unfold

    D   Trigger the crisis at an earlier, suitable, time   **(2 marks)**

46.10 Which one of the following is the most important attribute a change agent must posses?

    A   An awareness of politics within an organisation

    B   Negotiation skills

    C   Ability to gain support for change from all involved

    D   An understanding of relevant business processes   **(2 marks)**

(Total = 20 marks)

47 Objective test questions: Managing change   36 mins

Required

Each of the sub-questions numbered **36.1** to **36.5** below require a brief written response. Each sub-question is worth 4 marks. The response should be in note form and should not exceed 50 words.

47.1 Explain the term 'external change trigger' and state four headings under which external change triggers can be categorised.   **(4 marks)**

47.2 Some managers may not favour change. Explain four barriers managers may use to limit or reject change.   **(4 marks)**

47.3 Explain what is meant by 'adaptive change'.   **(4 marks)**

47.4 Explain why a phased system change-over for a computer development might help employees cope better with technological change.   **(4 marks)**

Pilot paper

47.5 Change occurs when there is organisational growth through takeover. Certain basic 'rules' for takeovers to succeed have been suggested which need to be considered before the takeover occurs. Identify what these rules are for an organisation considering a takeover.   **(4 marks)**

11/05

(Total for these sub-questions = 20 marks)

If you struggled with the MCQ and OT questions in Q45-Q47, go back to your BPP Study Text for Paper P4 and revise Chapters 13 and 14 before you tackle the longer questions on Managing Change.

48 Question with analysis: Introducing change   54 mins

Following a benchmarking exercise, the recently appointed Chief Executive Officer (CEO) of B Company, a steel manufacturer, decided that several changes were required in order to maintain competitiveness. He has made it clear that costs are too high and productivity too low. The changes included:

- A change in structure in order to improve the focus on particular products and customers
- Tighter control of costs
- The introduction of a more entrepreneurial culture

Having decided that these changes were necessary, the CEO e-mailed all heads of departments indicating that during the following few months, the company would move from a functional structure to a divisional structure.

Existing functional heads would be interviewed for senior posts in the newly-created divisions in open competition with other applicants. The job specification for the new divisional heads included a requirement that the new heads would drive the changes, including a rapid transition to a more entrepreneurial culture and the implementation of new control mechanisms to contain costs.

The CEO delegated the change programme implementation into the hands of the head of human resources and went off on a two-week overseas business trip asking that he be kept informed of progress. The CEO returned from the business trip to find that no progress had been made towards the changes requested.

The head of human resources informed the CEO that heads of departments were reluctant to discuss the intended changes and that some had even talked about resignation from the company.

The trade union that represents the steel workers in B Company is well-organised and has promised the workers that it will defend their wage levels and working conditions.

Required

(a)   Describe the key mistakes made by the CEO in the way he went about introducing the proposed changes in B Company.   **(10 marks)**

(b)   Identify the forces for change and causes of resistance in B Company and classify these according to whether they can be considered as deriving from internal or external sources.   **(10 marks)**

(c)   Given the situation on the CEO's return, advise him what he should do in order to ensure the changes can be successfully implemented.   **(10 marks)**

(Total = 30 marks)

48 Question with analysis: Introducing change   54 mins

Following a benchmarking exercise, the recently appointed Chief Executive Officer (CEO) of B Company, a steel manufacturer, decided that several changes were required in order to maintain competitiveness. He has made it clear that costs are too high and productivity too low. The changes included:

| Are these changes consistent with each other? |

- A change in structure in order to improve the focus on particular products and customers
- Tighter control of costs
- The introduction of a more entrepreneurial culture

| Such a significant change requires organisation wide consultation, not just an email. |

Having decided that these changes were necessary, the CEO e-mailed all heads of departments indicating that during the following few months, the company would move from a functional structure to a divisional structure.

Existing functional heads would be interviewed for senior posts in the newly-created divisions in open competition with other applicants. The job specification for the new divisional heads included a requirement that the new heads would drive the changes, including a rapid transition to a more entrepreneurial culture and the implementation of new control mechanisms to contain costs.

| Unlikely that he has sufficient understanding of operations to undertake this. |

The CEO delegated the change programme implementation into the hands of the head of human resources and went off on a two-week overseas business trip asking that he be kept informed of progress. The CEO returned from the business trip to find that no progress had been made towards the changes requested.

| Not surprising given the lack of consultation |

The head of human resources informed the CEO that heads of departments were reluctant to discuss the intended changes and that some had even talked about resignation from the company.

The trade union that represents the steel workers in B Company is well-organised and has promised the workers that it will defend their wage levels and working conditions.

Required

| Ensure you follow the requirement exactly |

(a)   Describe the key mistakes made by the CEO in the way he went about introducing the proposed changes in B Company.   **(10 marks)**

(b)   Identify the forces for change and causes of resistance in B Company and classify these according to whether they can be considered as deriving from internal or external sources.   **(10 marks)**

(c)   Given the situation on the CEO's return, advise him what he should do in order to ensure the changes can be successfully implemented.   **(10 marks)**

| There is no one correct answer to this |

(Total = 30 marks)

| Important to repair damage already done and then move forward with consultation. |

49 Question with helping hand: Implementing change: types of change (Pilot paper – original) 36 mins

(a) Using prescriptive, planned change theory, as outlined by *Lewin* and others, describe how any major new organisational initiative can be successfully implemented. **(10 marks)**

(b) Zed Bank operates in a fiercely competitive market and has decided to implement a number of important initiatives, including:

- Enhancing its current services to customers by providing them with on-line internet and telephone banking services

- Reducing costs by closing many of its rural and smaller branches (outlets)

In an attempt to pacify the employee representatives (the Banking Trade Union) and to reduce expected protests by the communities affected by branch closure, a senior Bank spokesperson has announced that the changes will be 'incremental' in nature.

In particular, she has stressed that:

- The change will be implemented over a lengthy time period

- There will be no compulsory redundancies

- Banking staff ready to take on new roles and opportunities in the on-line operations will be retrained and offered generous relocation expenses

For customers, the Bank has promised that automatic cash dispensing machines will be available in all the localities where branches (outlets) close. Customers will also be provided with the software needed for Internet banking and other assistance necessary to give them quick and easy access to banking services.

The leader of the Banking Trade Union is 'appalled' at the initiatives announced. He has argued that the so-called 'incremental' change is in fact the start of a 'transformational' change that will have serious repercussions, not only for the Union's members but also for many of the Bank's customers.

Required

Distinguish incremental change from transformational change. Explain why the Bank spokesperson and the trade union leader disagree over their description of the change. **(10 marks)**

(Total = 20 marks)

Helping hand. Don't be put off by the use of academic language in the requirement for part (a). *Lewin's* simple three stage theory of change provides an excellent framework for your answer.

---

50 Question with helping hand: Implementing change: types of change (Pilot paper – amended)　54 mins

(a)　Using prescriptive, planned change theory, as outlined by *Lewin* and others, describe how any major new organisational initiative can be successfully implemented.　**(10 marks)**

(b)　Zed Bank operates in a fiercely competitive market and has decided to implement a number of important initiatives, including:

- Enhancing its current services to customers by providing them with on-line internet and telephone banking services

- Reducing costs by closing many of its rural and smaller branches (outlets)

In an attempt to pacify the employee representatives (the Banking Trade Union) and to reduce expected protests by the communities affected by branch closure, a senior Bank spokesperson has announced that the changes will be 'incremental' in nature.

In particular, she has stressed that:

- The change will be implemented over a lengthy time period

- There will be no compulsory redundancies

- Banking staff ready to take on new roles and opportunities in the on-line operations will be retrained and offered generous relocation expenses

- Banking staff will be offered financial and non-financial incentives

For customers, the Bank has promised that automatic cash dispensing machines will be available in all the localities where branches (outlets) close. Customers will also be provided with the software needed for Internet banking and other assistance necessary to give them quick and easy access to banking services.

The leader of the Banking Trade Union is 'appalled' at the initiatives announced. He has argued that the so-called 'incremental' change is in fact the start of a 'transformational' change that will have serious repercussions, not only for the Union's members but also for many of the Bank's customers.

Required

Distinguish incremental change from transformational change. Explain why the Bank spokesperson and the trade union leader disagree over their description of the change.　**(10 marks)**

(c)　Discuss the effectiveness of financial incentive schemes as motivators for employees.　**(10 marks)**

(Total = 30 marks)

Helping hand. Don't be put off by the use of academic language in the requirement for part (a). *Lewin*'s simple three stage theory of change provides an excellent framework for your answer.

---

51 Job reductions: resistance to change (5/05 – original)

36 mins

R & L is a large manufacturing firm that is well known as a 'good employer'. Over the past few years, R & L has experienced difficult times with reducing sales and mounting losses. In desperation it employed management consultants to analyse its situation. The consultants have concluded that the downturn in sales is permanent and that R & L needs to reduce its workforce by 50% over the next year in order to survive. Reluctantly, R & L's board of directors has accepted these findings, including the need to reduce the number of staff. The directors have also agreed to act as honestly and as fairly as possible, but realise that any changes they propose will be unpopular and may meet with resistance.

Required

(a)   Discuss what initiatives R & L can take to achieve the job reductions needed given the company's reputation for being a good employer. (Your answer should include reference to appropriate support for any individuals affected.)   **(10 marks)**

(b)   Discuss the potential strategies available in order to overcome resistance to change, and identify those strategies that would be most suitable for R & L.   **(10 marks)**

(Total = 20 marks)

52 Job reductions: resistance to change (5/05 – amended)

54 mins

R & L is a large manufacturing firm that is well known as a 'good employer' especially with regard to its performance appraisal system and policies on employee empowerment. Over the past few years, R & L has experienced difficult times with reducing sales and mounting losses. In desperation it employed management consultants to analyse its situation. The consultants have concluded that the downturn in sales is permanent and that R & L needs to reduce its workforce by 50% over the next year in order to survive. Reluctantly, R & L's board of directors has accepted these findings, including the need to reduce the number of staff. The directors have also agreed to act as honestly and as fairly as possible, but realise that any changes they propose will be unpopular and may meet with resistance.

Required

(a)   Explain the purpose and objectives of a performance appraisal system.   **(5 marks)**

(b)   Explain the meaning and possible benefits of employee empowerment.   **(5 marks)**

(c)   Discuss what initiatives R & L can take to achieve the job reductions needed given the company's reputation for being a good employer. (Your answer should include reference to appropriate support for any individuals affected.)   **(10 marks)**

(d)   Discuss the potential strategies available in order to overcome resistance to change, and identify those strategies that would be most suitable for R & L.   **(10 marks)**

(Total = 30 marks)

53 Total learning experience   54 mins

Background

Total Learning Experience (TLE) is a training organisation that provides a wide range of training courses both locally and nationally. TLE operates from a city centre premises with six training rooms, a student common room and three administrative offices.

Staff

TLE employs 10 full-time tutors and also uses 8 freelance tutors. Seven of the 10 full-time tutors and all the freelance tutors are based at home. Most of the tutors have their own computers at home.

All administration staff are based permanently in the TLE offices. This includes the office manager, who is responsible for course management, timetabling and course materials management, and the Finance Manager who is responsible for all financial and management accounting activities and general IT issues.

Information technology position 1995 to 2002

Prior to 1995, all business records (including the accounts) were paper-based manual systems. In 1996, TLE invested in an IBM minicomputer (for administrative functions) and a standalone desktop PC (for use by tutors, of which there were 5 in 1995). In addition, a black-and-white ink-jet printer was purchased and shared between the two computers. Both the minicomputer and the PC were equipped with basic applications software including word processing, spreadsheet and desktop publishing facilities.

At this time, all student records were input into a 'student file', the business client data into a 'client file' and course data into a 'courses file' (each of these were separate word processing documents.) Timetabling information was transferred onto a number of spreadsheet files.

Information technology position 2002 to 2005

In June 2002 the most up-to-date versions of the operating system and application packages were installed. Three additional PCs were purchased: one for the administration assistant, one for the accounts clerk and one for the Finance Manager. An off-the-shelf accounting package was installed onto the accounts PC, to carry out the basic accounting and financial reporting functions. An off-the-shelf database software package was also installed on all computers, but it is rarely used. Additional purchases included one fax machine and one photocopier. All of the computers were standalone.

The three office-based tutors share the use of the original office PC bought in 1995 to prepare course material but often complain about the lack of computer availability. They often resort to using the administration and accounts computers early in the morning or at the end of the teaching day. There are no password systems currently in use on any of the administrative or accounts computers.

Timetable management

The usage of the six TLE training rooms is planned and timetabled several months in advance. This information is kept on a large whiteboard and highlights the rooms in use, by which course, at what time and by which tutor. This information is used to produce a weekly usage forecast spreadsheet for each room, which is produced each Friday and posted on the door of each room on Monday morning. (Note: a timetabling software package is available, but office staff consider the whiteboard system and spreadsheets are sufficient.)

Timetabling of staff is done by means of a diary system. Each tutor has his or her own diary which is kept by the administration assistant. She is responsible for filling in the diary for each tutor and then sending this monthly (one month in advance, so the teaching diary for January is sent out in December) to each home-based tutor by post or fax. It is the responsibility of all tutors to let the administration assistant know which days they are unavailable

BPP)))
LEARNING MEDIA

(such as holiday commitments) at least six weeks in advance. Ideally, the administration assistant should call all tutors at least once a week, but often (due to pressures of time) this is not done.

Course booking system

Professional courses

Six weeks prior to the start of a professional course, standard pre-printed booking forms (produced by a local firm of printers) are sent to all students currently listed on the student file. Other booking forms are sent as and when requested (by phone or by a posted tear-off slip included in local newspaper advertisements or leaflets posted to all registered students in the local area).

On receipt of completed booking forms, new and updated student details are entered onto the student file which is then used to update the course file and produce the course register. The administration assistant prints and copies the updated student file and passes it to the accounts clerk who enters the details into the accounts customer file to provide information for billing.

Business management skills and specialist courses

Business management training courses are normally delivered at the specific request of the client organisation. Course details are discussed between the client organisation and TLE, using the tutor diaries kept by the administration assistant to check tutor availability. On agreement, tutor diaries are updated, client files are updated and the information is passed to the accounts clerk for invoicing.

During the weeks when the training rooms are not being used by professional accounting courses, TLE utilises the time by offering a range of specialist training courses. These are timetabled and agreed with the freelance tutors some months in advance of delivery. They are advertised in specialist journals and magazines, in the local and national press and by advertising mail shots sent to organisations such as banks, solicitors, consultants and insurance companies. Booking forms are issued when a client rings the advertised telephone number or returns a tear-off slip from the mail shot.

Recent problems

Although TLE has maintained a strong reputation for high-quality course delivery, in the last year there have been a number of problems, including the two below.

- A presentation skills course due to be delivered to a new client at their premises had to be cancelled at short notice because of double booking of the tutor. The client has refused to use TLE again.

- A number of past students were sent invoices for courses which they did not attend. Their details were entered onto the sales ledger incorrectly after the student file was copied by the administration assistant to the accounts clerk. There have been a number of billing queries, mainly due to the difference in the information held by accounts and administration about clients and students.

Required

Write a report to the Finance Manager that provides:

(a) An evaluation of the current hardware facilities. **(5 marks)**

(b) An evaluation of the software facilities. **(5 marks)**

(c) An evaluation of the current course booking system. **(5 marks)**

(d) An evaluation of the current timetable management system. **(5 marks)**

(e) A description of the new hardware required for the new information system you believe would suit TLE.

(5 marks)

(f) A description of the new software that would facilitate the new information system at TLE. **(5 marks)**

Note. Your report should not exceed one page per topic.

(Total = 30 marks)

54 S&C software project (5/06)

54 mins

S & C is a medium sized firm that is experiencing rapid growth evidenced by increased turnover. It has been able to develop a range of new consultancy and specialist business advisory services that it offers to its growing customer base. To cope with these developments several organisation-wide initiatives have been launched over the past two years.

The existing financial systems are struggling to cope with these developments, but replacement software is due to be installed within the next six months. The new system was justified partly because it could reduce costs although precise details have not been given. The application software does not fit existing business processes exactly. However, it has the clear advantage of giving S & C access to an industry best practice system and is identical to that used by all its main competitors and some of its clients.

A three-person project steering group has recommended that a phased approach to introduction should be used and has undertaken most of the project planning. A programme of events for implementing the system has been agreed but is not yet fully operational. This group has not met for a while because the designated project manager has been absent from work through illness.

You are Head of S & C's Central Support Unit. You also serve on the project steering group.

A partners' meeting is due to take place soon. The firm's senior partner has asked you to prepare a PowerPoint presentation to other partners on implementation issues. You understand that partners are conscious that system implementation represents a form of further organisational change. They are asking questions about the approach that will be taken to the introduction of the new system, likely changes to practices, critical areas for success, system testing, support after implementation, system effectiveness, etc.

Required

You are required to produce **outline notes** that will support your eventual PowerPoint presentation. These notes should:

(a) Discuss the options to overcome the fact that the software does not fit existing business processes exactly.

(5 marks)

(b) Explain why a phased approach to introducing the system is, in this case, more suitable than a direct 'big bang' approach. **(5 marks)**

(c) Discuss the ways in which particular individuals and groups within S & C are important for implementation to succeed. **(5 marks)**

(d) Explain how users should be involved in the implementation phase of the project. **(5 marks)**

(e) Describe the training that should be given to targeted groups within S & C. **(5 marks)**

(f) Explain the aims of a post-implementation review. **(5 marks)**

Note. Your notes should not exceed one page per topic.

(Total = 30 marks)

BPP
LEARNING MEDIA

55 Tracey plc

54 mins

Tracey plc manufactures and sells garden equipment via mail order. The Board of Tracey plc are about to consider investing in a new computer system for the marketing department, which will include an updated marketing database and broadband Internet access.

The existing database was implemented 10 years ago, and due to lack of training and knowledge of pre-Windows programmes, only the marketing manager can currently use the programme. This database only provides a list of marketing contacts which can be printed using key fields of name or geographical region.

As a result of the implementation, the marketing department staff will be reduced from 26 to 21 employees – the 5 middle managers will be made redundant. The rationale behind this move is that all staff in the marketing department will be able to use the new computer system, freeing up time for the marketing manager to actually manage staff rather than process all requests through the computer.

The new marketing database will hold information about customers and potential customers, clearly identifying:

- Name and address
- Company products information requested on.
- Promotion method that the customer used to contact the company.
- Product enhancements requested
- Amount of sales made
- Date of last sale / amendment of contact details
- Narrative of discussions with the customer.

The marketing database is only one of the initiatives currently being followed with Tracey plc; many other databases and computer systems are being upgraded. This means that a data controller will have to be recruited with key responsibilities for managing data across the whole of the company. This person will need to negotiate with all departmental managers to ensure that databases conform to Tracey plc standards and that access is provided for appropriate personnel.

The Board of Tracey plc want to know more about the proposed change, with specific reference to how that change will be managed and the benefits of the new database. As the management accountant in the company, you have been asked to make a presentation to the Board on the change.

Required

Prepare briefing notes for the management accountant's meeting with the Board of Tracey plc covering the topics below. Your briefing notes should take no more than one page for each topic.

(a) Recommend a formal procedure, with brief explanation of the key stages, that can be followed to change from the old to the new database system. **(5 marks)**

(b) Explain the 4 P's of the marketing mix, showing how the new database provides additional information on these factors. **(5 marks)**

(c) Describe the new marketing information that can be obtained from the database. **(5 marks)**

(d) Evaluate the extent to which marketing information can be used to determine production strategy. **(5 marks)**

(e) Explain the effect of the new database on the organisational structure and culture of the marketing department. **(5 marks)**

(f) Provide job competences for the new data controller. **(5 marks)**

(Total = 30 marks)

56 Question with answer plan: Zircon company   54 mins

The Zircon Company sells holidays to customers from 29 'travel agent' shops in one country. Each shop sells a range of holiday 'packages' – that is specific locations with fixed travel dates and standard activities and amenities in each location.

The philosophy of the company has always been to offer personal service to customers, hence it has not moved into other selling media such as Internet and sending out catalogues in the post, which its competitors have done. Unfortunately, profits have been declining in recent years, indicating that this strategy may not be appropriate.

Zircon management have also noted the trend of customers wanting to amend its standard holiday packages to their own specific requirements, and a move to booking holidays just before they are taken, rather than planning months in advance. As Zircon cannot always offer 'tailored' holidays, this trend has had a negative effect on its profits. Management have allowed staff to work more independently, but without changing the product itself. Independent working involves discussing holiday requirements with individual customers up to and including completing the sale. Previously, staff were required to check with a manager that the all details of the holiday had been correctly recorded prior to confirming the sale with the customer.

One option being investigated by management of Zircon is the purchase of aircraft and hotels to be run within the Zircon Company. This action would enable Zircon to be more flexible in offering different holiday dates and activities as well as not be reliant on third parties for supply of services. Zircon has been criticised in the past for customers missing holidays due to overbooking of seats on aircraft, although this was not the fault of Zircon.

Required

(a)   Identify and explain the change triggers that suggest Zircon needs to amend its business model to incorporate other methods of selling holidays.   **(5 marks)**

(b)   Explain the advantages of vertical integration to the Zircon Company.   **(5 marks)**

(c)   Explain the principle of Total Quality Management and whether the TQM-related theory of six sigma is appropriate to Zircon.   **(5 marks)**

(d)   Discuss the factors the Zircon will need to consider when setting a price for the enhanced holiday package.
                                                                                                                                               (5 marks)

(e)   Describe the marketing strategies available to Zircon, stating whether or not each strategy should be used by Zircon.   **(5 marks)**

(f)   Discuss the extent to which providing staff with more independence in booking a holiday will improve their motivation at work.   **(5 marks)**

Note. Your answers should not exceed one page per question part.

                                                                                                                        (Total = 30 marks)

57 Zodiac plc

54 mins

Zodiac plc manufactures 'outerwear' clothing (e.g. coats, boots, fleeces etc.) from about 250 different inputs. Clothing is sold by mail order direct to the customer. When orders are received, they are entered into a customer ordering system, which is based on generally available software. On order fulfilment, details are transferred electronically to the sales ledger system.

The re-order and production systems are based on ensuring that sufficient stock is always available to manufacture the required clothing. This means that the production controller normally orders large quantities of stock to try and avoid stockouts. However, the system which is based on the controller 'guessing' how much stock is required, does not always work. This means that 'emergency' orders have to be processed taking up valuable time of the controller.

Manufacturing systems include the use of CAD / CAM, particularly in the cutting of cloth ready for manufacture into coats etc. However, this is a stand alone system using standard software; there are no links to any other computer systems in Zodiac.

Quality of the production system is currently measured under the headings *customer, internal operations, innovation* and *learning* and *financial.*

The board of Zodiac are currently considering whether to implement a Materials Requirements Planning (MRP) system. This will be used to control materials requirements (by having links to production and order databases) including automatically issuing orders to suppliers based on materials usage. Some orders will be sent via Electronic Data Interchange (EDI) with other suppliers having direct access to the MRP via an Extranet to see precisely what stock is required in Zodiac.

Given Zodiac's lack of experience with MRP systems, the board are considering whether or not to outsource the setup and maintenance of this system.

Following the implementation of the MRP, the production controller will continue to be in charge of production, although without the responsibility for ordering stock. He will continue to report to the senior management accountant and be responsible for the overall quality of goods being produced.

Required

(a)   Evaluate the feasibility of the Materials Requirement Planning (MRP) system in Zodiac under appropriate headings.   **(5 marks)**

(b)   Explain the benefits of implementing a MRP system for Zodiac plc.   **(5 marks)**

(c)   List and explain the reason for a series of questions that can be used by the board of Zodiac to assist in making the decision on whether or not to outsource the new MRP system.   **(5 marks)**

(d)   List the performance measures that can be used to check the quality of production under the headings currently used by Zodiac. Note changes that can be expected in these measures with the implementation of the MRP system.   **(5 marks)**

(e)   Explain the term market segmentation and discuss whether segmenting the clothes market would be beneficial to Zodiac.   **(5 marks)**

(f)   Outline the steps of an appropriate appraisal system for the production controller.   **(5 marks)**

   Note. Your answer should not exceed one page per question part.

(Total = 30 marks)

58 Services marketing

54 mins

Required

Using a financial service of your choice, discuss the possible implications of the following four characteristics of services in the context of marketing.

(a)	Perishability.	**(5 marks)**
(b)	Intangibility.	**(5 marks)**
(c)	Inseparability.	**(5 marks)**
(d)	Heterogeneity.	**(5 marks)**

Explain the importance of the following two elements of the extended marketing mix in the context of marketing financial services.

(e)	People.	**(5 marks)**
(f)	Process.	**(5 marks)**

Note. All answers should not exceed one page per question part.

(Total = 30 marks)

59 Question with helping hand: Hubbles (Pilot paper)   54 mins

Hubbles, a national high-street clothing retailer has recently appointed a new Chief Executive. The company is well established and relatively financially secure. It has a reputation for stability and traditional, quality clothing at an affordable price. Lately, however, it has suffered from intense competition leading to a loss of market share and an erosion of customer loyalty.

Hubbles has all the major business functions provided by 'in house' departments, including finance, human resources, purchasing, strategy and marketing. The Strategy and Marketing Department has identified a need for a comprehensive review of the company's effectiveness. In response, the new Chief Executive has commissioned a review by management consultants.

Their initial findings include the following:

- Hubbles has never moved from being sales-oriented to being marketing-oriented and this is why it has lost touch with its customers;

- Hubbles now needs to get closer to its customers and operate a more effective marketing mix;

- Additional investment in its purchasing department can add significantly to improving Hubbles' competitive position.

The Chief Executive feels that a presentation of interim findings to senior managers would be helpful at this point. You are a member of the management consultancy team and have been asked to draft a slide presentation of some of the key points. The Chief Executive has identified six such points.

Required

Prepare a slide outline, and brief accompanying notes of two to three sentences, for each of the Chief Executive's key points identified below. Do not exceed one page per question part.

(a)   Describe the difference between a company that concentrates on 'selling' its products and one that has adopted a marketing approach.   **(5 marks)**

(b)   Explain how Hubbles might develop itself into an organisation that is driven by customer needs.   **(5 marks)**

(c)   Explain what is meant by the 'marketing mix' (include the 4 traditional elements and 'people' as the fifth part of the mix).   **(5 marks)**

(d)   Identify examples of ways in which the management of Hubbles could make use of the marketing mix to help regain its competitive position. **(5 marks)**

(e)   Describe the main areas in which Hubbles' Human Resources Department might reasonably contribute to assist the Purchasing Department. **(5 marks)**

(f)   Explain how an efficient Purchasing Department might contribute to effective organisational performance. **(5 marks)**

(Total = 30 marks)

Helping hand. Remember, marketing in this context is a business philosophy rather than a separate function concerned only with traditional marketing activities such as advertising and PR. Likewise, you should also consider all aspects of purchasing (including supplier relationships) rather than focussing on administrative aspects.

---

60 Round the table (11/05) 54 mins

You are a researcher employed by a topical business discussion television show 'Round the Table'. Next week's discussion is about managing supply to achieve quality and customer satisfaction. Invited guests will be leading academic, public and private sector senior managers and the chief executive of a car producer. You have been asked to prepare an outline briefing that will give some background information to the show's presenter.

Your researcher shows that the automobile industry is highly competitive and globally suffers from 'overcapacity'. In certain countries however, there is unfulfilled demand for specialist makes and models, implying some under capacity 'hot spots'. You understand that for any organisation, whether producing goods or services, effective capacity management is vital. It ensures that customers' needs are more fully met and that there are fewer unfulfilled delivery date promises. There are several ways of dealing with variations in demand and matching production capacity including:

*   concentrating on inventory levels (a 'Level capacity' strategy)
*   concentrating on demand (a 'Demand' strategy)
*   adjusting levels of activity (a 'Chase' strategy)

As part of your investigation you note that distinctive issues exist for service organisations (such as those found in the public sector) compared with manufacturing organisations (such as car producers).

Required

As the show's researcher you are required to produce guidance notes to support the show's presenter which:

(a)   Discuss why a level capacity strategy might be difficult for a firm wishing to adopt a just-in-time (JIT) philosophy. **(5 marks)**

(b)   Discuss the impact of demand strategies on an organisation's marketing practices. **(5 marks)**

(c)   Discuss the relationship between chase strategies and the flexible organisation. **(5 marks)**

(d)   Identify the ways that service organisations differ from manufacturing organisations when considering capacity management. **(5 marks)**

(e)   Describe the types of software applications a manufacturing firm might introduce to improves its inbound logistics. **(5 marks)**

(f)   Describe the types of computerised assistance that could be used by those involved in selling cars and wanting to improve demand. **(5 marks)**

Note. (a) to (d) should have particular regard to quality, capacity and other organisational issues. Do not exceed one page per question part.

(Total = 30 marks)

61 V (5/05)

54 mins

V is an innovative company run according to the principles of its entrepreneurial owner. V operates a package distribution service, a train service, and sells holidays, bridal outfits, clothing, mobile telephones, and soft drinks. V is well known for challenging the norm and 'giving customers quality products and services at affordable prices and doing it all with a sense of fun'. V spends little on advertising but has great brand awareness thanks to the 'visibility' of its inspirational owner.

V has just announced the launch of 'V-cosmetics' to exploit a gap in the market. The cosmetic range will be competitively priced against high street brands and have the distinctive V logo.

You work for a market analyst who is about to appear on a radio discussion of V's business interests. You have been asked to provide a clear, short briefing for the market analyst on the thinking behind V-cosmetics. Your research of the V-cosmetics range identifies innovative marketing proposals. V-cosmetics will not be on sale in shops, instead it will use two approaches to promotion and selling, namely:

- The use of 'cosmetic associates'. Individuals may apply to become an associate and, if accepted, will be required to buy a basic stock of every V-cosmetic product. The associate will then use these products as samples and 'testers'. After initial training associates organise parties in the homes of friends and their friends where they take orders for products at a listed price. Associates receive commission based on sales.

- The Internet and mobile telephone technology will also be heavily used to offer V cosmetic products to the public.

Required

Prepare brief notes containing bullet points and no more than two to three sentences for each of the key points identified below. Do not exceed one page per question part.

(a)	Explain how the proposed approach can be understood within the context of the marketing mix.	**(5 marks)**
(b)	Explain the human resource implications of using 'cosmetic associates'.	**(5 marks)**
(c)	Explain the concept of direct marketing.	**(5 marks)**
(d)	Explain the advantages of the Internet as a marketing channel.	**(5 marks)**
(e)	Describe how V might use Internet and mobile phone technology as part of its marketing approach.	**(5 marks)**
(f)	Identify the main ethical issues associated with the proposal to market V cosmetics.	**(5 marks)**

(Total = 30 marks)

Answers

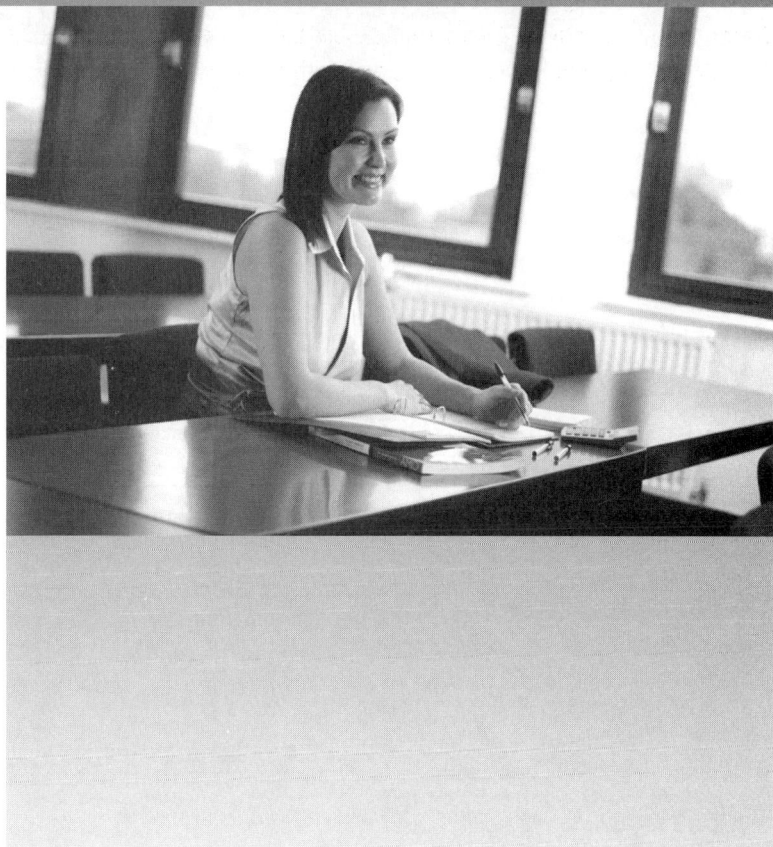

1 Multiple choice questions: Information systems 1

1.1 C   A and B are incorrect, and while data transfer times may be slow, the main problem is loss of data on power failure.

1.2 C   Within a database, data redundancy refers to incidences when the same data item is stored in more than one place.

1.3 B   ROM is memory can only be read from, and not written to.

1.4 B   The other three options are all advantages of distributed processing.

1.5 C   Statement (ii) is nonsense.

1.6 A   The environment is the external elements of a system. B is clearly incorrect, C refers to the system itself while D is a brief definition of processing.

1.7 A   The correct answer is touch screen – the user selects options by touching the required button on screen.

1.8 A   The server provides services such as access to shared printers. Data can be stored on client PCs which also means that centralised backup (D) is not always available. Client PCs can also run their own application software rather than being dependent on the server.

1.9 C   The system boundary is the outside edge of a system; therefore it does not relate to the boundaries within a system itself.

1.10 A   The other explanations relate to effector (B), standard (C) and sensor (D).

2 Multiple choice questions: Information systems 2

2.1 A   When a system is cut off from its environment and does not react with its environment, it is said to be a closed system. There are degrees of 'closed-ness' and 'openness' in systems. Closed systems tend to deteriorate over time.

2.2 A   The law of requisite variety is a principle rather than a law, but it draws attention to the need for sufficient flexibility and variety in its features to enable it to react efficiently and effectively to inputs from and influences of its environment. If a system does not have sufficient flexibility and variety, it will not survive.

2.3 D   Negative entropy is new inputs or new information put into a system from its environment. An example is a company whose business is declining because it has not responded sufficiently to the requirements of its markets and customers, or the pace of technological change. Negative entropy is needed, and might take the form of new management with new ideas, updated products or the introduction of updated technology.

2.4 B   Filtering is the process of removing 'impurities' such as excessive detail from data as it is passed along the information chain. Here the mass of news data is filtered initially by the media scanners, then by their supervisor, then by the client liaison officer, so that only some news reports reach the client.

2.5 A   A data dictionary is a form of technical documentation of the data in a database. It is used in systems analysis and systems maintenance. A dictionary specifies the structure of data items (field names and lengths, data codes and their meaning, entity, attribute and relationship types and so on).

2.6 C   A database is interrogated using a query language (eg SQL).

2.7 B A data flow diagram is constructed to show entities, data flows, data processes and data stores. An entity is a source or destination of data that is outside the system under development, from which or to which data or information will flow. For example, in an on-line stock broker system, entities will include clients of the stockbroker and market dealers in securities with which the broker makes transactions on behalf of clients.

2.8 D Boxes in a DFD represent processes. The nature of the process will be shown as the text in the lower part of the box. The number 7 in the top left-hand corner shows that this is data process number 7 in this diagram.

2.9 A The four quadrants in a decision table are condition stub, condition entry, action stub, action entry.

2.10 D The purpose of an entity relationship model (also known as an entity model or a logical data structure) is to show the logical data requirements of the system independently of the system's organisation and processes.

3 Multiple choice questions: Information systems 3

3.1 A These are all hardware input devices.

3.2 A A LAN is, by definition, used over a limited geographical area.

3.3 A Entropy refers to the effect randomness or disorder has on a system.

3.4 B An intranet provides a storage and distribution point for information accessible to staff.

3.5 D Data integrity and the elimination of duplicated data are two advantages of a database management system.

3.6 A An expert system could be described as a database built on knowledge and experience.

3.7 A The operating system is software – for example Microsoft Windows.

3.8 C The five elements of a computer system are hardware, software, procedures, data and people.

3.9 C Three common network topologies are star, ring and tree

3.10 B As the direct approach involves the old system ceasing operation completely at a given time, this approach is the most risky.

4 Objective test questions: Information systems 1

4.1 A database is a collection of structured data. The data is held in a way that allows it to be accessed and used by a number of applications. This is an example of data independence, as data is able to be used in a number of different ways (to suit user requirements). A well planned database therefore provides data independence.

4.2 With centralised processing, processing is carried out in one location. Uses a mainframe with large amounts of memory and data storage (eg airline booking systems). Under distributed processing, data is processed locally on individual PCs. Processed data can be shared using a Local or Wide Area Network.

4.3 Interviews obtain direct response from users and allow follow-up questions. Observation allows the analyst to see how a system works in reality. Flowcharts provide a graphical representation of the system, improving overall understanding. Questionnaires are used where many responses are required – numeric answers makes analysis easier.

4.4 The following factors should be taken into account when choosing hardware.

- The cost and whether this is justified in relation to expected benefits, and versus the cost of other similar systems.

- Compatibility with relevant software and other hardware.

- Specification and user requirements (eg are required transaction processing speeds met?).
- Reliability, security features and availability of parts/replacement systems.

4.5 Corrective maintenance is carried out to correct system errors or bugs. Perfective maintenance aims to make enhancements or improvements to systems. Adaptive maintenance takes account of anticipated changes in the processing environment – for example new taxation rates.

5 Objective test questions: Information systems 2

5.1 Information systems that are developed in-house should match the needs of users as they are written for specific situations. Close co-operation between users and developers should be possible, which should result in users feeling a sense of ownership of the system – resulting in high levels of user acceptance.

5.2 An extranet is an intranet that is expanded to allow access to authorised outsiders such as business partners. Advantages include:

- Encourages information sharing
- Facilitates quick communication and information exchange
- Enhances co-operation and encourages co-dependability
- Allows electronic data interchange and e-procurement
- Strengthens relationships (eg with customers and suppliers)

5.3 Open systems interact with the external environment. Adaptive maintenance amends a system to take into account environmental changes. If a system did not interact with the environment adaptive maintenance would not be required – and if adaptive maintenance was not carried out, an open system would lose effectiveness over time.

5.4 A direct approach may be preferred because:

- A suitable quiet time is available
- There is complete confidence in the new system
- To overcome a reluctance to 'let the old system go'
- Cheaper and more convenient than running two systems
- The change may be implemented before staff are able to object

5.5 Reasons manual records may continue to be used include:

- Reliability – computer systems may have downtime
- A reluctance to accept change
- Cultural resistance to IT
- Lack of confidence in new system
- New system too complex
- Efficiency of manual system
- Ineffective communication, training and support

6 Entity relationship model

Text reference. Chapter 2 covers the entity relationship model and entity life histories.

Top tips. The type of question in parts (a) to (d), testing your knowledge of a modelling technique, is more likely to appear in the exam than a question requiring you to draw a diagram.

(a) An **entity** is an item about which information is to be stored. An entity could be a department, a person a product, a service, a role – anything considered significant enough to be labelled and treated as an entity. An entity is shown on an entity-relationship model by a rectangle with the name of the entity placed inside it.

Common examples of entities include customers, suppliers and employees.

Attributes are facts or characteristics related to the entity. Attributes are sometimes shown in a table that accompanies some entity relationship models.

For example, attributes recorded relating to customers could include name, address and purchase history.

Relationships show the links between different entities. There are three types of relationship that could be shown.

- A **one- to-one** relationship means there is only one link between two particular entities. For example, entity 'Employee' would have a one-to-one relationship with the entity 'Employee current salary' (as an employee has only one current salary). This relationship is shown by a straight line joining the two entities.

- A **one-to-many** relationship means one entity has more than one link to another entity. For example, an entity 'Organisation' would have a one to many relationship with an entity 'Department'. A single line departing from one entity but branching into three before it reaches the second entity shows this relationship.

- A **many-to-many** relationship means that two entities could have many links to each other. For example an entity 'Product' is likely to have a many-to-many relationship with an entity 'Customer'. The line between each entity in this situation is branched at both ends showing the many to many relationship.

(b) Four **attributes** likely to be recorded for the entity 'Student' are:

- Name
- Address
- Date of birth
- Date of enrolment

(*Note*. A wide range of answers are acceptable for this question)

(c) (i) B Limited and Department; one to many.
(ii) Department and Employee; one to many.
(iii) Department and Departmental Manager; one to one.
(iv) Managerial Board and Departmental Managers; one to many.
(v) Weekly payroll to employee; one to many.

(d) The **purpose** of an **Entity Life History** is to show, for each individual entity, how that entity is created, what modifies the entity, and finally how that entity is deleted from a system.

The **notation** or format of an Entity Life History is a series of rectangles arranged in an hierarchical manner. The **first level** contains one rectangle which contains the **name of the entity** being described, such as sales invoice or despatch note.

The **second level** contains three rectangles, which are all linked to the first level rectangle. These rectangles describe the **creation, amendment** and **deletion** of the entity. If there is only one event that can give rise to each action, such as a despatch note resulting in a sales invoice being produced, then this event is stated in the appropriate rectangle. If there is more than one event, then these are described in the third level of the Entity Life History.

The **third level** of the Entity Life History is used where there is **more than one event** for the creation, amendment or deletion of an entity. The different events are linked to the appropriate second level rectangle. Where the events are 'either/or', a small circle is placed in the event rectangle. Where an event can occur more than once, such as a customer address changing, then an asterisk is placed in the event rectangle.

(e)

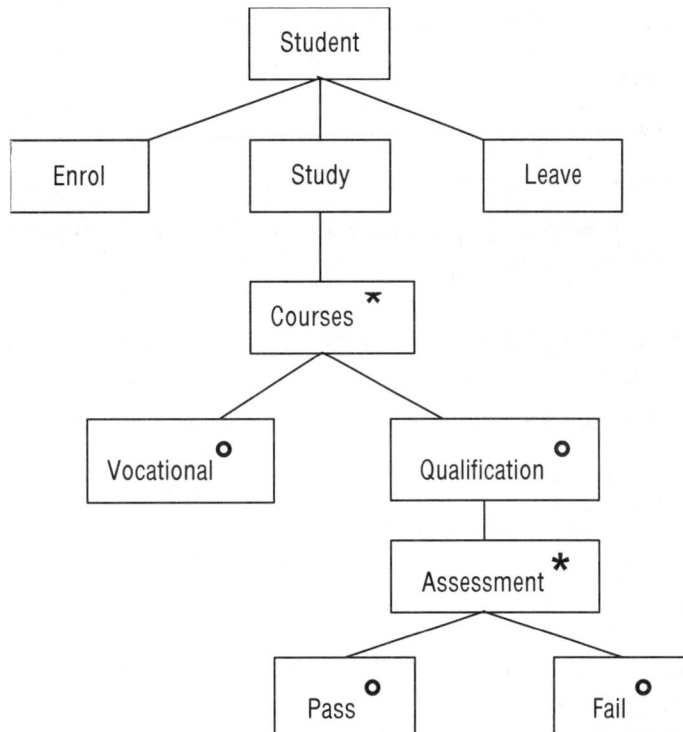

7 Data flow diagram errors

> **Text reference.** Data flow diagrams are covered in Chapter 2.
>
> **Top tips.** Use the structure of the question to provide a structure to your answer. There are four techniques to cover, and for each you are required to explain the technique and how it helps the systems analyst.
>
> There are therefore eight separate areas to cover.

(a) **Data Flow Diagrams (DFDs)** describe the flow of data between entities, processes and data stores. Data is shown being transferred to and from entities such as customers, suppliers and different departments. Within each department, the flow of data in terms of the processing required and the storage of that data identifies how data is changed within each department.

By showing the flow of data, the DFD helps the systems analyst understand how data needs to move around the organisation without having to be concerned about the physical representation of that system in terms of computers, document flows etc. The logical data flow is identified; the actual physical requirements can be determined to follow the required flow, rather than the physical requirements being implemented and the logical flow having to follow these.

Entity Relationship Models (ERMs) are used to show the links between different items of entities, primarily in the context of database design. In this context, an entity can be a person, document, location etc. about which information is stored. The links between entities are expressed in terms of relationships, with the diagram categorising those links. For example, one customer can be related to many sales invoices, but each sales invoice only relates to one customer.

ERMs are used to plan database structures. The relationships help the analyst build the logical structure for the database, which will then be turned into the physical database by programmers. Providing the logical structure in the ERM helps to ensure that database meets the functional requirements of the organisation.

Entity Life Histories (ELHs) show the main events that occur in the life of an individual entity. Basically three events are always recognised: creation, amendment and termination. The ELH will show how each of the three events can occur eg creation of a new student record at a university by that student enrolling. The student record gets amended by the student taking courses. The record is then terminated either when the student graduates or occasionally when the student resigns from their course.

The ELH is used to ensure that all changes that can occur to an entity are documented. These can then be used to ensure that other documentation such as ERMs are complete prior to physical system design being started.

Decision tables show the processing of logic in a system. Each table has four sections:

- The condition section shows the events affecting a decision.

- The condition entry section shows all possible combinations of the different conditions so the effect of each combination can be determined.

- The action section shows the possible outcomes from the conditions entered in the condition section

- The action entry shows which output a given combination set of conditions provides.

Decision tables are used to show the logic of a problem, clearly stating the conditions and resulting actions. For example, the credit limit for a customer will depend on factors such as the amount purchased and type of customer, while the actions will be different discount amounts. The decision table confirms the logic of the situation and then provides the programmer with the information needed to write the logic of the computer programme to follow the actual processing required. The time taken to amend incorrect programme logic should be reduced.

Top tips. Start a question like this by looking for the obvious errors.

A quick scan of all the entities in the diagram include one named 'invoice'. This is an obvious error (if you know what an entity is!).

Look at the diagram as a whole to gain an understanding of what it is attempting to show – then focus on the detail to spot the errors.

(b) **Errors in the Data Flow Diagram**

(i) The interview information states that the order details are checked to ensure that the product and payment-type are valid. This means that the two stores are checked with data flowing from the store to process 1. However, the data flow on the diagram shows data being written to the payment type store. This arrow needs reversing to show data going from the store to process 1.

(ii) The interview information also states that the despatch-date is noted on the order file. However, on the DFD, data is shown going from the order file to process 2 only. Another data flow is needed to show the despatch date being added to the order file.

(iii) At the end of the week, invoices are raised and sent to the *customer*. However, the DFD shows invoice data being sent to an external entity called Invoice. The name of this entity needs replacing with *customer*. Also, as the external entity customer is now duplicated, a line or similar duplication symbol needs added to both occurrences of the entity to identify this duplication.

(c) Data flow diagrams are used during the **analysis stage** of development.

8 Decision table and software testing

Text reference. Chapter 2 shows how decision tables are constructed. Overcoming resistance to change is covered in Chapter 14.

Top tips. To produce an accurate table you must first identify the conditions the table should contain.

Read through the narrative and ask what are the factors that impact upon the action or decisions taken. These are the conditions.

Then ensure you identify all possible actions in the bottom half of your table.

In Part (e) you will get marks for reasonable points. You do not need to quote the theory that is presented.

BPP marking scheme

			Marks
(a)	1 mark for identifying each condition (two conditions)	2	
	1 mark for identifying each action (three actions)	3	
	1 mark for identifying each column (four columns)	4	9
(b)	1 mark for each valid point – to a maximum of 3 marks.		3
(c)	1 mark for each valid point – to a maximum of 3 marks.		3
(d)	1 mark for each valid point – to a maximum of 3 marks.		3
(e)	1 mark for identifying each technique	6	
	1 mark for describing each technique	6	12
			30

(a)

	1	2	3	4
Car garaged?	Y	Y	N	N
Willing to pay £250 excess?	Y	N	Y	N
Standard quote	X	X	X	X
5% increase on quote		X		X
£100 addition to quote			X	X

(b) Decision tables are used to improve the thoroughness of software testing as they ensure:

- **All possible combinations of conditions are tested**. By following the rules of decision table construction, every combination of conditions is identified. In this example there are four (as 2*2=4) possible combinations.

- **Required outcomes are established for each combination**. To be sure that the system is operating correctly, it is necessary to know what the correct outcome is for each combination. Constructing an accurate decision table ensures the correct outcomes are specified before the test is executed.

(c) The role of **volume** or **performance testing** is to evaluate the compliance of a system or component with specific performance requirements.

Volume testing is concerned with the number/frequency of transactions or other activity that the system can cope with.

Testing is usually carried out to ensure the system can meet defined performance objectives (such as a two-second response time) given expected data volumes and network traffic.

Volume testing involves increasing the volume of transactions input within a given timeframe to establish the volume of transactions or data the system can handle.

The technical specifications of the system provide some indication, but testing in the actual operating environment is required to establish a more accurate picture.

(d) The role of **user acceptance testing** is to establish how well the system meets user needs and to identify any problems with the system in a realistic environment.

User acceptance testing is vital as a system may look great on paper and perform well when tested by analysts and programmers, but prove **inefficient** when used by users in the required operating environment.

User acceptance testing is concerned with the system performing as **users expect** (eg output/results are correct) and also with ease of use (usability).

Users could identify **errors of logic**, or identify relatively small changes (eg screen layout) that would enhance the **user friendliness** of the system.

Users acceptance testing should ultimately conclude with **user sign-off** – users accepting the system.

(e) Kotter and Schlesinger (1979) identify six techniques:

(i) **Education and Communication**

- Small group briefings
- Newsletters
- Management development
- Training

(ii) **Participation and Involvement**

- Small groups
- Delegates and representatives

(iii) **Facilitation and Support**

- One-on-one counselling
- Personal development
- Provision of organisational resources

(iv) **Negotiation and Agreement**

- Provision of rewards
- Collective bargaining

(v) **Manipulation and Co-optation**

- Influence staff that are positively disposed
- Buy-off informal leaders
- Provide biased information

(vi) **Explicit and implicit coercion**

- Threaten staff with penalties
- Create sense of fear
- Victimise individuals to send message to the rest

9 Question with student answer: System development

Student answer

Text reference. Systems development is covered in Chapter 2.

BPP commentary. This is a 20 mark question covering system development. There are five stages identified within the question – you should provide sufficient explanation of each stage to earn the marks on offer. On the other hand, avoid the temptation to write everything you know about system development.

The key is to remain focussed on the question asked. The BPP answer does this through the use of headings and short paragraphs clearly related to the question requirement.

The main problem with the student answer below is a lack of explanation to earn the marks on offer and a failure to take into account the different mark allocation for different stages.

The student answer below represents a marginal pass for this question.

BPP marking scheme

	Marks
Explain planning and feasibility activities; up to 2 marks for each explained point	4
Explain analysis activities; up to 2 marks for each explained point	4
Explain design activities; up to 2 marks for each explained point	4
Explain development activities; up to 2 marks for each explained point	2
Explain implementation activities; up to 2 marks for each explained point	6
	20

[Not necessary to reproduce this, won't earn a mark]

Developing a computerised information system is a complex process involving the following stages.

- Planning and feasibility
- Analysis
- Design
- Development
- Implementation

[Points lack explanation. Too many points in a single paragraph]

Planning and feasibility starts with the identification of a problem or opportunity. It involves an analysis of the organisation's information requirements. The feasibility study will involve a review of existing systems and identify of a range of possible alternative solutions. A feasible (technical, operational, economic, social) solution will be selected – or a decision not to proceed made. Assuming a decision is taken to proceed, an outline plan will be developed covering the remainder of the development process.

[Good, but points need to be 'fleshed out'.]

The analysis stage starts with an investigation into the existing system to obtain details of data volumes, response times and other key indicators. The workings of the existing system are analysed to examine why current methods are used, what alternatives might achieve better results. Existing systems may be drawn using techniques such as Data Flow Diagrams.

During the design stage existing procedures are looked at (computerised and manual), including inputs, outputs, program design, file design and security. The performance criteria required from a system are established and a specification of the new system is produced.

[Accurate, but lacks explanation]

<table>
<tr><td>This is just about adequate to earn the 2 marks available</td><td>*Development involves building the system. It includes acquisition (or writing) of software and program testing. Programmers will liase with analysts and users and may need to look at drawings made during the analysis and design stages.*</td></tr>
<tr><td>This part was worth 6 marks. Far more explanation required</td><td>*Implementation activities include file conversion or set-up, buying and installation of hardware and system changeover. An important question during this stage is which method of changeover will be used.*</td></tr>
</table>

BPP answer

The main activities relevant at each of the five stages are identified and explained below.

Planning and feasibility

At this early stage the organisation investigates the need and role of a possible new system. The trigger for this may have been dissatisfaction with existing systems or the realisation that it's likely a more effective system is possible. Initial investigations into possible future systems are undertaken to establish the possibilities.

It is important that this stage results in an overview of what is required and what is available. Then issues such as cost/affordability and possible impact upon working practices must be considered. The scope and detail required of a feasibility study will depend to a certain extent upon the size and nature of the system.

A steering committee may be set up to oversee the development process. This should draw upon areas of expertise from across the organisation (eg financial, technical and human resources) to ensure all relevant issues are considered (eg cost, capacity and training needs).

Compare the amount of explanation provided here with the student answer

Analysis

This stage focuses on establishing how the existing system operates and how a possible new system could operate. User interviews, a review of existing documentation (eg user manuals, procedures manuals, system logs) and the production of system diagrams (eg data flow diagrams) are carried out during this stage.

It is important that a good understanding of how the system works, what it is used for and how people interact with it is established. This knowledge is essential to avoid oversights in the design of the new system. User input into the development process is essential at this early stage if expensive re-work is to be avoided later in the process.

Again, no extra knowledge was required than used in the student answer – but the explanation provided would earn more marks

Design

The design stage involves using the information gathered during the analysis stage and using this to design a suitable system that will meet the needs of users.

Diagrammatic techniques such as data flow diagrams and entity life histories may also be used at this stage to represent the way data and information will be held and communicated in the new system.

The proposed design should be developed with user consultation and reviewed by user representatives.

At the end of this stage a system specification document should exist that clearly outlines the new system design (including hardware and software requirements).

Good use of layout to distinguish the points made. Encourage the marker to give you marks!

Development

The development stage involves doing whatever is necessary to take the new system off the 'drawing board' and bring it into existence.

For bespoke systems this will involve programmers writing and testing code for the new software. If software is to be purchased off-the-shelf, the final selection and purchase will be made.

Less explanation provided and fewer points made reflecting the mark allocation

Implementation

Implementation involves installing and introducing the system into use. Installation includes the five steps explained below.

A greater number of points (with explanation) reflecting the mark allocation

- File conversion involves ensuring data to be held in the new system is in a suitable format. This process is likely to involve the conversion of data held in both existing computer and manual files.

- Installation involves installing the hardware and software that comprise the system. This should be performed by IT specialists.

- Testing the system in the 'real' environment is essential – including user acceptance testing. Some problems may only become apparent in the 'live' environment.

- Training users to ensure they are able to utilise the full potential of the system. Users should be trained before changeover!

- Changing over from the old system to the new. The method of changeover is a key consideration (eg direct, parallel, phased or pilot). The most appropriate method will depend upon the individual circumstances (eg the trade-off between cost and risk).

User support in the period after changeover is essential to ensure the smooth running and acceptance of the system.

10 Multiple choice questions: Operations management 1

10.1 A   ISO 14001 covers issues related to an organisation's environmental performance.

10.2 B   This theory was produced by *Ouchi* in 1981.

10.3 C   The 5-S model describes operations management practices of structurizse, systemize, sanitize and self-discipline. It does not describe internal analysis or a form of six sigma.

10.4 C   A and D refer to continuous inventory systems , while B refers to periodic inventory (or bin) systems.

10.5 D   Strategic benchmarking is a form of competitive benchmarking, but its purpose is directed towards strategic action and organisational change.

10.6 A   To gain ISO accreditation an organisation is required to submit documentation to show that their processes meet ISO requirements.

   The other options are not necessarily required.

10.7 D   An important aspect of TQM is achieving customer satisfaction for both external and internal customers (eg other departments). Consistency is important because customers need to know what they are 'going to get' – the standard of output must be reliable and provide customer satisfaction. Another aspect of TQM is continuous improvement: there is always scope for further improvements, however small. TQM is also based on the concept of getting things right first time – avoiding sub-standard output before it is produced.

10.8 D   The five S words are: Seiri or Structurise; Selton or Systemise; Seiso or Sanitise; Seiketsu or Standardise and Shitsuke or Self-discipline.

10.9 A   Kaizen seeks to improve quality by small, incremental steps. It does not seek radical changes (options B and C) and is not a problem solving technique (option D).

10.10 A   TQM aims to eliminate the costs of poor quality – not just reduce them. It is not possible to eliminate all quality-related costs without ceasing production. TQM does not aim to reduce the workforce – although changes in working methods may be required to improve quality.

11 Multiple choice questions: Operations management 2

11.1 D SPC may help eliminate poor quality but doesn't on its own, SPC measures processes rather than output such as products and SPC doesn't necessarily require 24 hour supervision – it requires the process to be monitored whenever its operating (usually using a computer).

11.2 B Fewer (preferably none) internal failures means less time lost correcting problems and therefore more time engaged in production. The other options are false; internal failures cause delays in delivery, improving process quality should reduce the testing required and inspecting finished goods is expensive as it means re-producing sub-standard production rather than focusing efforts on producing high quality output first time.

11.3 D TQM focuses on 'getting things right first time' rather than on inspecting completed output. The other options aren't directly related to TQM.

11.4 A Kaizen is originally a Buddhist term but was adopted by the Japanese (and now by other nations) to represent continuous improvement. The other options may involve or imply some elements of continuous improvement but have different meanings.

11.5 C Because of this, lean manufacturing is sometimes referred to as the Toyota Production System (TPS).

11.6 A The other options appear on the strategic supply wheel but not in the centre (the wheel also includes 'organisation structure' and 'performance measures' – not included in this question).

11.7 D The other options do not refer to recognised, formal supply sourcing strategies.

11.8 D Under a level capacity plan activity is maintained at a constant level.

11.9 A Under a chase demand capacity plan, the activity level responds to changes in demand.

11.10 B Five S (5-S) practice encourages standardised procedures to improve both the physical environment and environmental factors relevant to employee attitudes and thought.

12 Multiple choice questions: Operations management 3

12.1 D World-class manufacturing involves a strong customer focus and the flexibility to enable changes to be made to meet customer requirements.

12.2 B In this paper, you should have studied ABC as an inventory management method that concentrates effort on the most important items.

12.3 A Corrective work, the cost of scrap and materials lost are examples of internal failure costs.

12.4 D Economies of scope refers to economically producing small batches of a variety of products with the same machines (eg using Computer Aided Manufacturing that allows settings to be changed to produce different products).

12.5 A *Reck* and *Long*'s strategic positioning tool identifies an organisation's purchasing approach.

12.6 D Inbound logistics is a primary activity that refers to receipt, storage and inward distribution of raw materials.

12.7 B Supply chain partnerships grow out of recognising the supply chain and linkages in a value system.

12.8 C Training workers in methods of statistical process control and work analysis is part of a quality management approach.

12.9 C JIT means goods are only produced when needed, so stock-outs are more likely than with traditional production (although if the JIT system operates correctly stock-outs should be avoided).

12.10 B Quality control systems improve quality within the organisation. The other options may be part of such a system.

13 Objective test questions: Operations management 1

13.1 Quality control systems involve comparing actual quality with desired or expected quality. This allows corrective action to be taken if required. Quality assurance systems attempt to ensure quality by focussing on product design, production materials, methods and processes – rather than focussing quality checks on output.

13.2 Operations Management

Concerned with developing processes within an organisation that turn inputs, such as materials and labour, into outputs, such as products and services.

Technostructure

Co-ordinates work through standardising processes, outputs and skill. Involves expert advice and work-study.

Relationship

OM = Operating core that finances the technostructure which improves its effectiveness.

13.3 Continuous inventory systems

Continually monitor stock levels. When levels fall below a predetermined amount an order is sent to replenish it. A minimum buffer stock is held regardless of demand.

These systems go against JIT philosophy that goods should only be delivered when needed (stockless production) and waste should be eliminated.

13.4 Examples of external failure costs

- Delivery of faulty products and replacements
- Operating a customer services section
- Repair or replacement

Significance

- Loss of 'quality' reputation
- Loss of future custom
- Damaged staff morale
- Potential loss of ISO accreditation if a member
- Bad PR

13.5 Automation usually involves assisting employees to carry out the same task but more efficiently. Rationalisation involves not only the automation of a process but also efficient process design. Automation and rationalisation usually offer modest returns and little risk. Business process re-engineering involves fundamental changes in the way an organisation functions.

14 Objective test questions: Operations management 2

14.1 Just-in-time (JIT) systems minimise inventory holdings as items are produced or delivered 'just-in-time' for production. This means very little cash is tied-up in unnecessary stocks. JIT should therefore improve organisational cash flow (compared to traditional production).

14.2 A manufacturing organisation could use Computer Aided Design (CAD) software to improve the efficiency in the design process. Computer Assisted Manufacturing (CAM) software could be used to ensure the production process results in products that meet the required specification. Also, statistical software could be used to monitor the production process.

14.3   Quality control focuses on the inspection of work already completed to check it meets the required standards. Quality circles involve groups of employees meeting to share ideas and discuss ways in which problems could be solved and quality improved.

14.4   Total Productive Maintenance (TPM) reduces breakdowns and helps ensure production consistency. This helps ensure uniform output, reduces waste and therefore lowers the cost of quality. TPM also improves the accuracy of production schedules and therefore facilitates on-time order delivery – an important aspect of customer service quality.

14.5   Total Quality Management (TQM) embraces continuous improvement, employee involvement and the need for a customer focus to achieve customer satisfaction. The customer focus required under TQM should result in a refocusing of all areas of customer satisfaction (for example through quality circles) – and a commitment to long-term quality improvement.

15 Virtual companies and purchasing

Text reference. Virtual companies, virtual supply chains and purchasing are covered in Chapter 5.

Top tips. Don't be put off by the jargon used. 'Virtual' in this context simply means web-based.

Easy marks. The definition required in part (a). Ensure you provide sufficient detail to earn the 2 marks available.

(a)   A **virtual company** is a collection of separate companies, each with a specific expertise, who work together, sharing their expertise to compete for bigger contracts/projects than would be possible if they worked alone.

(b)   Within the last five years it has become increasingly common for combinations of organisations and individuals to combine in the form of a virtual company and **virtual supply chains**. Virtual companies enable people such as executives, engineers, researchers and others, based in a number of locations, to collaborate on a particular venture.

This trend has been made possible by the widespread use of **remote networking** which is now available at relatively low cost to organisations of all sizes. The collaborators are able to utilise technology to work together and present themselves as a single virtual entity to potential clients.

Virtual companies and members of virtual supply chains tend to utilise the Internet and related technologies such as **intranet** and **extranet**. To be successful the partners involved must do more than establish virtual links. They must provide complimentary areas of expertise, and develop a close relationship based on mutual need and trust.

A virtual company may be the best way to implement business strategies particularly strategies that require **close collaboration** with others. For example, in order to exploit a new opportunity, business partners may be required to move fast. Establishing a virtual company may enable these partners to quickly establish a united entity to pursue the opportunity. Establishing traditional 'bricks and mortar' links would take considerably longer – increasing the risk of competitors grasping the opportunity first.

Top tips. Your ability to deal with Part (c) really depends on your awareness of what a purchasing department does. When you move on to explain how purchasing can contribute to organisational performance, think of wider issues such as partnerships with suppliers and ensuring quality.

(c)   The purchasing department is responsible for the **acquisition** of the physical (as opposed to human and financial) resources that the organisation requires in order to operate. It will co-operate with other departments in order to deploy an effective purchasing strategy. This can **increase profit** in three ways.

- Obtaining best value for money
- Helping to meet quality targets
- Minimising stock holding costs

BPP
LEARNING MEDIA

There are four components to the purchasing mix.

Quantity. Quantities ordered will depend on three things: economic order computations; if a computerised automatic re-order trigger level is used, the level this is set at; and whether or not JIT is used.

The EOQ approach balances the administrative costs of dealing with purchase orders against the cost associated with holding stock. The JIT approach, however, aims to minimise stock holdings as an over riding priority, since the cost of holding stock, in working capital terms alone, is seen as highly wasteful. Automatic ordering can be set up to use either approach and will produce constant order quantities. Where there is manual ordering, there may be more variation.

Quality. The purchasing officer will liaise with R&D, purchasing and marketing about the quality of inputs. Technical specifications may be modified in the light of experience: the principle considerations should be what is acceptable to the ultimate customer. Purchasing from ISO 9000 approved suppliers can reduce the burden of acceptance inspection.

Price. It will be a major responsibility of the purchasing officer to ensure value for money over time, but the pursuit of discounts above all else may lead to over-stocking (to obtain quantity discounts) and may damage relationships with suppliers.

Delivery. Inputs must be made available as they are needed by the production process. This requires consideration of order lead times. Where a JIT system is installed, the scheduling of deliveries must be integrated with the scheduling of production. This is usually achieved by the use of a Kanban or pull system.

It is now common for the purchasing department to undertake control of the entire **inbound logistics** function, including quality matters and stores management. The advent of the JIT approach to procurement has extensive implications for these matters. Order quantity and delivery have been mentioned above. Quality is particularly important. Where a bare minimum of material is delivered to support current production, consistent quality becomes vital: there are no spares available if an item is rejected.

This has led to an increased degree of co-operation between purchasing businesses and their suppliers. It is common for purchasers to enter into a kind of **partnership** with their suppliers, abandoning the adversarial approach designed to secure the lowest price by playing one supplier off against another. Through co-operation, purchasers can improve the quality of the goods delivered, by assisting their chosen suppliers to improve their output. They can also secure their supplies, by guaranteeing a **long-term relationship**.

Under such a system, suppliers become more or less integrated into the purchaser's **value chain**, with significant benefits accruing to both parties. Both parties can plan for smooth production and minimise the costs associated with selling on the one hand and purchasing on the other.

16 TQM and sourcing

Text references. Chapter 6 covers TQM whilst Chapter 15 features sourcing strategies.

Top tips. If you memorise these seven principles of TQM using the bold headings you will have a ready made structure to answer similar future questions.

(a)   In a nutshell, **Total quality management** (TQM) is a management philosophy, aimed at **continuous improvement** in all areas of operation.

A TQM initiative aims to achieve continuous improvement in quality, productivity and effectiveness. It does this by establishing management responsibility for processes as well as output.

Principles of TQM

(i)   **Prevention**

Organisations should take measures that prevent poor quality occurring.

(ii)   **Right first time**

A culture should be developed that encourages workers to get their work right first time. This will save costly reworking.

(iii) **Eliminate waste**

The organisation should seek the most efficient and effective use of all its resources.

(iv) **Continuous improvement**

The Kaizan philosophy should be adopted. Organisations should seek to improve their processes continually.

(v) **Everybody's concern**

Everyone in the organisation is responsible for improving processes and systems under their control.

(vi) **Participation**

All workers should be encouraged to share their views and the organisation should value them.

(vii) **Teamwork and empowerment**

Workers across departments should form team bonds so that eventually the organisation becomes one. Quality circles are useful in this regard. Workers should be empowered to make decisions as they are in the best position to decide how their work is done.

Top tips. This is a question that may appear daunting at first, but if you go through and deal with each element in turn it should not prove too difficult to earn a pass.

Ensure you provide justification for the changes you recommend.

(b) **Aluminium foil** is obtained from a single supplier – a sourcing strategy termed 'single sourcing'. The advantages of this strategy include:

- Easy to develop and maintain a relationship with a single supplier – which is especially beneficial when the purchasing company relies on that supplier.

- A supplier quality assurance program can be implemented easily to help guarantee the quality of products – again mainly because there is only one supplier.

Economies of scale may be obtained from volume discounts.

However, the **disadvantages** of this strategy are:

- PicAPie is dependent on the supplier – providing significant supplier power. Issues such as quality assurance may not be addressed quickly because the supplier is aware that there are few alternative sources of supply.

- PicAPie is vulnerable to any disruption in supply.

Given that there are few suppliers in the industry this strategy may be appropriate. However, there is no guarantee that the current supplier will not go out of business so the directors of PicAPie could look for alternative sources of supply to guard against this risk.

The **pastry shell flour** is obtained a number of suppliers – a strategy known as **multi-sourcing**. The advantages of this strategy include:

- Ability to switch suppliers should one fail to provide the flour. Having suppliers in different countries is potentially helpful in this respect as poor harvests in one country may not be reflected in another.

- Competition may help to decrease price.

Disadvantages include:

- It may be difficult to implement a quality assurance program due to time needed to establish it with different suppliers.

- Suppliers may display less commitment to PicAPie depending on the amount of flour purchased making supply more difficult to guarantee.

PicAPie appears to have covered the risk of supply well by having multiple sources of supply. The issue of quality remains and PicAPie could implement some quality standards that suppliers must adhere to in order to keep on supplying flour.

A third party is given the responsibility for obtaining **meat and vegetables** – this is termed **delegated sourcing**. Advantages of this method include:

- Provides more time for PicAPie to concentrate on pie manufacture rather than obtaining inputs. Internal quality control may therefore be improved.

- The third party is responsible for quality control checks on input – again freeing up more time in PicAPie. Where quality control issues arise, PicAPie can again ask the third party to resolve these rather than spending time itself.

- Supply may be easier to guarantee as the specialist company will have contacts with many companies.

Disadvantages are:

- Quality control may be more difficult to maintain if the third party does not see this as a priority.

- There will be some loss of confidentiality regarding the products that PicAPie uses, although if there are no 'special ingredients' then this may not be an issue.

Given the diverse sources of supply, PicAPie are probably correct using this strategy.

The **plastic film** is obtained from two different sources utilising two different supply systems. This is termed **parallel sourcing**. The advantages of this method include:

- Supply failure from one source will not necessarily halt pie production because the alternative source of supply should be available.

- There may be some price competition between suppliers.

Disadvantages include:

- PicAPie must take time to administer and control two different systems.

- Quality may be difficult to maintain, and as with multiple sourcing, it will take time to establish supplier quality assurance programmes. Given that some stock is surplus to requirements from other sources, quality control programmes may not be possible anyway.

The weakness in the supply strategy appears to be obtaining film from the Internet site – in that quality control is difficult to monitor. Changing to single sourcing with a supplier quality assurance programme would be an alternative strategy to remove this risk.

17 Operations management

Text references. Managing capacity and demand is covered in Chapter 5, the 'lean' concept and six sigma can be found in Chapter 6.

Top tips. To be able to score any marks on Part (a) of this question you must understand the three planning and control activities referred to. This shows the importance of ensuring you have studied all of the BPP Study Text. Any topic from the P4 syllabus could appear in an examination question.

Note the mark allocations in Part (b). Don't waffle, a short, punchy answer will earn the marks on offer within the time available.

(a)   (i)   **Loading** is the amount of work that is allocated to an operating unit. The term is frequently applied to the allocation of workloads to a machine or group of machines, although it has more general application than just machines. In theory, a machine can operate for 24 hours each day, seven days a week. In practice, this is not realistic. Machines cannot be in operational use if they are being cleaned, serviced or repaired. A hairdressing salon could open on a 24/7 basis but it is unlikely that customers would want their hair done at, say, 3 o'clock in the morning.

- **Finite loading** occurs when work is allocated to an operating unit up to a set limit, and then no further work is allocated to that unit. Finite loading is particularly appropriate when it is necessary to limit the load. An aircraft, for example, has a maximum load capacity and there is a limit to the number of passengers, for safety reasons.

- **Infinite loading** occurs when there is no set limit to the loading of an operating unit, which is expected to deal as well as it can with any unexpected surge in demand. Infinite loading is particularly appropriate where it is not possible to limit the load (eg refugees should not be turned away from a refugee camp) or when it is not necessary to limit the load (eg in a fast-food outlet, customers will often be prepared to wait for some time in a queue if they cannot get immediate service).

(ii)   Whether loading is finite or infinite, decisions have to be taken when work comes in about the order in which different jobs will be done or different orders fulfilled. This planning and control activity is called **sequencing**. The sequencing of operations will be decided according to a set of rules or guidelines, which could be any of the following.

- Customer priority
- Due date
- Last in first out
- First in first out
- Longest operation time first (LOT)
- Shortest operation time first (SOT)

The preferred sequencing criteria should be the one that **optimises** operational performance.

Once work has been sequenced and jobs put in order for completion, it might then be necessary to prepare a detailed timetable that schedules the work required in a way that meets customer demand (an activity known as **scheduling**).

In some operations, scheduling is impracticable, and the operation must simply react to orders as they arrive. This is more likely in service industries such as hairdressing, petrol stations and restaurants.

Forward scheduling means starting work as soon as it arrives. **Backward scheduling** means starting a job at the latest time necessary to complete it by the latest acceptable time.

(iii)   Having loaded, sequenced and scheduled the work, management must **monitor** the operation to make sure that the work is carried out as planned. Any deviation from the plan should be identified as soon as a problem becomes apparent so that corrective measures can be taken (**control action**), or so that the work can be re-scheduled.

The terms '**push control**' and '**pull control**' refer to when control action is taken to manage the flow of work. With push control, the focus is on pushing work through each stage of the process, regardless of whether the next stage is ready to receive it. Push control is characterised by centralised scheduling and control. There are likely to be inventories at each stage, queues and idle time.

With pull control, the focus is on each stage of the process calling for work to be delivered from the previous process when it is needed. The work is not delivered from the previous process until it is needed, and the customer (internal or external) acts as the stimulus for the supplier to do the work. An example of pull control is a **just-in-time** purchasing and production system. With pull control, there should be less inventory in the system.

Top tips. Lean and six sigma are relatively new techniques/theories and remain fairly topical. As such, they are likely to feature regularly in the P4 exam. This question and answer provides good revision of them. Remember you may have to apply this knowledge if these topics are tested in a scenario question.

(b)   (i)   The **Lean concept** means eliminating waste. Waste means any activity that does not create value for the customer. 'Waste' activities include:

- Rework
- Waste of material and labour
- Over-production
- Waiting or idle time

Lean emphasises workplace organisation through use of the '**5Ss**' – as explained below.

- Seiri\Sort – remove any disorder
- Seiton\Straighten – organise the work environment
- Seiso\Shine – clean the work environment on an ongoing basis
- Seiketsu\Standardise × be consistent in your approach
- Shitsuke\Sustain – maintain the improved state

A Lean process is one that has eliminated waste and focuses all activity on creating value for the customer. Lean achieves greater speed, reduced costs, and employees who are more highly motivated because they understand their role and its importance.

(ii)   **Six Sigma** is a method for improving quality by removing defects and their causes in business processes. Six Sigma is normally executed by people known as Green Belts (part time), Black Belts (full time) and Master Black Belts (full time trainers and coaches).

Six Sigma is all about **reducing** the **variation** of a process. It requires an understanding of the relationship between input variables (Xs) and the dependent output variable (Y). 6 Sigma equates in percentage terms to 99.9997% accuracy or to 3.4 defects per million.

Which Sigma Level to strive for is dependent upon market conditions, competitors' performance and customer expectations. A good example is the airline industry, where it would be inconceivable that only 99% of flights landed safely. In contrast, most airline baggage handling processes are generally performing at 3 Sigma (93% accuracy).

Six Sigma has evolved into a powerful business philosophy and an instrument for driving **cultural change**. As is the case with Lean, Six Sigma also relies on the application and deployment of best management practice in a structured manner.

A common tool used in Six Sigma is **DMAIC** (explained below).

- **D**efine the customer requirements that are Critical to Quality (CTQ) and map the process at a high level.

- Establish a valid **M**easurement system, collect the data and describe the distribution of the process data.

- **A**nalyse. Determine the process capability and identify and validate root causes of variation using statistical tools.

- **I**mprove. Develop and implement solutions.

- **C**ontrol. Establish ongoing process controls to avoid the problem recurring by implementing control charts, assigning clear process ownership and documenting the improved workflow.

18 Benchmarking and quality costs

Text references. Benchmarking and quality costs are covered in Chapter 6.

Top tips. There are a large number of areas to cover in part (a). It's clear you must cover the aims, operation and limitations of internal benchmarking carefully. Read the requirement carefully and note that you must also cover these areas for external benchmarking. Part (b) can be answered from 'textbook' knowledge.

(a)   **Benchmarking** refers to the establishment of targets and comparators used to identify relative levels of performance. By the adoption of identified best practice, performance should improve. Benchmarking therefore **aims to achieve** competitive advantage by learning from others' experiences and mistakes, finding best practice and bringing this best practice into use.

Internal benchmarking involves comparing the performance of one part of a business with that of a different part of the same business with the aim of establishing best practice throughout an organisation. Some external benchmarking may be required, however, in order to establish best practice.

External benchmarking involves comparing the performance of an organisation with that of a direct competitor acknowledged to be the 'best in class' (competitive benchmarking) or comparing the performance of an internal function with those of the best external practitioners of those functions, regardless of the industry within which they operate (functional benchmarking). Given that the benchmark is the 'best' in a particular field, it provides a meaningful target towards which the organisation should aim.

Approach or operation

The basic approach to internal benchmarking is the collection of data from other functions within the organisation and are the analyse of this to establish any transferable 'best ways of working' that can be spread throughout the organisation.

For external benchmarking, 'best in class' organisations need to be identified and performance data collected. Data from non-competitors might be fairly easy to obtain; companies engaged in different industries might agree to collaborate and exchange data on, for example, debt collection as this would not place their competitive advantage in jeopardy. Obtaining data from competitors for the purposes of competitive benchmarking might be more difficult, however. Customer and supplier interviews and any publicly available data (such as promotional material and advertising, inter-firm comparison reports and information from credit rating agencies) can be used. Benchmarking 'clubs' exist, run by firms of management consultants, trade associations and professional bodies.

Any changes suggested by the internal or external exercise should be implemented, and their success monitored.

Limitations

The **principal limitations of internal benchmarking** centre on the relevance of findings in one area to the other part of the business.

- The amount of resources devoted to the units may differ.

- There may be local differences.

- Inputs and outputs may be difficult to define.

- Comparisons will only be valid if the figures reported are utterly reliable, but this is highly unlikely in practice.

- The possibility of the manipulation of figures must be considered.

Limitations associated with external benchmarking include the following.

- Deciding which activities to benchmark

- Identifying which organisation is the 'best in class' at an activity

- Persuading that organisation to share information

  (i)   If it is a direct competitor, there is little incentive for it to give away its secrets or reveal its weaknesses. Worse, it may provide information that is not authentic.

  (ii) Even if it is not a direct competitor, a rapport needs to be built up between the organisations and this will take time.

- There is little point in comparing performance with an organisation that is not 'best in class' since it will only lead to complacency.

- Practices that get good results in one organisation may not transfer successfully to another organisation: they may depend on the talents or knowledge of particular individuals or on a particular culture.

Despite these limitations, however, many benefits have been reported from the use of benchmarking, both internal and external.

(b)   **Briefing note: Categories of quality costs**

The four categories of quality costs are outlined below.

- **Prevention costs** are costs that are incurred to prevent defects before the production process is complete. An example relevant to an electrical goods manufacturer would be the cost of staff time spent double checking machine settings before commencing a production run.

- **Appraisal costs** are costs associated with establishing whether quality has been achieved. At an electrical goods manufacturing plant, an example of an appraisal cost would be the detailed inspection of a number of components from every batch produced.

- **Internal failure costs** are those costs incurred fixing a sub-standard product before the product or service is delivered. An example at an electrical goods manufacturer would be the reworking of a batch of components found to have been produced using slightly incorrect machine settings (assuming the problem was discovered on inspection before delivery to the customer).

- **External failure costs** are those costs incurred fixing a sub-standard product after the product or service has been delivered. An example relevant to an electrical goods manufacturing operation would be paying for a sub-standard batch of components to be transported back from the customers' premises to KCC, and the cost of producing a replacement batch.

19 Multiple choice questions: Managing human capital 1

19.1 B Taylor believed individuals were motivated by material reward and that efficiency in the workplace was vital.

19.2 D Expectancy theory and equity theory are both types of process theory. Process theory explores the processes through which outcomes become desirable.

19.3 A This is *Maslow*'s hierarchy.

19.4 C 360 degree feedback includes appraisal 'from all angles'; subordinates, peers, line manager and possibly external parties.

19.5 D CIMA's ethical guidelines require members to act responsibly, honour any legal contract of employment and conform to employment legislation.

19.6 A Job candidates are assessed at an assessment centre.

19.7 D Employee compliance is typically based on tight formal controls.

19.8 C Motivation is difficult to measure or judge so targets are rarely set (except informally).

19.9 B Option B shows *Honey* and *Mumford*'s four learning styles.

19.10 C The crucial difference between personnel management and HRM is the degree of integration with overall strategic management. A, B and D are all tactical activities.

20 Multiple choice questions: Managing human capital 2

20.1 C This tends to break the link between performance and reward.

20.2 A Such questions allow fair comparability between candidates.

20.3 A In a climate of learning, experimentation should be encouraged.

20.4 B This ability is a general behavioural or personal competence applicable to a wide range of roles.

20.5 A *Taylor* assumed that workers are rational so would try to obtain the highest remuneration for the least effort.

20.6 B A whistleblower exposes unethical conduct.

20.7 C The overall trend is towards shorter periods of employment with each employer.

20.8 A All possible solutions are potential weaknesses of interviewing as a selection technique. Contagious bias occurs when the interviewee 'catches' the drift of a meaning in the interviewer's words or gestures, and tries to respond in a way he or she thinks the interviewer will want to hear. The interview then fails to serve its purpose of finding out about the interviewee.

20.9 D All of the options shown are likely to result from efforts to ensure diversity in an organisation.

20.10 B Professional accountants must not be party to anything which is deceptive or misleading. This is specified in CIMA's Ethical guidelines and goes further than simply 'not telling lies'.

21 Multiple choice questions: Managing human capital 3

21.1 D Induction involves a new employee familiarising themselves with their new role and environment.

21.2 D Appraisal should be a participative, problem-solving process.

21.3 C The motivating potential score assesses job content.

21.4 B Job rotation involves individuals moving from post to post.

21.5 C Grievance procedures are established to allow employees to formally raise issues of perceived ill treatment.

21.6 C An 'assessment centre' approach is used in the selection process.

21.7 B A test that doesn't produce similar results if taken more than once by the same candidate is unreliable.

21.8 D The so-called 'psychological contract' is a notion that is based on the expectations the organisation and employee have of one another.

21.9 A According to *Douglas McGregor* 'Theory X' people dislike work, need direction and avoid responsibility.

21.10 C The purpose of a person specification is to provide details of personal characteristics, experience and qualifications expected of a candidate.

22 Multiple choice questions: Managing human capital 4

22.1 D Charles Handy's 'shamrock organisation' consists of a three-leaf structure of core, contractual and flexible part-time employees.

22.2 D Job family structures involve jobs in a function or discipline that are similar in terms of activities performed or skills required, but are differentiated by the level of skill, competence or responsibility expected.

22.3 A Maslow's theory of motivation describes a hierarchy of needs from physical needs up to self-actualisation.

22.4 B The process where new employees are familiarised with an organisation is called their induction.

22.5 C Recruitment describes the process attracting suitable candidates to apply for selection. Options A and B include selection methods. Option D is irrelevant.

22.6 C Three hundred and sixty (360) degree feedback is used in appraisal processes where appraisals from those senior and junior to an individual, or even from customers, are collected. It s not relevant to the other options.

22.7 B Job analysis forms the basis of job descriptions and person specifications. These may be used later (after an employee has performed the role) in the performance appraisal process.

22.8 C Content theories of motivation (eg *Maslow*, *Hertzberg*) focus on the needs of the individual.

22.9 D An organisational development initiative usually involves an independent third party as facilitator for the change. Therapy groups and confrontation may also be involved.

22.10 A In a redundancy situation, outplacement consultants are sometimes used to help redundant employees retrain and/or find a new job.

23 Objective test questions: Managing human capital 1

23.1 *Schein's* categories of worker:

- Rational economic man – motivated by the pursuit of self-interest and gain.

- Social man – pay attention to people's needs.

- Self-actualising man – self-fulfilment is the main driving force.

- Complex man – has a 'psychological contract' with the organisation. Could be seen as a combination of the other three categories.

23.2 Advantages:

- Tailored to organisation's specific requirements.
- Cost effective when provided by in-house staff.

Disadvantages:

- Participants may be distracted by on-going work issues.
- More likely to cancel due to lack of a cancellation fee.

23.3 Possible questions:

- Does it motivate employees?

- Does it measure the performance of employees accurately?

- Does it encourage productivity gains – and do employees understand how productivity can be improved?

- Does it accommodate change? The system needs to change as work patterns change.

23.4 Human Resources cycle:

- Selection process: obtain people with appropriate skills.

- Appraisal process: set individual performance targets in line with organisational goals.

- Training and development: fill any skill gaps and check the organisation retains appropriately skilled people.

- Reward system: to motivate and retain employees.

23.5 Appraisal purposes:

- Reward review – measuring the extent to which employee bonuses or pay increases are deserved.

- Performance review – for identifying training and development needs and validating training methods.

- Potential review – planning career development by assessing the employee's long term capability.

24 Objective test question: Managing human capital 2

24.1 *Lawrence and Lorsch's* contingency theory is based upon the premise that the management approach should be tailored to the situation. They concluded that organisations in a stable environment are more effective if they have detailed procedures and centralised decision-making while organisations in an unstable environment should have decentralisation and less emphasis on standard procedures.

24.2 Recruitment involves employing people from outside the organisation. It includes finding applicants, communicating opportunities and information and generating interest. Selection is the process of choosing who is offered the job. Selection involves procedures to choose the successful candidate from those made available through the recruitment process.

24.3 *Herzberg* identified hygiene factors as factors that don't provide motivation when present, but that cause dissatisfaction if not present. An example is wage or salary level. The argument is that employees who feel poorly rewarded could be demotivated, but that monetary reward (on its own) does not provide consistent motivation.

24.4 Potential benefits to the employer are increased employee motivation and productivity, increased employee commitment, ability to attract high performing individuals, reduced absenteeism and reduced staff turnover. Potential benefits to the employee include easier balancing of personal and professional priorities and feeling valued – which could lead to increased job satisfaction.

24.5 Stages in developing a HR plan.

1   Forecast supply of resources

- Existing
- Estimated changes (natural wastage/turnover)

2   Forecast demand

Use corporate plan to estimate requirements

3   State supply/demand in HR plan

4   Develop plan to reconcile demand/supply at target dates

Use recruitment, selection, redeployment or redundancies

25 Maslow

Text reference. Chapter 8 contains Maslow's theory while appraisals are covered in Chapter 9.

Top tips. This question is typical of many scenario questions in that it starts by testing your knowledge then moves on and requires you to apply this knowledge.

Ensure that you don't simply repeat yourself in the second part of your answer – the theory provides a framework but does not need to be repeated.

Easy marks. If you have studied the material on Maslow's hierarchy in the BPP Text, part (a) provides a chance to earn 8 marks for reproducing the relevant parts of this material.

(a)   Maslow identified that individuals are motivated by different needs – and as each need is fulfilled in a hierarchy, then other needs become dominant. **Maslow's hierarchy** of needs (starting at the bottom) is:

- **Physiological** – food and shelter
- **Safety** – security and freedom from threat
- **Love/social** – relationships and belonging
- **Esteem** – independence, recognition etc.
- **Self-actualisation** – fulfilment of personal potential

As physiological needs are satisfied, so safety needs become dominant – and so on up the hierarchy. While the theory appears to have some intuitive appeal, **criticisms** Include:

- **Empirical evidence** is hard to obtain – physiological and safety needs are not always dominant.

- **Research** also does not confirm that needs become less powerful as they are fulfilled.

- **Application of the theory is difficult** – for example, money can be used to fulfil most of the levels of the hierarchy.

- Criticism for being **too vague** and **based on western values** only.

(b)   The general purpose of any **assessment** or **appraisal** is to improve the efficiency of the organisation by ensuring that the individual employees are performing to the best of their ability and developing their potential for improvement. Performance appraisal may be defined as 'the regular and systematic review of performance and the assessment of potential with the aim of producing action programmes to develop both work and individuals.'

The **common objectives** of a formal performance appraisal system include the following:

- To **enable a picture** to be drawn up of the human 'stock' of an organisation – its strengths and weaknesses, enabling more effective personnel planning

- To **monitor** the undertaking's initial selection procedures against the subsequent performance of recruits, relative to the organisation's expectations

- To **establish** what the individual has to do in a job in order that the objectives for the section or department are realised

- To **assess** an individual's current level of-job performance. This can be used both as a base line against which performance can be measured in future and as a means of deciding how the individual has improved since the last performance appraisal. It allows managers and subordinates to plan personnel and job objectives in the light of performance

- To **identify weaknesses** in an individual's performance and identify training needs. Actual performance is compared with pre-defined objectives; shortcomings in performance are then used as indicators of the training required to achieve improvements. Training needs may arise for reasons other than the capabilities of individuals, such as new demands made by changing legislation, new technology and so on. Once training has taken place, performance appraisal enables some evaluation of training effectiveness

- To **assess** the level of **reward** payable for an individual's efforts, eg, in merit payment systems. It represents an opportunity to provide positive feedback to employees on their performance and to set new targets and challenges for the coming period along with the a reminder of possible rewards

- To **assess potential**. At the organisational level this permits career and succession planning. At the individual level it permits appraiser and person being appraised to assess the most effective development plan.

(c)   **Weaknesses** in the proposed PRP scheme include the following.

A simple **increase in earnings may not be an incentive** to some individuals. MMC's wage rates are already above industry averages, indicating that employees are meeting their basic physiological and safety needs, in terms of Maslow's theory. **Other incentives** besides increased wages **should be offered**, such as reduction in overtime working. This will enable employees to meet their love/social needs (in the context of Maslow) by providing more leisure time.

A **Performance Related Pay (PRP)** scheme would provide an incentive to produce more to obtain more income. However, the scheme suffers from two problems; some workers may not place obtaining additional income high on their list of requirements – and the scheme applies to the whole factory meaning individual workers are not in control of their PRP. Factors such as machine breakdown will limit PRP results and workers cannot control this.

If possible, the PRP scheme should be based on **individual worker performance**. This will encourage an increase in output as well as meeting esteem needs in terms of Maslow. Workers will be more in control of their job, providing greater self-esteem.

Some workers may find **additional income** (ie **money**) to be an incentive, especially where this enables them to meet higher Maslow needs in terms of self-esteem or self-actualisation. For example, having met all needs up to esteem, some people enjoy expensive holidays and they do not meet their personal potential without these. Unfortunately, working harder may result in **quality** assurance issues. The PRP scheme therefore needs to be linked to production quality to ensure this is maintained. The scheme could therefore pay some bonus based on both quantity and quality.

Having such a **long period of time between reviews** of the PRP scheme (18 months) may hinder motivation as any weaknesses in the new scheme will not be resolved until after this period. Providing a review date in say three months would allow sufficient time to note any problems and allow these to be rectified in a timely manner.

26 HR division and strategy – original

Text reference. Human resource management is covered in Chapter 7.

Top tips. Before starting your answer for part (a), consider what you will write for part (b). There is potential for overlap in these two parts – but you will not score marks for making exactly the same point twice. The two parts are different; part (a) covers the *role of the HR division* and part (b) *aspects of the HR strategy*. In part (b), start by thinking of areas that would be covered by the HR strategy – then think of how these may be affected by the recent changes at NS.

Easy marks. In part (a) you could pick up a couple of easy marks for briefly discussing the difference between a narrow personnel function and a wide HR function.

Examiner's comments. This was not a popular choice and few attempting this question performed to a high standard. A substantial number of scripts were muddled and lacked structure and cohesion.

OUTLINE NOTES: HEAD OF HR CANDIDATE INTERVIEW – HR DIVISION AND HR STRATEGY

To: Divisional director   **From:** Divisional accountant

Date: November 23 20X5

(a)   Following the new corporate initiative the HR division will have a wide ranging role. Some of the most important aspects of the role are explained below.

    (i)   The HR Division should take a **strategic approach** to employment, development and management of human recourses at NS. It is important that all aspects of people/employment issues at NS are **integrated**. A **long term** perspective, rather than the short-term firefighting approach typical of personnel departments, should be taken.

    (II)   The HR Division has a role to play in the empowerment and continuous improvement initiatives. The division could help set up **quality circles** to suggest improvements that ultimately result in improved service to customers.

    (iii)   The HR Division should represent the organisation's central value system or culture. At NS, all aspects of HR should be geared ultimately towards providing exceptional **customer service** – in line with the **customer focus** of NS. HR policies and procedures must be developed with **quality** (from a customer perspective) in mind.

(iv)   The changes at NS, and the need to improve customer service to policy holders is likely to mean longer operating hours in some areas (eg call centre staff dealing with policy renewals, claims etc). This is likely to require **new ways of working**, such as **flexible shift patterns**. The HR Division has an important role to play in devising these arrangements (eg establishing best practice in, and/or **benchmarking**, call centre operation).

(v)   The HR Division also has an important role to play in **managing the change process** (eg staff consultation, 'selling' the change, possibly providing a 'champion of change'). It is likely that **resistance to change** will occur – the HR team have an important part to play in overcoming this (eg by rewarding compliance and emphasising the need for and benefits of the change).

(b)   The HR strategy aims to ensure we have the **people** required to **successfully implement the** overall **corporate plan**. The following aspects of the HR strategy will change significantly as a result of recent developments.

(i)   **Recruitment and selection**. The 'new NS' will require pro-active, customer focussed employees right throughout the organisation. This will significantly impact the recruitment and selection strategy. A potential employee's technical skills are likely to be seen as less important – as these can be taught. The recruitment and selection process should aim to employ individuals with the personal traits/attitude required.

(ii)   **Training, induction and mentoring**. NS aims to distinguish itself from the competition by providing superior customer service. This may require more employees (eg to reduce waiting times on call centre lines) and will also require all customer facing employees to be highly efficient and to deliver exceptional service. To be able to do this, employees must have a clear understanding of the role they perform and all associated procedures. This requires thorough training (including induction and possibly mentoring).

(iii)   **Appraisal**. Employees should now be judged not only on their technical knowledge and proficiency but also on 'softer' areas such as displaying initiative and general attitude/helpfulness to both external customers and colleagues (internal customers). 360 degree appraisal could be considered.

(iv)   **Rewards**. Employee reward schemes in the 'new NS' should encourage co-operation, initiative and a focus on customer satisfaction. A bonus system linked to customer satisfaction feedback should be implemented – this should include an individual element (to encourage initiative) and a team element (to encourage co-operation between team members).

(v)   **Job design/job descriptions**. Narrow job descriptions and strict task demarcation have no place in the new NS. Employees should now be encouraged to learn a wide range of skills to enable greater flexibility in the workforce. For example, call centre employees should not specialise in one area – they should be skilled in dealing with new policy enquiries, policy renewals and claims handling.

27 HR division and strategy – amended

> **Text reference.** Human resource management is covered in Chapter 7.
>
> **Top tips.** Part (a) requires a straightforward explanation of HRM, make sure you answer the question set. Before starting your answer for part (b), consider what you will write for part (c). There is potential for overlap in these two parts – but you will not score marks for making exactly the same point twice. The two parts are different; part (a) covers the *role of the HR division* and part (b) *aspects of the HR strategy*. In part (b), start by thinking of areas that would be covered by the HR strategy – then think of how these may be affected by the recent changes at NS.
>
> **Easy marks.** In part (a) you could pick up easy marks for briefly stating objectives of HRM and why it is important. You should be able to pick up most of the marks from your general knowledge.
>
> **Examiner's comments.** This was not a popular choice and few attempting this question performed to a high standard. A substantial number of scripts were muddled and lacked structure and cohesion.

(a)   (i)   Four possible answers are listed here, you were any required to provide two.

- To **develop** an effective **human component** for the organisation which will respond effectively to change.

- To **obtain** and **develop** the **human resources** required by the organisation and to use and **motivate** them effectively.

- To **create** and **maintain** a co-operative climate of **relationships** within the organisation.

- To **meet** the organisation's **social** and **legal responsibilities** relating to the human resource.

(ii)   Large organisations such as NS Insurance employ a wide range of staff of differing cultures, social groups and academic ability. HRM is important to develop their talents and to provide human capital that meets the objectives of the organisation this can be achieved in a number of ways.

- By **increasing productivity**. Developing employee skills might make employees more productive, hence the recent emphasis on public debate on the value of training.

- By **enhancing group learning**. Employees work more and more in multi-skilled teams. Each employee has to be competent at several tasks. Some employees have to be trained to work together (ie in teamworking skills).

- By **reducing staff turnover**. Reducing staff turnover, apart from cutting recruitment costs, can also increase the effectiveness of operations. In service businesses, such as hotels, or retail outlets, reductions in staff turnover can be linked with repeat visits by customers. As it is cheaper to keep existing customers than to find new ones, this can have a significant effect on profitability.

- By **encouraging initiative**. Organisations can gain significant advantage from encouraging and exploiting the present and potential abilities of the people within them.

OUTLINE NOTES: HEAD OF HR CANDIDATE INTERVIEW – HR DIVISION AND HR STRATEGY

To: Divisional director   **From:** Divisional accountant

Date: November 23 20X5

(b)   Following the new corporate initiative the HR division will have a wide ranging role. Some of the most important aspects of the role are explained below.

(i) The HR Division should take a **strategic approach** to employment, development and management of human recourses at NS. It is important that all aspects of people/employment issues at NS are **integrated**. A **long term** perspective, rather than the short-term firefighting approach typical of personnel departments, should be taken.

(ii) The HR Division has a role to play in the empowerment and continuous improvement initiatives. The division could help set up **quality circles** to suggest improvements that ultimately result in improved service to customers.

(iii) The HR Division should represent the organisation's central value system or culture. At NS, all aspects of HR should be geared ultimately towards providing exceptional **customer service** – in line with the **customer focus** of NS. HR policies and procedures must be developed with **quality** (from a customer perspective) in mind.

(iv) The changes at NS, and the need to improve customer service to policy holders is likely to mean longer operating hours in some areas (eg call centre staff dealing with policy renewals, claims etc). This is likely to require **new ways of working**, such as **flexible shift patterns**. The HR Division has an important role to play in devising these arrangements (eg establishing best practice in, and/or **benchmarking**, call centre operation).

(v) The HR Division also has an important role to play in **managing the change process** (eg staff consultation, 'selling' the change, possibly providing a 'champion of change'). It is likely that **resistance to change** will occur – the HR team have an important part to play in overcoming this (eg by rewarding compliance and emphasising the need for and benefits of the change).

(c) The HR strategy aims to ensure we have the **people** required to **successfully implement the** overall **corporate plan**. The following aspects of the HR strategy will change significantly as a result of recent developments.

(i) **Recruitment and selection**. The 'new NS' will require pro-active, customer focussed employees right throughout the organisation. This will significantly impact the recruitment and selection strategy. A potential employee's technical skills are likely to be seen as less important – as these can be taught. The recruitment and selection process should aim to employ individuals with the personal traits/attitude required.

(ii) **Training, induction and mentoring**. NS aims to distinguish itself from the competition by providing superior customer service. This may require more employees (eg to reduce waiting times on call centre lines) and will also require all customer facing employees to be highly efficient and to deliver exceptional service. To be able to do this, employees must have a clear understanding of the role they perform and all associated procedures. This requires thorough training (including induction and possibly mentoring).

(iii) **Appraisal**. Employees should now be judged not only on their technical knowledge and proficiency but also on 'softer' areas such as displaying initiative and general attitude/helpfulness to both external customers and colleagues (internal customers). 360 degree appraisal could be considered.

(iv) **Rewards**. Employee reward schemes in the 'new NS' should encourage co-operation, initiative and a focus on customer satisfaction. A bonus system linked to customer satisfaction feedback should be implemented – this should include an individual element (to encourage initiative) and a team element (to encourage co-operation between team members).

(v) **Job design/job descriptions**. Narrow job descriptions and strict task demarcation have no place in the new NS. Employees should now be encouraged to learn a wide range of skills to enable greater flexibility in the workforce. For example, call centre employees should not specialise in one area – they should be skilled in dealing with new policy enquiries, policy renewals and claims handling.

28 Question with answer plan: Human resource plan and activities – original

Answer plan

Quickly note down points you believe could be relevant and organise them into a coherent pan. You may decide to exclude some points noted from your answer – and to add offers when writing your answer. The plan provides a flexible framework.

(a)   Steps in the plan

- Strategic review
- Current position
- Required position
- Plan to move

Flesh out with explanation in the answer

(b)   Important activities

- How paid /rewarded
- How judged/appraisal
- Wider employment issues
- Flexibility of employment

(a)   **Outline of a Human Resource Plan**

Section 1: Strategic review

Relevant issues include

- Level of taxi service
- Expansion of the tyre fitting service
- Develop the electronic wheel alignment

Section 2: The current HR position

Staffing

•	Owner/manager	1
•	Taxi drivers	8
•	Reception/Taxi co-ordinator	1
•	Tyre fitter	1

Skills

Skills gap re wheel alignment

Section 3. The required HR position (taking into account the new way of working)

Staffing recruitment required

•	Replace taxi drivers	2 (plus some flexibility in the busy season)
•	Appoint co-ordinator	1
•	Appointment of tyre fitter (with wheel alignment skills)	1 (also to train existing fitter in wheel alignment)

Section 4. Action plan to move from the current HR position to the required HR position

- Advertise, select and recruit two taxi drivers
- Recruit a tyre fitter capable of training others
- Training of taxi drivers
- Training of tyre fitters
- Review the human resource situation and the HR plan

Explanation of outline HR plan

Section 1: Strategic review

Overall business strategy will influence the HR strategy. It is necessary to establish what the strategy of the organisation is, so that the HR strategy can help this be achieved. The expansion of the tyre fitting service is a good opportunity, but has important HR implications.

Section 2: The current HR position

An audit of the existing staff and skills is necessary to establish the current HR position. In this case, staff numbers are small so this will be a fairly simple exercise.

Section 3. The required HR position (taking into account the new way of working)

Any change in strategy has HR implications. The new ways of working should be documented and staffing requirements worked out.

In this case it seems likely that staff with tyre fitting and wheel alignment skills are required (whether through recruitment, training of existing staff or a combination of both). Additional staff may be required to cope with the co-ordination of the taxi service and reception work. Also, two drivers are required to replace the two who have just left.

Section 4. Action plan to move from the current HR position to the required HR position

The required position is then compared with the current position, and plans drawn up to 'close the gap' between the two positions. In this case it may be necessary to recruit people with the specific skills required (for example the use of wheel alignment equipment). They could then pass these skills onto existing employees – building a flexible, multi-skilled workforce.

Top tips. To get the most out of a workforce, workers must be motivated and capable. Recruitment and training relate to employee capabilities – which the note to the requirement says to exclude from your answer. Therefore, your answer should cover issues related to worker motivation – appraisal and reward are two important aspects.

(b)   The important human resource activities to which attention should be paid in order to get the most out of the workforce are the reward system, an appraisal system and working arrangements.

Reward

The reward system refers to how workers are compensated for the work they do. This includes wages, bonuses and any other rewards. The company might also make use of incentive payments to reward productivity. For example, taxi drivers could be rewarded by being entitled to a percentage of all fares in excess of a basic amount per week, tyre fitters may earn a bonus based on both the quantity of work completed and the quality (eg no customer complaints).

Appraisal

Performance appraisal involves evaluating the performance of each employee including plans on how to improve performance. The appraisal gives employees the opportunity to have some input into how they see their future career development – they may be content to continue in their current role which is not necessarily a bad thing. Appraisal may also help in decisions relating to promotion or poor performance. The process also helps identify training and development needs.

Working arrangements

Working arrangements will impact upon worker performance. Issues include shift patterns, team-work, priority setting and covering holidays and sickness. Health and safety is also an important consideration. Some of these issues are related to the reward and appraisal system – for example employees are unlikely to work as a team and help others if this would adversely impact upon their own recorded output, which in turn affects their bonus.

29 Question with answer plan: Human resource plan and activities – amended

Text references. Recruitment and selection and HR plans are covered in Chapter 7. Other HR activities are in Chapter 8.

Top tips. Always note the mark allocation of the different question parts. Part (a) of this question is worth only 4 marks, part (b) is worth 14. You should therefore spend approximately 7 minutes on part (a), and 29 minutes on part (b). The requirement for part (c) is split in two. You are asked to produce an outline HR plan and then to explain each aspect of the plan. To ensure your answer is clear and focussed, provide the outline plan first, then use the same section headings to structure your explanation.

Easy marks. Four easy marks are on offer in part (a) for providing definitions of recruitment and selection. Phrase your answer in a way that makes the difference between the two clear. When you are asked to produce a document such as a 'human resource plan', start by writing the headings or steps your answer will include (with space in between). This 'pro-forma' provides a framework for your answer and ensures you pick up the easy marks on offer for the main points.

Answer plan

Quickly note down points you believe could be relevant and organise them into a coherent pan. You may decide to exclude some points noted from your answer – and to add others when writing your answer. The plan provides a flexible framework.

(a) Define recruitment
     Define selection
     Highlight the difference

(b) Define policies
     Flesh out typical recruitment and selection policy contents
     How recruitment policies can be improved
     Flesh out Importance of selection and how it can be improved

(c) Steps in the plan

     –   Strategic review
     –   Current position
     –   Required position | Flesh out with explanation in the answer |
     –   Plan to move

(a) **Recruitment**: is the part of the process concerned with finding the applicants: it is a positive action by management which involves going into the labour market (internal and external), and communicating opportunities and information and generating interest.

Selection: is part of the employee resourcing process which involves choosing between applicants for jobs: it is largely a negative process, eliminating unsuitable applicants.

(b) **Recruitment policy and practice**

Policies are general guidelines that govern how certain organisational situations will be addressed. For example the human resource management department maintains policies that govern sick leave, and benefit options.

A **typical recruitment policy** might deal with the:

- Internal advertisement of vacancies

- Efficient and courteous processing of applications

- Fair and accurate provision of information to potential recruits

- Selection of candidates on the basis of abilities related to the position, without discrimination on any grounds

Given the changes in the labour market over the past few decades and the move towards **flexibility** and **multi-skilling**, this has required modern organisations to be more acutely aware of gathering market intelligence as part of an organisation's manpower planning process.

Organisations need therefore to look at their **overall priorities** and requirements for labour and to put into place policies that recognise and meet any changes in the labour market.

There is also a need to focus not on the needs of sub-systems such as individual departments, but on the needs of the organisation and its future **growth** and **development**, particularly if the organisation has an international strategy in place.

Selection policy and practice

The selection of employees must be approached **systematically**. The recruiting officers must know what the organisation's **requirements** are, and must measure each potential candidate against those requirements. For example the selection policy may be to advertise all new posts externally with a view to introducing new blood into the organisation. In such a case the organisation's policy on selection will evident to all members of the organisation whether they be internal or external applicants.

Although this policy may be unpopular with some members of the organisation, it clearly **defines** how candidates will be selected. Any organisation must however be aware that it should review and monitor both the recruitment and selection process in order to meet the challenges and changes that will affect the business.

(c) **Outline of a Human Resource Plan**

Section 1: Strategic review

Relevant issues include

- Level of taxi service
- Expansion of the tyre fitting service
- Develop the electronic wheel alignment

Section 2: The current HR position

Staffing

*   Owner/manager   1
*   Taxi drivers   8
*   Reception/Taxi co-ordinator   1
*   Tyre fitter   1

Skills

*   Skills gap re wheel alignment

Section 3. The required HR position (taking into account the new way of working)

Staffing recruitment required

*   Replace taxi drivers   2 (plus some flexibility in the busy season)

*   Appoint co-ordinator   1

*   Appointment of tyre fitter   1 (also to train existing fitter in wheel alignment)
    (with wheel alignment skills)

Section 4. Action plan to move from the current HR position to the required HR position

*   Advertise, select and recruit two taxi drivers
*   Recruit a tyre fitter capable of training others
*   Training of taxi drivers
*   Training of tyre fitters
*   Review the human resource situation and the HR plan

Explanation of outline HR plan

Section 1: Strategic review

Overall business strategy will influence the HR strategy. It is necessary to establish what the strategy of the organisation is, so that the HR strategy can help this be achieved. The expansion of the tyre fitting service is a good opportunity, but has important HR implications.

Section 2: The current HR position

An audit of the existing staff and skills is necessary to establish the current HR position. In this case, staff numbers are small so this will be a fairly simple exercise.

Section 3. The required HR position (taking into account the new way of working)

Any change in strategy has HR implications. The new ways of working should be documented and staffing requirements worked out.

In this case it seems likely that staff with tyre fitting and wheel alignment skills are required (whether through recruitment, training of existing staff or a combination of both). Additional staff may be required to cope with the co-ordination of the taxi service and reception work. Also, two drivers are required to replace the two who have just left.

Section 4. Action plan to move from the current HR position to the required HR position

The required position is then compared with the current position, and plans drawn up to 'close the gap' between the two positions. In this case it may be necessary to recruit people with the specific skills required (for example the use of wheel alignment equipment). They could then pass these skills onto existing employees – building a flexible, multi-skilled workforce.

30 HR plan and workforce flexibility – original

> **Text references.** HR plans and workforce flexibility are both covered in Chapter 7.
>
> **Top tips.** There is much to cover in part (a). Ensure you don't just focus on the stages involved in developing a HR plan – you are also required to describe the main issues to consider in this process.
>
> In part (b), mention the different types of workforce flexibility (eg numerical, task, financial) and suggest how these could be achieved at CX.
>
> **Easy marks.** In part (a), start with a brief explanation of the role of the HR plan. This should help focus your answer – as well as earning an easy mark.
>
> **Examiner's comments.** There was a real range of performance on this question from well-prepared candidates who successfully applied known theory to the scenario in a purposeful manner to those who merely reproduced their understanding of general HR issues.

(a)   **Human resource planning** involves developing a plan to recruit, utilise, develop and retain staff.

The CX buy-out involves three main initiatives; heritage 'real ale' tours, bottling beer for sales in supermarkets and employing a flexible but experienced workforce.

The HR plan associated with the buy-out must support these initiatives. The **main issues** involved in developing a HR plan for the CX buy-out are described below.

Workable. The plan must be realistic and suitable for implementation (taking into account cost and working practices).

Impact upon culture. CX has a long history and a national reputation for traditional 'real ale' production. Although CX wishes to change, the organisation and the people that work there should preserve this feeling and reputation as it is a source of competitive advantage. Therefore, the HR plan should encourage valued ex-employees back – it should **not** be a case of 'out with the old and in with the new'.

Specific issues the plan should address include:

- Budgets, targets and standards for staffing at all levels
- How the flexibility required within the workforce will be achieved
- The retraining required and how this will be addressed
- Remuneration and reward systems
- Responsibilities and procedures for implementing, monitoring and controlling the plan

There are four main **stages involved in developing a HR plan** for the CX buy-out.

Stage 1: Conduct an audit of existing human resources

As the brewery has closed, technically there are no existing human resources. However, as the shut down only occurred a month ago, and the workforce has specialist skills, it is highly likely that most ex-employees would be available for reemployment. The buy-out team should consult HR records and speak to key ex-employees to establish the current position.

Deciding who should be offered employment is a key task. Selection should take into account existing employee skills and the potential to develop any new skills required. A key consideration for re-employment would be a willingness to be flexible rather than simply 'I want my old job back'.

Stage 2: Forecast future demand for skills/labour

Past experience should provide a reasonable estimate of staff numbers required (including seasonal fluctuations).

New activities (eg bottling) will require new skills – and increased workforce flexibility also needs to be taken into account when estimating the numbers/skill mix required. Bottling may also impact upon seasonal fluctuations. Brewery tours will require significantly different skills.

All of these factors need to be considered and addressed – within a realistic, budget.

Stage 3: Assess the external labour market and forecast supply

In this situation, the external market is somewhat blurred with the internal market (as Stage 1 of this plan included ex-employees). Supply for many positions/skills is likely to be able to be satisfied from the pool of ex-employees – but areas such as bottling and brewery tours may require specialist knowledge and skills that may need to be found from other sources. Teaching ex-employees new skills is another option.

Information relating to ex-employees will be available using CX HR records. These should provide a wide range of information including positions held, age, training undertaken and performance levels.

Stage 4: Establish a plan reconciling demand and supply

When a realistic estimate of employee numbers and skills has been established, the next step is to produce action plans that will result in the recruitment and training of a workforce that will meet the demands of CX.

The plan should ensure steps are taken to ensure all required positions and skills are accounted for. Key employees should be identified by name. There may also need to be contingencies built into the plan to allow for circumstances where expected 'first options' are unavailable.

The four steps outlined above will not run completely sequentially – in reality many aspects of the plan will span more than one stage.

(b) Before the shut-down, **seasonal fluctuations** in sales were large – an indicator that labour flexibility has always been important.

Logic dictates that as the old CX was ultimately unsuccessful the new CX must do something different. Changes in working practices will therefore be required. This is why the CX buy-out team have identified **workforce flexibility** as a key aspect of their plan.

Although the introduction of brewery tours and bottled beers may help smooth seasonal fluctuations, they will also introduce the need for new skills and probably new working hours. Flexibility is therefore essential.

For CX, the flexibility required would include **numerical**, **task** and **financial**.

Numerical flexibility. This is key to deal with seasonal fluctuations and for different demand levels during the day and or week eg for tours.

The development of a numerically flexible workforce will involve the use of temporary and part time workers supplementing full time employees (eg *Handy's* Shamrock). Another option is the outsourcing of non-core functions.

Task or functional flexibility. This involves recruiting and developing multi-skilled staff able to perform a range of tasks. This helps reduce overall numbers and provides ready made cover in cases of absence.

At CX, an employee may for example be able to help with brewing, carry out maintenance and conduct a brewery tour all on the same day.

Financial flexibility. This is achieved most often through performance related reward system.

At CX, staff payments should be linked to output (eg litres brewed, bottles produced, feedback scores from brewery tours or achieving financial targets related to sales figures and profitability).

31 HR plan and workforce flexibility – amended

(a)   **Human resource planning** involves developing a plan to recruit, utilise, develop and retain staff.

The CX buy-out involves three main initiatives; heritage 'real ale' tours, bottling beer for sales in supermarkets and employing a flexible but experienced workforce.

The HR plan associated with the buy-out must support these initiatives. The **main issues** involved in developing a HR plan for the CX buy-out are described below.

Workable. The plan must be realistic and suitable for implementation (taking into account cost and working practices).

Impact upon culture. CX has a long history and a national reputation for traditional 'real ale' production. Although CX wishes to change, the organisation and the people that work there should preserve this feeling and reputation as it is a source of competitive advantage. Therefore, the HR plan should encourage valued ex-employees back – it should **not** be a case of 'out with the old and in with the new'.

Specific issues the plan should address include:

- Budgets, targets and standards for staffing at all levels
- How the flexibility required within the workforce will be achieved
- The retraining required and how this will be addressed
- Remuneration and reward systems
- Responsibilities and procedures for implementing, monitoring and controlling the plan

There are four main **stages involved in developing a HR plan** for the CX buy-out.

Stage 1: Conduct an audit of existing human resources

As the brewery has closed, technically there are no existing human resources. However, as the shut down only occurred a month ago, and the workforce has specialist skills, it is highly likely that most ex-employees would be available for reemployment. The buy-out team should consult HR records and speak to key ex-employees to establish the current position.

Deciding who should be offered employment is a key task. Selection should take into account existing employee skills and the potential to develop any new skills required. A key consideration for re-employment would be a willingness to be flexible rather than simply 'I want my old job back'.

Stage 2: Forecast future demand for skills/labour

Past experience should provide a reasonable estimate of staff numbers required (including seasonal fluctuations).

New activities (eg bottling) will require new skills – and increased workforce flexibility also needs to be taken into account when estimating the numbers/skill mix required. Bottling may also impact upon seasonal fluctuations. Brewery tours will require significantly different skills.

All of these factors need to be considered and addressed – within a realistic, budget.

Stage 3: Assess the external labour market and forecast supply

In this situation, the external market is somewhat blurred with the internal market (as Stage 1 of this plan included ex-employees). Supply for many positions/skills is likely to be able to be satisfied from the pool of ex-employees – but areas such as bottling and brewery tours may require specialist knowledge and skills that may need to be found from other sources. Teaching ex-employees new skills is another option.

Information relating to ex-employees will be available using CX HR records. These should provide a wide range of information including positions held, age, training undertaken and performance levels.

Stage 4: Establish a plan reconciling demand and supply

When a realistic estimate of employee numbers and skills has been established, the next step is to produce action plans that will result in the recruitment and training of a workforce that will meet the demands of CX.

The plan should ensure steps are taken to ensure all required positions and skills are accounted for. Key employees should be identified by name. There may also need to be contingencies built into the plan to allow for circumstances where expected 'first options' are unavailable.

The four steps outlined above will not run completely sequentially – in reality many aspects of the plan will span more than one stage.

(b) Before the shut-down, **seasonal fluctuations** in sales were large – an indicator that labour flexibility has always been important.

Logic dictates that as the old CX was ultimately unsuccessful the new CX must do something different. Changes in working practices will therefore be required. This is why the CX buy-out team have identified **workforce flexibility** as a key aspect of their plan.

Although the introduction of brewery tours and bottled beers may help smooth seasonal fluctuations, they will also introduce the need for new skills and probably new working hours. Flexibility is therefore essential.

For CX, the flexibility required would include **numerical**, **task** and **financial**.

Numerical flexibility. This is key to deal with seasonal fluctuations and for different demand levels during the day and or week eg for tours.

The development of a numerically flexible workforce will involve the use of temporary and part time workers supplementing full time employees (eg *Handy's* Shamrock). Another option is the outsourcing of non-core functions.

Task or functional flexibility. This involves recruiting and developing multi-skilled staff able to perform a range of tasks. This helps reduce overall numbers and provides ready made cover in cases of absence.

At CX, an employee may for example be able to help with brewing, carry out maintenance and conduct a brewery tour all on the same day.

Financial flexibility. This is achieved most often through performance related reward system.

At CX, staff payments should be linked to output (eg litres brewed, bottles produced, feedback scores from brewery tours or achieving financial targets related to sales figures and profitability).

(c) Five benefits of employing ex-employees to the new organisation and local community.

Benefits to the new organisation

(i) **Knowledge and skill base**

By re-employing skilled staff, CX will save money on training new employees. Their experience will be vital to keep the brewery operating, as the business grows.

(ii)   **Local support**

The local population may get behind the new venture and offer it support by going on tours or purchasing the beer. This support may be enough to see the venture through its early stages.

Benefits to the local community

(i)   **Influx of cash**

The influx of cash from employment and visitors to the area will benefit other local businesses who may find their sales improve due to a knock-on effect.

(ii)   **Flexible working**

Employees and their families may benefit from the flexible working practices on offer. Older employees can enjoy semi-retirement and younger ones can fit the job around their family commitments.

(iii)   **Local tradition/history**

The local area will retain an important part of its history and tradition that would otherwise be lost through property development.

32 Motivation and reward– original

Text reference. Herzberg's theory and reward schemes are covered in Chapter 8.

Top tips. Herzberg's theory gives you a good structure to set out your answer. We recommend splitting your answer between motivators and hygiene factors, you should then look for examples in the scenario for each.

Easy marks. There are few easy marks in this question. However you would gain credit for sensible factors suggested in Part (b)

Examiner's comments. A wide range of performance on this question. Part (a) was an opportunity for candidates who were familiar with this motivation theory to sc ore heavily. Strangely, some who opted for this question confused the theory with the work of another and scored poorly as a result. Others rehearsed a number of motivation theories instead of answering the question.

(a)   **Frederick Herzberg** developed a two factor theory to analyse the causes of satisfaction and dissatisfaction of employees in the workplace

This research required 203 Pittsburgh engineers and accountants to recall events that made them feel good or bad about their work. He identified two factors that influenced their feelings – **motivation** and **hygiene factors**.

The factors stem from two separate 'need systems' that individuals have.

Firstly the **need for personal growth (motivators)**. Motivators include factors such as status, recognition, achievement and growth. When these factors are present they are capable of motivating an individual's performance and effort.

The second **need is to avoid unpleasantness (hygiene factors)**. Such factors are unable to motivate individuals if present, however, their absence will cause dissatisfaction. Hygiene factors include salary, quality of supervision, interpersonal relations and working conditions.

Herzberg noted that an **absence** of motivators results in employees focussing on hygiene factors and demanding more pay (for example) to make up for their dissatisfaction. Hygiene satisfaction is often short-lived and individuals will demand more later on.

The **two new initiatives** from CQ4's chief executive **address both** the motivation and hygiene requirements of Herzberg's theory.

Motivators

- **Achievement** – from individual performance contract targets.

- **Recognition** – that SBU managers have a significant role to play.

- **Advancement** – of 'star achievers' to senior positions on a fast track scheme.

- **Responsibility** – SBU managers are to manage in the way they deem most appropriate.

- **Challenge and autonomy** – managers will become autonomous but will be assessed by their profitability.

Hygiene factors

- Improved **remuneration** package with bonuses linked to profitability.

- Supervision of SBU managers is reduced as 'central interference' is replaced by **autonomy** and **responsibility**.

- **Working conditions** should improve as the SBU managers can organise themselves in a way most appropriate to them.

The initiatives should improve the motivation of the SBU managers.

(b)   Factors the HR department should consider when redesigning the remuneration and reward package of the SBU managers include the following.

Payroll budget

The HR department should ensure the package it offers is consistent with any budget or other restrictions in place. Particular care should be taken when calculating expected bonuses – any under-estimate may cause bonus payments to exceed any allowance in the budget.

Attractiveness to managers

Revised remuneration packages should be attractive and motivate the SBU managers. Whilst pay is a key motivator, other components may be equally as motivating. For example, managers who may be earning a good salary already may prefer additional holiday instead of extra money. The HR department should consider the needs of the managers and consider introducing an element of flexibility into the packages.

Equity and relativity

As a pan-European company, there is likely to be a wide spread of remuneration package benefits and salaries across the organisation. The HR department should ensure the new packages offer equity (a fair rate for the job) and relativity (fair differential pay according to the economic conditions of the specific country the manager resides, as well as their status and competences). Failure to ensure these could be demotivating to managers who consider that they deserve higher rates of pay than others.

Calculation of bonuses

Bonuses should be based on the results that an individual can directly influence if they are to be effective. When designing the bonus scheme, the HR department should take into account factors outside an individual's control. For example, it would be unfair to include the cost of the 'enabling' services in an SBU's profit calculation as the manager can no longer control them.

Quantifying performance

Whilst profitability is relatively simple to quantify through financial performance, non-financial performance such as innovation is harder to calculate. Quantifying innovation is a subjective process performed by senior management – this may cause resentment if managers feel their ideas are snubbed. Care should be taken to design performance criteria that all can understand and feel is fair.

33 Motivation and reward – amended

Text references. Appraisal systems can be found in Chapter 9. Herzberg's theory and reward schemes are covered in Chapter 8.

Top tips. You should be able to attempt Part (a) from your common sense even if your knowledge of appraisal systems is minimal – just make sure it is related to the scenario.

Herzberg's theory gives you a good structure to set out your answer. We recommend spitting your answer between motivators and hygiene factors, you should then look for examples in the scenario for each.

Easy marks. There are few easy marks in this question. However you would gain credit for sensible factors suggested in Part (c)

Examiner's comments. A wide range of performance on this question. Part (a) was an opportunity for candidates who were familiar with this motivation theory to sc ore heavily. Strangely, some who opted for this question confused the theory with the work of another and scored poorly as a result. Others rehearsed a number of motivation theories instead of answering the question.

(a) A problem with many appraisal schemes is that they **reinforce hierarchy**, and are perhaps unsuitable to organisations where the **relationship between management and subordinates is fluid** or participatory.

Appraisal systems, because they target the individual's performance, tend to **ignore the organisational and systems context of that performance**. For example, if any organisation is badly led, no matter how able the employees, it is likely to be unsuccessful. Appraisal schemes focus on personal characteristics and performance, rather than the wider picture.

The effectiveness of an **appraisal system** could be hindered by:

- The effort line managers put into the appraisal process

- The integrity of line managers

- A tendancy of line managers to favour people who have a similar personality and background

- A lack of congruence between what the organisation actually wants and the behaviours it is prepared to reward

The effectiveness of any appraisal system relies heavily on the **quality** and **reliability of assessment**. Variations in the consistency of reporting standards can quickly lead to a feeling of dissatisfaction and injustice.

To improve the appraisal system at CQ4, the new system should have the following characteristics.

(1) It is not possible to apply a completely objective approach to every unique situation. The system should therefore always **allow for at least a degree of discretion and personal judgement**.

(2) Although reviewing past performance is an integral part of an appraisal system, it is also important to concentrate attention on the changes required to bring about **an improvement in future performance**.

(3) The HR department should learn from other organisations who have recognised the problems associated with performance appraisal and have taken steps taken to limit their detrimental effect. For example:

- **Competence-based frameworks**, that focus on the performance rather than on the qualities of the appraisee, could increase the objectivity of the appraisal.

- Schemes of **integrated performance management** could be introduced, incorporating appraisal within a wider, structured approach to the management of human resources.

(b) **Frederick Herzberg** developed a two factor theory to analyse the causes of satisfaction and dissatisfaction of employees in the workplace

This research required 203 Pittsburgh engineers and accountants to recall events that made them feel good or bad about their work. He identified two factors that influenced their feelings – **motivation** and **hygiene factors**.

The factors stem from two separate 'need systems' that individuals have.

Firstly the **need for personal growth (motivators)**. Motivators include factors such as status, recognition, achievement and growth. When these factors are present they are capable of motivating an individual's performance and effort.

The second **need is to avoid unpleasantness (hygiene factors)**. Such factors are unable to motivate individuals if present, however, their absence will cause dissatisfaction. Hygiene factors include salary, quality of supervision, interpersonal relations and working conditions.

Herzberg noted that an **absence** of motivators results in employees focussing on hygiene factors and demanding more pay (for example) to make up for their dissatisfaction. Hygiene satisfaction is often short-lived and individuals will demand more later on.

The **two new initiatives** from CQ4's chief executive **address both** the motivation and hygiene requirements of Herzberg's theory.

Motivators

- **Achievement** – from individual performance contract targets.

- **Recognition** – that SBU managers have a significant role to play.

- **Advancement** – of 'star achievers' to senior positions on a fast track scheme.

- **Responsibility** – SBU managers are to manage in the way they deem most appropriate.

- **Challenge and autonomy** – managers will become autonomous but will be assessed by their profitability.

Hygiene factors

- Improved **remuneration** package with bonuses linked to profitability.

- Supervision of SBU managers is reduced as 'central interference' is replaced by **autonomy** and **responsibility**.

- **Working conditions** should improve as the SBU managers can organise themselves in a way most appropriate to them.

The initiatives should improve the motivation of the SBU managers.

(c) Factors the HR department should consider when redesigning the remuneration and reward package of the SBU managers include the following.

Payroll budget

The HR department should ensure the package it offers is consistent with any budget or other restrictions in place. Particular care should be taken when calculating expected bonuses – any under-estimate may cause bonus payments to exceed any allowance in the budget.

Attractiveness to managers

Revised remuneration packages should be attractive and motivate the SBU managers. Whilst pay is a key motivator, other components may be equally as motivating. For example, managers who may be earning a good salary already may prefer additional holiday instead of extra money. The HR department should consider the needs of the managers and consider introducing an element of flexibility into the packages.

Equity and relativity

As a pan-European company, there is likely to be a wide spread of remuneration package benefits and salaries across the organisation. The HR department should ensure the new packages offer equity (a fair rate for the job) and relativity (fair differential pay according to the economic conditions of the specific country the manager resides, as well as their status and competences). Failure to ensure these could be demotivating to managers who consider they deserve higher rates of pay than others.

Calculation of bonuses

Bonuses should be based on the results that an individual can directly influence if they are to be effective. When designing the bonus scheme, the HR department should take into count factors outside an individual's control. For example, it would be unfair to include the cost of the 'enabling' services in an SBU's profit calculation as the manager can no longer control them.

Quantifying performance

Whilst profitability is relatively simple to quantify through financial performance, non-financial performance such as innovation is harder to calculate. Quantifying innovation is a subjective process performed by senior management – this may cause resentment if managers feel their ideas are snubbed. Care should be taken to design performance criteria that all can understand and feel is fair.

34 Multiple choice questions: Marketing 1

34.1   C   A shakeout would occur between market growth and market maturity (shaking some of the weaker 'players' out of the market).

34.2   A   Distribution channels, transport, warehouse and sales outlets are examples of the 'place' component in the marketing mix. Promotion usually describe advertising and physical evidence usually describes the product's environment in a service industry. Option D is irrelevant as it refers to a service organisation – the locations in the question relate to traditional consumer goods.

34.3   A   Purchasing a fast-moving consumer good involves personal choice and involves relatively low financial outlay (eg washing powder).

34.4   C   Market segmentation involves subdividing a market into distinctive subgroups of customers.

34.5   C   Market segments must be measurable (so its size can be ascertained), accessible (so the company can enter it) and substantial (so profits can be made). The other options are not supported by conventional marketing theory.

34.6   B   One aim of Electronic Data Interchange (EDI) is to replace conventional documentation (eg invoices) with structured electronic data.

34.7   B   Business-to-business marketing involves initiators, influencers, buyers and users in the buying decision.

34.8   D   The marketing strategy follows the business planning process – not drive the company objectives (A) or productive capacity (B). C is incorrect because it fails to consider the requirements of the consumer.

34.9   D   A marketing orientation involves structuring an organisation's activities around the needs of the customer.

34.10   B   Effective product promotion is centres on customers and communication. The other options focus on the internal business rather than the consumers.

35 Multiple choice questions: Marketing 2

35.1   D   The aim of segmentation is to allow marketing efforts to be identified and targeted more effectively by grouping customers by identifiable characteristics relevant to buying behaviour.

35.2   D   Costs, competition and demand are the three main influences on an organisation's price setting strategy.

35.3   D   The correct answer is business to business.

35.4   C   Perishability refers to the fact that services can not be stored – for example an appointment at a hair salon. This makes anticipating and responding to levels of demand crucial.

35.5   A   Customer Relationship Management (CRM) systems enable marketers to utilise the information they hold about customers.

35.6   D   A cookie is a small file used to identify a user/computer. Cookies allow certain elements of websites to be personalised to individual users.

35.7   D   Accepting orders on-line is only the first step – the challenge then is to deliver the product or service ordered. For this to occur, efficient back-office procedures are vital.

35.8   A   The correct answer is primary data is collected specifically for the purpose of the research in question. Secondary data is data not collected specifically for one research project.

35.9   D   Quantitative data is easily measurable using numbers. Qualitative data relates more to feelings and opinions.

35.10 B   Stratified sampling involves first dividing the population into strata or categories. With multistage sampling the population is first divided into quite large groups, then a small sample of these groups is selected at random and subdivided into smaller groups and again, a smaller number of these is selected at random. This process is repeated until a random sample of individuals in each of the smallest groups is taken.

36 Multiple choice questions: Marketing 3

36.1   A   Differentiated marketing involves offering different products to different segments of the market.

36.2   C   M-marketing is used to describe any marketing activity that utilises mobile phones.

36.3   B   The correct stages and sequence of the product life cycle are introduction, growth, maturity and decline.

36.4   D   Direct marketing is sometimes referred to as a zero level channel.

36.5   A   Market segmentation is a technique based on the belief that every market consists of potential buyers with different needs.

36.6   D   Lifestyle, gender and age are three examples of bases for market segmentation.

36.7   C   FMCG is an abbreviation of fast moving consumer good.

36.8   D   Marketing is a broad concept including all aspects that affect how a product (or service) is perceived or experienced. This will include advertising, packaging and much more besides.

36.9   B   Product orientated organisations focus on product features.

36.10 A   Penetration pricing is used to establish or increase market share.

37 Objective test questions: Marketing 1

37.1 Push policies focus on 'pushing' goods into retail outlets and are used by producers to get their goods into the shops.

Promotion is by the final seller in the value chain.
Pull policies create consumer demand that 'pulls' goods into shops.
Promotion is shared between the manufacturer and final seller.

37.2 Product life cycle:

- Introduction – the new product starts production. Low demand and high advertising expenditure.
- Growth – demand and profitability improve; competitors produce similar products.
- Maturity – mainly repeat purchases, new features added, static demand.
- Decline – demand falls, product superseded.

37.3 Positioning products and services in the market involves differentiating products from competitors. Undifferentiated positioning involves targeting the entire market with a single marketing mix. Differentiated positioning involves applying a different marketing mix to each segment. Concentrated positioning means targeting one market segment with hopefully the ideal product for that segment.

37.4 Sales potential is an estimate of the part of the overall market within possible reach of a product. Influences include:

- Price – a higher price restricting the market.
- Promotional expenditure – may broaden the market.
- Overall size of the market.

37.5 PESTEL factors are influences in the environment. Political, Economic, Social/Cultural, Technological and Legal factors all impact upon markets and customers. Therefore, marketers take these factors into account when planning marketing activities. For example, economic conditions affect purchasing power and technological developments may provide product development opportunities.

38 Objective test questions: Marketing 2

38.1 Strategic marketing covers long-term decisions such as which market to operate in.
Example: a retailer decides to set up an outlet in a new country.

Tactical marketing covers short-term decisions relating to the marketing mix.
Example: a retailer decides to cut prices to clear space for new stock.

38.2 Fulfilment means actually delivering goods ordered over the web. Customers expect the goods they order to arrive within acceptable time limits. Customers also need to be convinced that any problems with the goods received will be addressed efficiently. If this is not done, customers will place future orders elsewhere.

38.3 Product orientated organisations focus on product development particularly product features. Production orientated organisations focus on production efficiency and minimising costs. Both production and product orientated organisations place little emphasis on market research or customer needs – and producing products takes precedence over identifying customers.

38.4 Demography relates to the composition of the population. It includes factors such as age, location, occupation and social classification. Demographic factors suggest the size and purchasing power of customer groups. Different demographic groups may be suitable for market segmentation eg an aging population may result in targeting older people.

38.5 *Ansoff's* matrix shows possible strategies for products and markets.

Market penetration – increasing sales of existing products in existing markets.
Market development – expansion into new markets using existing products.
Product development – changing existing products or introducing new ones into existing markets.
Diversification – both new products and new markets.

39 Marketing action plan – original

Text references. The 4 Ps are covered in Chapter 10, job descriptions in Chapter 7.

Top tips. Use the various aspects of the requirement to part (a) to structure your answer. This approach makes it clear that you should provide 3 to 4 marks of information each relating to the marketing action plan in the areas of product, place and promotion. Breaking the requirement down like this should make the question less daunting – and should reduce the temptation to waffle!

Easy marks. In part (b) ensure your answer is presented in the format of a job description – you should head the document up appropriately and use a realistic layout with appropriate headings. Also, don't miss out on the easy marks on offer for including aspects of the expanded role specified in the scenario information.

Examiner's comments. This was a popular question and most candidates answered Part (a) in particular, well. Part (b) however, exposed a basic lack of knowledge of the structure and content of a job description.

(a) The changes at SX (increased use of technology, increased customer focus, new preparation and packaging equipment and more drivers) have implications for the marketing action plan. These implications are discussed below.

(i) **Product related issues relevant to the marketing action plan**

- SX sandwiches are currently perceived as fresh and high quality, and SX snacks as 'home baked'. Increased automation and packaging may require SX products to be more **standardised** (eg consistent sizes to allow automated packaging).

- How these changes will affect **coffee** and **fruit juice sales** also needs to be considered. For example, could SX branded packaged juice be introduced? This may have other implications, for example antagonising other packaged juice suppliers who may attempt to influence retailers.

- What are our **sales targets/objectives** (both in total and for different products – and across different market sectors)?

(ii) **Place related issues relevant to the marketing action plan**

- Distribution is an essential element of the marketing mix for SX. To ensure **freshness**, products have to be delivered as soon as possible following production.

- The earlier in the day products are delivered the more likely they are to sell (due to **increased shelf time**).

- Satellite navigation software including vehicle positioning could be installed at the depot and in vehicles to allow **delivery/driver tracking**. Customers could be given the opportunity to access this information via an extranet.

- How will we set **distribution targets/objectives** and how will we measure them? Asking drivers to gather feedback and increase sales is likely to reduce the number of deliveries each driver can perform.

(iii) **Promotion related issues relevant to the marketing action plan**

- Increased automation and packaging may mean SX products need to be **repositioned** slightly – for example as **good quality and good value**. Home baked snacks may not be consistent with the increased use of food preparation equipment.

- How will the **new format products be promoted** – is a launch required? If so, what should this entail?

- Who should SX aim their promotional effort at (retailers, 'final customers' or both?) and **what promotion channels** are appropriate (eg radio, TV, newspaper, brochures, websites). Different channels may be required for **different target audiences** (eg trade magazine for petrol station operators).

- What are our **targets/objectives for promotion** and how will we measure them? Isolating and measuring the effect of different promotional activities is difficult.

(b)

Job description (draft)	Prepared May 23, 20X5
Job title	Driver
Reporting to	Distribution manager
Staff responsible for	None
Overall purpose of the role	The timely delivery of SX produce to retail outlets (currently mainly petrol stations)
Main duties	The role includes (but is not limited to) the following duties: • Delivering sandwiches, snacks, coffee and fruit juices • Gathering customer feedback • Expanding the number and range of outlets stocking SX products
Technical skills required	• Clean driving licence (essential) • Knowledge of retail food and beverage dispensing (desirable) • Some 'selling' skills (desirable)
Personal skills/qualities required	• Ability to prioritise and to use initiative • Friendly, approachable and customer focussed • Ability to work alone and as part of a team • Reasonably physically fit
Location/base	Drivers start and end their delivery runs at the SX central depot
'Standard' hours	6.00 am – 12.00 am (with a 30 minute break taken any time between 8.30am and 9.30am) Some flexibility is required Refer to your employment letter for details overtime payments
Note	Terms and conditions of employment are set out in the SX handbook (available on the company intranet) and in your employment letter

40 Marketing action plan – amended

(a)   The changes at SX (increased use of technology, increased customer focus, new preparation and packaging equipment and more drivers) have implications for the marketing action plan. These implications are discussed below.

(i)   **Product related issues relevant to the marketing action plan**

- SX sandwiches are currently perceived as fresh and high quality, and SX snacks as 'home baked'. Increased automation and packaging may require SX products to be more **standardised** (eg consistent sizes to allow automated packaging).

- How these changes will affect **coffee** and **fruit juice sales** also needs to be considered. For example, could SX branded packaged juice be introduced? This may have other implications, for example antagonising other packaged juice suppliers who may attempt to influence retailers.

- What are our **sales targets/objectives** (both in total and for different products – and across different market sectors)?

(ii)   **Place related issues relevant to the marketing action plan**

- Distribution is an essential element of the marketing mix for SX. To ensure **freshness**, products have to be delivered as soon as possible following production.

- The earlier in the day products are delivered the more likely they are to sell (due to **increased shelf time**).

- Satellite navigation software including vehicle positioning could be installed at the depot and in vehicles to allow **delivery/driver tracking**. Customers could be given the opportunity to access this information via an extranet.

- How will we set **distribution targets/objectives** and how will we measure them? Asking drivers to gather feedback and increase sales is likely to reduce the number of deliveries each driver can perform.

(iii) **Promotion related issues relevant to the marketing action plan**

- Increased automation and packaging may mean SX products need to be **repositioned** slightly – for example as **good quality and good value**. Home baked snacks may not be consistent with the increased use of food preparation equipment.

- How will the **new format products be promoted** – is a launch required? If so, what should this entail?

- Who should SX aim their promotional effort at (retailers, 'final customers' or both?) and **what promotion channels** are appropriate (eg radio, TV, newspaper, brochures, websites). Different channels may be required for **different target audiences** (eg trade magazines for petrol station operators).

- What are our **targets/objectives for promotion** and how will we measure them? Isolating and measuring the effect of different promotional activities is difficult.

(b)

Job description (draft)		*Prepared May 23, 20X5*
Job title	Driver	
Reporting to	Distribution manager	
Staff responsible for	None	
Overall purpose of the role	The timely delivery of SX produce to retail outlets (currently mainly petrol stations)	
Main duties	The role includes (but is not limited to) the following duties: <ul><li>Delivering sandwiches, snacks, coffee and fruit juices</li><li>Gathering customer feedback</li><li>Expanding the number and range of outlets stocking SX products</li></ul>	
Technical skills required	<ul><li>Clean driving licence (essential)</li><li>Knowledge of retail food and beverage dispensing (desirable)</li><li>Some 'selling' skills (desirable)</li></ul>	
Personal skills/qualities required	<ul><li>Ability to prioritise and to use initiative</li><li>Friendly, approachable and customer focussed</li><li>Ability to work alone and as part of a team</li><li>Reasonably physically fit</li></ul>	
Location/base	Drivers start and end their delivery runs at the SX central depot	
'Standard' hours	6.00 am – 12.00 am (with a 30 minute break taken any time between 8.30am and 9.30am) Some flexibility is required Refer to your employment letter for details overtime payments	
Note	Terms and conditions of employment are set out in the SX handbook (available on the company intranet) and in your employment letter	

(c) *Note*. We have explained seven possible pricing strategies, you were only required to explain four.

(i) **Market penetration**: here the organisation sets a **relatively low price** for the product or service in order to **stimulate growth of the market and/or to obtain a large share** of it. This strategy was used by Japanese motor cycle manufacturers to enter the UK market. UK productive capacity was virtually eliminated and the imported Japanese machines could then be sold at a much higher price and still dominate the market.

(ii) **Market skimming**: Skimming involves **setting a high initial price for a new product in order to take advantage of those buyers who are ready to pay a much higher price for a product.** A typical strategy would be initially to set a premium price and then gradually to reduce the price to attract more price sensitive segments of the market. This strategy is really an example of **price discrimination over time**. It may encourage competition, and growth will initially be slow.

(iii) **Early cash recovery**: Under this method the objective is to recover the investment in a new product or service as quickly as possible and achieve a minimum payback period. The price is set to facilitate this objective.

(iv) **Product line promotion**: This pricing strategy is focuses on **profit from the range of products** which the organisation produces **rather than to treat each product as a separate entity**. The product line promotion objective will look at the whole range from two points of view.

(v) **Cost-plus pricing**. A firm may set its initial price by marking up its unit costs by a certain percentage or fixed amount.

(vi) **Target pricing**. A variant on cost-plus where the company tries to determine the price that gives a specified rate of return for a given output.

(vii) **Price discrimination**. Different prices are given to different buyers. However, the danger is that price cuts to one buyer may be used as a **negotiating lever** by another buyer.

Given the circumstances, a policy of **market penetration** is recommended. As the market is price sensitive, lowering prices should increase sales. As unit costs fall as sales increases SX can afford to reduce its prices to achieve it.

The lower prices set could be enough to put off the potential competitor from entering the market.

41 Question with analysis: Consumer buying decision making process

Text references. Chapter 11 covers all aspects of buyer behaviour. Benefits of marketing can be found throughout Chapters 10, 11 and 12.

Top tips. Don't worry if your answer is based around a different decision making process – there is no one single correct process. If your answer is reasonable, logical and answers the question asked you will score well.

In part (b), you may have identified a wide range of factors. Again, don't worry if your answer does not match ours as many different answers could earn good marks on this question.

(a) Five decision making steps are explained below.

The steps address the need to explain the process – ie this answer includes a 5 step process

Step 1 **Need recognition**. The customer perceives a want or a problem that must be satisfied. In this situation, due to a change in circumstances (children playing musical instruments and the need for more luggage) Mr P needs to obtain a larger car.

Step 2   **Search**. This is a search for information on solutions to the problem identified in step 1.

Mr P knows that a larger car is required. When insufficient information is found on the internal memory search then an external search commences. The extent of the external search depends on the urgency of need and the individual characteristics of the customer. As Mr P needs a larger car quite quickly, then the external search will take place shortly after the internal search. An initial visit to the PCW Company is part of the search.

> The explanation provided with each step includes an example as stated in the requirement

Step 3   **Alternative evaluation**. The search process identifies various ways in which the problem can be solved. These alternatives are evaluated against the internal evaluation criteria and may also lead to changes in preferences regarding different brands or functionality of products, depending on information obtained in step 2. The option which fits the internal evaluation criteria the best will be selected leading onto an intention to purchase that option.

> Could Mr P walk to work, and if so does he still need a new car?

In the scenario, Mr P could visit other dealers to investigate other makes and models of car. Within PCW, sales representatives can move Mr P towards an intention to purchase by providing more details about specific cars and offering services such as a test drive to ensure Mr P likes the car and it does fulfil his internal evaluation criteria.

Step 4   **Purchase**. The intention to purchase is translated into action unless unforeseen circumstances intervene to prevent or postpone the purchase decision.

Mr P will purchase the car.

Step 5   **Outcomes**. After purchase, the customer will use the product and continue to compare performance against expectations. If the item does not live up to expectations, then additional searches may take place to obtain more information about the product. Customers like to think they have made a correct decision, hence the post purchase evaluation.

Mr P will therefore start driving the new car, effectively evaluating the car post purchase. Hopefully the purchase decision will be justified, although additional clarification on features in the car may be requested.

(b)   There are four main groups of factors that will influence a buyer such as Mr P.

1.   **Social factors**. Social factors relate to social groupings which a consumer belongs to as well as trends in society which influence buying patterns. Social factors will include the buyer's peer group and the effect of mass media.

> The requirement asks you to identify and explain – this answer does both very well

For Mr P the main social factors are his perceptions of the different makes of car and those of his peer group at the golf club regarding what is an acceptable car to drive. Other factors influencing the decision will include whether the car provides an appropriate status and image.

2.   **Cultural factors**. Cultural factors include the values attitudes and beliefs held by people that help them function within society. Cultural factors change between different countries, eg smoking is accepted in restaurants in some countries but not in others. There are many different cultural factors such as religion, language, law and politics and social organisations. Depending on the beliefs and principles held in each of these areas, different individuals will make different purchase decisions.

Mr P may well be influenced by the look and feel of the car – hence the test drive to show him how the car drives. His environmental concerns may result in him choosing a car with low exhaust emissions.

3. **Personal factors**. Personal factors include things such as age, family including number and age of children, economic circumstances and lifestyle.

    Family obviously affects Mr P – this is the main reason for purchasing a different car. Mr P's economic circumstances indicate he can afford a large car while other lifestyle benefits such as being able to transport his golf clubs easily will reinforce the decision by showing other personal benefits of a large car.

4. **Psychological factors**. The buyer will be also be influenced by:

    - **Motivation** – that is how much the purchase needs to be made. The theories of *Maslow* and *McGregor* discuss this area in more detail. Mr P will be motivated because his children will be reminding him of the need to change his car.

    - **Perception** – that is the way purchasers view a specific product, which is in turn influenced by their past experience. For example, Mr P is interested in purchasing a Yotoda car, presumably because he thinks that is a good brand.

    - **Beliefs** – the thoughts held about an object or brand. Mr P may well believe that some makes of car are more reliable.

> Good – brief links to relevant theories

> If Mr P really is concerned about environmental damage, he could walk the three kilometres to work

> **Top tips.** This answer explores the broader concept of marketing going further than the traditional view of product and profitability. Your answer should develop the benefits of marketing to a wider audience of stakeholders.

(c)   **Benefits of marketing to business organisations, consumers and society**

> Introduction sets the context of the answer

Marketing is directed at **satisfying needs** and wants through **exchange processes**. Marketing combines many activities – marketing research, product development, distribution, pricing, advertising, personal selling and others – designed to sense, serve and satisfy consumer needs whilst meeting the organisation's goals. The core concepts of marketing are needs, wants, demands, products, exchange, transactions and markets that will benefit the individual, consumers and society at large, organisations and national and international governments.

Marketers must be able to manage the **level, timing** and **composition** of **demand** from these different beneficiaries to satisfy their needs and wants. For instance IKEA and McDonald's have adopted the broader marketing concept on a global scale through understanding and responding to the changing needs of their customers.

> Good use of examples

Modern marketing is guided by a number of converging philosophies. The production concept holds that the **consumer** favours products which are available at **low cost** and that marketing's task is to improve production efficiency and bring down prices. The marketing concept holds that a **company** should **research** the needs and wants of a well defined target market and deliver the desired satisfactions, which is accompanied by long-run **societal well being**.

In marketing led organisations all employees share the belief that the **customer** is all important and that building lasting relationships is key to customer retention. A company's sales are derived from content existing customers and attracting new customers and this benefits the livelihoods of the employees and suppliers and their staff.

Successfully adopting a marketing approach should improve **customer retention** and minimise additional costs. A satisfied customer buys more, stays loyal longer, talks favourably to others, pays less attention to competing brands and is less price sensitive. These benefits are transferred into gains for **consumers** and ultimately **society** at large as success breeds success. IKEA and McDonald's divert much of their energies to ensuring that customers repeatedly return to them satisfied and content with their offering.

42 Marketing and information technology

Text references. The use of technology in marketing is covered in Chapter 12.

Top tips. To produce a good answer, you need to stick closely to the question asked – ways in which the Internet is being used (and will be used) by suppliers, customers and internally. Your answer must relate the information you provide to these specific points.

(a)　**What is the Internet?**

The Internet enables computers across the world to be linked together so that users can search for and access data and information provided by others. **Websites** are points within the network created to provide an information point and often the facility to enter into a **transaction**.

Current uses and development issues

Some of the most **common uses** of the Internet are:

- Information provision
- Product development (eg feedback facility)
- Facilitating transactions (e-commerce)
- Fostering dialogue and relationships with different stakeholders (eg e-mail groups, chat rooms)

Internet based communication has the following **beneficial attributes**.

- High speed of interaction
- Low cost provision and maintenance
- Ability to provide mass customisation
- Global reach and wide search facilities
- Instant dialogue
- Multi-directional communications (eg: to suppliers, customers and regulators)
- High level of user control
- Customer (visitor) driven
- Moderate level of credibility

Use with customers

The use of the Internet by organisations has generally been focussed upon the business-to-business sector. Websites have become increasingly sophisticated and are a useful means of meeting the needs of customers and organisations.

Businesses can communicate more cost-effectively with their customers and provide a wide range of facilities. The volume of customer traffic that can be handled is far larger and quicker than through traditional means. Sales literature, ideas, price lists, queries, complaints, sales promotions such as competitions, and orders and sales can all be undertaken over the Internet.

The objectives are essentially two-fold. The first is to generate the first steps of a relationship (or maintain one already established). The second is the collection of customer profile information. Names, addresses and other demographic and psychographic data can be collected and collated in a database.

The execution of financial transactions over the Internet was initially a stumbling block, due to the fear of fraud. More secure systems and protection devices are now available and this has spurred the growth of purchasing activities. For example, Tesco and Sainsbury's home shopping initiatives have been successful.

Use with suppliers

The use of the Internet with suppliers will provide a more dynamic form of communication facilitating:

- Problem identification
- Formation of solutions, including tailored product modifications
- Constant dialogue opportunities

These factors enable suppliers to forge closer relationships in the marketing channel.

Marketing communications opportunities will arise where, for example, new products can be presented to suppliers much more quickly, sales literature and product specification data can be relayed instantly and advertising materials presented more effectively.

Use within and between organisations: intranets and extranets

Internally, Internet technology has been used in the development of intranets. The provision of internal website-like communication networks allows for the rapid dissemination of corporate and marketing information. For global organisations this represents a tremendous step forward, as an intranet can overcome time barriers and allow for the transmission of materials to all parts of a company. The development of and interest in internal marketing has been assisted by the growth of intranets. The involvement of staff, and the motivational opportunities afforded by intranet technology, enable employees and management to work more closely together.

The opening up of intranets to authorised outsiders (eg suppliers) allows efficient sharing of information. An intranet open to some people from outside the organisation is known as an extranet.

Future of the Internet

The future of the Internet is likely to involve greater integration between web-based and internal systems. The result of this is likely to be more opportunities for stakeholders to interact with organisations for information, education, entertainment, products, services and financial transactions quickly and efficiently.

(b) ### Use of Information Technology in Marketing Research

The use of information technology is now common place in marketing research. This is because vast amounts of information relating to markets are **held in computer systems** (both internal and external eg customer databases, websites/search engines). This answer relates to a supermarket attempting to gather information on customers to enable better targeting of future marketing campaigns.

Primary data can be collected using **EPOS** equipment in combination with **loyalty** cards. This data shows who is buying what (and when). The data will be held in a **database** to enable future interrogation looking for significant patterns and trends. This types of data is known at quantitative – as it is suitable for statistical analysis.

Online shopping transactions could also feed into this database – and provide an additional source of information (eg through user registration and 'cookies').

General **demographic** and **economic** trends will influence the purchasing power of supermarket customers. Many **government agencies** publish their reports on the Internet, business reports are also available online and often also on CD-ROM. Competitors' **websites** can be viewed to establish their strategies.

IT can also be employed in collecting qualitative information. Examples of this approach could involve the use of **chat rooms** and online focus groups with webcams etc. There are now also a number of computer packages which can analyse qualitative data.

Analysis of information is another important area where IT could help. The use of computer software to analyse data with such packages as spreadsheets (eg Excel), can be used to statistically evaluate quantitative data. Indeed, online questionnaires are often set up with a database for responses which can be immediately analysed as soon as the respondents reply.

IT helps the production of **professional looking reports** that incorporate graphs, graphics and other relevant illustrations. The distribution of information worldwide quickly and cheaply is also facilitated (eg send via e-mail and/or post on a website for viewing by head-office staff based in another country).

43 Environmental change and marketing – original

Text references. This question covers many syllabus areas. You need a good understanding of marketing (Chapters 10, 11 and 12), organisational development (Chapter 13), Human Resource management (Chapter 7) and IT systems (Chapter 3).

Top tips. To answer both parts, you must read the information given and make realistic points. Do not provide a general discussion about not responding to environmental change.

Easy marks. Jot down any issues that leap out at you when reading the scenario. They are there for a reason and you should be able to slot them into your answer at some point.

Examiner's comments. There was a range of performance on this question. Those candidates who diligently applied their knowledge to the scenario scored well, whilst those who attempted over-theoretical answers scored far less well. Some candidates obviously failed to interpret the causes of business failure from the clues in the scenario. Part (b) of the question was answered rather better than Part (a).

(a)   Everland banks have enjoyed an oligopoly-type position over the years (a small number of service providers have dominated the market with little competition). The new legislation opening up the market presents a threat to the established banks. The dangers, if the banks don't change, include the following.

- The banks may remain **complacent to the needs of the customer**, since they all offer similar products and are happy to maintain a 'satisfactory' service level. Customers in the new environment will be able to **seek better service at a different bank**.

- **Product development** is currently lacking. This could prove to be a key danger when the market is opened up for competition – **customers will seek providers whose products meet their needs**.

- New suppliers of banking services are likely to come from **customer-focussed organisations** with broad experience from other markets. It is highly likely that new entrants will develop products more closely related to the customers needs, causing the existing banks to **lose custom**. They may eventually drive them **out of business**.

- The existing banks have only to look to Utopia for evidence of how customer attitudes are changing. **Demand for better quality products** is likely to become a trend in Everland in the near future. If improved product design and marketing are not employed by the existing banks, but are by the new providers **demand for the old banks' services will be reduced**.

(b)   The banks of Everland need to make changes to their products, systems and marketing in order for them to improve their customer focus and to survive.

Marketing changes

- Products should be designed to meet customer needs. Market research is required to determine what the needs are.

- Market segmentation should be considered to focus certain products on specific groups.

- The use of customer service questionnaires or other methods of analysing satisfaction levels should be investigated to monitor how well customer needs are being met.

Organisational changes

- Structural changes should be made that reflect the need to provide improved customer service. For example, setting up of a customer services department.

- The strategic importance of marketing should be reflected by the inclusion of a marketing department, headed by a marketing director to co-ordinate resources and activities.

Human resources

- Marketing and customer service professionals should be recruited at the expense of traditional bankers.

- A broad range of skill sets and experience should be brought in by employing staff from markets outside banking.

- Recruitment, selection and promotion policies should reflect the new skills/experience mix. Senior management must also reflect this diversity to counter the lack of marketing, HR and customer service experience.

- Training should be given to promote customer focus and new marketing techniques.

Information technology systems

- Systems should be updated to focus on the need for customer focus and quality of information.

- New systems may be needed to monitor marketing and customer satisfaction.

- Systems should allow feedback from customers and marketing campaigns to be available to senior management who can use it to make strategic decisions.

- Systems should allow awareness of customer needs such as ethical behaviour or social responsibility to filter out to all staff.

44 Environmental change and marketing – amended

Text references. This question covers many syllabus areas. You need a good understanding of marketing (Chapters 10, 11 and 12), organisational development (Chapter 13), Human Resource management (Chapter 7) and IT systems (Chapter 3).

Top tips. To answer Parts (a) and (b), you must read the information given and make realistic points. Do not provide a general discussion about not responding to environmental change.

Part (c) could be answered even if you have little knowledge of ethics or social responsibility as many issues are in the news, TV programmes and internet. Don't be afraid to pull in your outside knowledge where appropriate.

Easy marks. Jot down any issues that leap out at you when reading the scenario. They are there for a reason and you should be able to slot them into your answer at some point.

Examiner's comments. There was a range of performance on this question. Those candidates who diligently applied their knowledge to the scenario scored well, whilst those who attempted over-theoretical answers scored far less well. Some candidates obviously failed to interpret the causes of business failure from the clues in the scenario. Part (b) of the question was answered rather better than Part (a).

(a) Everland banks have enjoyed an oligopoly-type position over the years (a small number of service providers have dominated the market with little competition). The new legislation opening up the market presents a threat to the established banks. The dangers, if the banks do not change, include the following.

- The banks may remain **complacent to the needs of the customer**, since they all offer similar products and are happy to maintain a 'satisfactory' service level. Customers in the new environment will be able to **seek better service at a different bank**.

- **Product development** is currently lacking. This could prove to be a key danger when the market is opened up for competition – **customers will seek providers whose products meet their needs**.

- New suppliers of banking services are likely to come from **customer-focussed organisations** with broad experience from other markets. It is highly likely that new entrants will develop products more closely related to the customers needs, causing the existing banks to **lose custom**. They may eventually drive them **out of business**.

- The existing banks have only to look to Utopia for evidence of how customer attitudes are changing. **Demand for better quality products** is likely to become a trend in Everland in the near future. If improved product design and marketing are not employed by the existing banks, but are by the new providers **demand for the old banks' services will be reduced**.

(b) The banks of Everland need to make changes to their products, systems and marketing in order for them to improve their customer focus and to survive.

Marketing changes

- Products should be designed to meet customer needs. Market research is required to determine what the needs are.

- Market segmentation should be considered to focus certain products on specific groups.

- The use of customer service questionnaires or other methods of analysing satisfaction levels should be investigated to monitor how well customer needs are being met.

Organisational changes

- Structural changes should be made that reflect the need to provide improved customer service. For example, setting up of a customer services department.

- The strategic importance of marketing should be reflected by the inclusion of a marketing department, headed by a marketing director to co-ordinate resources and activities.

Human resources

- Marketing and customer service professionals should be recruited at the expense of traditional bankers.

- A broad range of skill sets and experience should be brought in by employing staff from markets outside banking.

- Recruitment, selection and promotion policies should reflect the new skills/experience mix. Senior management must also reflect this diversity to counter the lack of marketing, HR and customer service experience.

- Training should be given to promote customer focus and new marketing techniques.

Information technology systems

- Systems should be updated to focus on the need for customer focus and quality of information.

- New systems may be needed to monitor marketing and customer satisfaction.

- Systems should allow feedback from customers and marketing campaigns to be available to senior management who can use it to make strategic decisions.

- Systems should allow awareness of customer needs such as ethical behaviour or social responsibility to filter out to all staff.

(c) **Responsibilities of the modern marketer**

Marketing reflects and influences **cultural values** and **norms**. The boundaries of marketing extend beyond economic considerations.

Marketing concepts and techniques are used to promote the **welfare of society** as a whole instead of the traditional approach of providing products that satisfy consumers' needs efficiently and profitably. This could encompass reduction in poverty, improved education and improved healthcare. For example, marketing tools are used in promoting healthier lifestyles through better diets, encouraging leisure activities and pursuits and social behaviour.

Social marketing suggests that a more **ethical** and **moral orientation** be incorporated into companies' marketing strategies. Marketers consider and incorporate the wider social implications of their products and services, such as natural conservation or labour exploitation in emerging countries.

Social marketing does not imply a replacement of the **traditional marketing concept** but it is an extension so as to recognise and encompass the wider needs of society at large.

Criticisms of marketing generally focus on **ethical issues** and the extent to which marketing is **responsible** for a variety of social and environmental problems. Whatever the reasons, voluntarily or otherwise, marketers have to consider ecological, environmental and consumer welfare issues together with their wider social role more frequently in their marketing plans and activities.

Effective and **aware marketers** have **responded** to these developments in a number of ways. For instance by producing recyclable products and packaging, reducing pollution generated by toxic products or from contamination and protecting consumers against harmful or hazardous products by modifying them or withdrawing them from sale.

45 Multiple choice questions: Managing change 1

45.1 A This is the correct sequence of crises in *Greiner's* growth model.

45.2 B Activities associated with organisational development require 'interventions' into the social processes of an organisational The other answers are not necessarily true.

45.3 A The organisation life cycle ('S' curve) follows this sequence.

45.4 A Lewin's Force Field analysis depicts two opposing forces, one driving the current state to an ideal position and on resisting change, trying to keep the current state of affairs.
The other options do not describe this theory.

45.5 B When an external shock constitutes an immediate threat to the organisation's continued existence (ie a crisis), resistance to change is likely to be subordinated to the need for survival.

45.6 B Planned change will involve action by management to adjust internal practices and attitudes that might be labelled the internal environment, of which culture would form part.

45.7 A B and C are other possible responses to change, while D is a made-up term.

45.8 B The final state in Lewin's three stage model of change is called refreezing and describes the process of fixing a certain behaviour into individuals or groups.

45.9 C The other options focus on some possible negative aspects of the work of the change agent.

45.10 D The other options are either disadvantages of acquisitions or an action that will take place after acquisition.

46 Multiple choice questions: Managing change 2

46.1   C   Culture may be a target for change and it may be, in *Lewin's* terminology, one of the forces restraining or driving change. However, it is not an aspect of the way in which change is undertaken.

46.2   D   During the growth through co-ordination phase formal systems and procedures are used to achieve greater co-ordination. However, procedures eventually take precedence over problem-solving and innovation – a crisis of red tape.

46.3   C   Tolerating failure encourages experimentation and creativity (not all ideas will work but people should feel their ideas are wanted).

46.4   C   Changing culture is a massive undertaking that could form part of the 'move' or 'change' phase.

46.5   D   An increase in rules and procedures is often seen as a way to co-ordinate a larger organisation.

46.6   B   A relates to incremental change, C is planned change and D is transformational change.

46.7   B   Transformational change involves an organisation acting outside its traditional way of thinking/operating.

46.8   A   Facilitation involves techniques such as counselling and discussion – a help line is an example of this.

46.9   B   This would mean leaving the problem until it is too late to resolve it. Option A would prepare the organisation for the crisis. By accepting the change in option C, plans can be made to adapt to it. Option D forces change before the real crisis occurs.

46.10   C   Change agents must be able to gain support from all involved. The other options would be useful, but the ability to gain support for the change is most important.

47 Objective test questions: Managing change

47.1   An external change trigger is an external event which results in the need for change. Categories include:

- Political – new government policies or legislation
- Economic – different exchange rates or interest rates
- Social – changes in education or values in society
- Technological – new inventions or processes

47.2   Four barriers that managers may use are:

- Excessive focus on costs, rejecting all change that increases costs
- Taking decisions that protect individual areas rather than co-operating with others
- Being overly risk adverse to avoid any possible blame for unsuccessful projects
- Focussing on problems without recognising benefits

47.3   Adaptive change involves slow, incremental changes in an organisation: it is change in little stages, and thus has the advantage of minimising the resistance faced at any one time. An example would be the slow demise of the UK's coal industry, with a long programme of incremental cut-backs.

47.4   A phased system changeover is less dramatic than an instant or direct changeover. This gives employees more time to adjust to the change, which should reduce levels of resistance. It also allows for increased time for training and means the impact of any problems found are restricted.

47.5   Considerations relevant when considering a takeover include:

- Contribution. How will the acquiring company enhance the acquired company?

- Common core. The companies should have some common markets, operations or technology.

- Value. The acquiring company should value the products, services and customers of the other company.

- Management. The acquiring company should have some top management capable of managing the acquired company.

- Linkage. Some managers should be able to 'cross over' between the companies.

48 Question with analysis: Introducing change

Text references. Managing change and organisational development are covered in Chapters 13 and 14.

Top tips. Common sense and a little experience of typical reactions of people in the workplace could earn you half marks on part (a), even with only limited knowledge of change theory. However, you would earn a much higher mark if you compared the CEO's behaviour with the elements of a formal programme of change management.

One important mistake

(a)   While the CEO's overall objectives and the enabling moves he wishes to put in place may be quite sensible, **the way he has introduced his change programme** has seriously compromised its potential for success.

Explanation linked to appropriate theory

The CEO's **first mistake** was to reach his own conclusions about the benchmarking exercise. Lewin and Schein's three stage model of change is useful here, beginning, as it does, with the process of **unfreezing** existing practices, attitudes and motivations. This stage requires considerable sensitivity to the current situation. People are unlikely to react well to a programme of organisational change that is imposed from above; they are much more likely to agree to the need for change and the details of what is to be done if they are involved in the decision-making process. For this reason, **consultation** is recommended as an important part of the change management process. In this case, the senior executives will certainly view the prospect of re-applying for employment as highly threatening. This alone may account for their lack of movement.

So far, the hostility aroused by the CEO is confined to his department heads, but only because they are the only staff who have been informed of the changes he proposes! If he had published his plans more widely, they would have attracted hostility from even more people – as **he has already decided what needs to be done**.

Another mistake

Another important error by the CEO was the way in which he informed his team of his plans. E mail is a useful and flexible system of communication, but hardly adequate for the CEO's purposes. The essentially **informal image** of e-mail compounds the error. No doubt feathers were further ruffled by the CEO's immediate departure on his long business trip. This would make protest or even comment far more difficult for those on the receiving end.

Good explanation

The CEO seems to be under the impression that he can introduce major change by simply issuing an instruction. In fact such a complex programme would require **extensive planning** and the commitment of significant **resources of cash and management time**. For example, the development of an entrepreneurial culture throughout the organisation would not be best achieved by department heads acting in an un-coordinated way according to their own ideas of what was needed and what they could get away with. Extensive training and development would be required, particularly for managers. Reporting and control systems would have to be examined and probably redesigned so that they supported rather than inhibited the required innovative, risk-taking culture.

Finishes with another mistake made by the CEO	The CEO has, knowingly or not, adopted a common approach – the appointment of a '**champion of change**' in the form of the head of human resources. Given the circumstances, even the best qualified champion would find it difficult to make any headway: not surprisingly, the head of HR has failed completely. It is not unusual for HR departments to take a prominent role in the management of change, however they should be part of a team that includes those with detailed knowledge of operations. This mistake has encouraged opposition to the change.

Top tips. This is simple if you know your *Lewin*! If you don't, you can probably get most of the marks by using information provided in the question. You need to make ten points in total.

(b) **Forces for change – internal**

- Forceful new CEO
- Poor operational performance
- High costs
- Low productivity

Forces for change – external

You must consider the nature of the industry and real-life developments	• Competition from foreign, subsidised steel-makers • Demanding customers **Forces resisting change – internal** • Unhappy department heads • The trade union's attitude **Force resisting change – external**

- Growing demand in developing countries may ease pressure to cut costs
- Customer focus is less important in homogenous products such as steel

Top tips. The problem with this part of the question is that it is almost a mirror image of part (a). It would be very easy to make too much of your answer to the first part and leave yourself with nothing to say in the second.

There is a general lesson of examination technique here: read the question all the way through before you start on the first part, looking out for this possibility. If you come across it, decide in advance what is going into each part.

Start by trying to reverse the mistakes made so far	(c) If the CEO wishes to introduce change successfully, he really has no choice but to **withdraw his existing plan and start again**. A top-down, coercive approach can work, but only in times of great crisis, such as when the very survival of the organisation is threatened. We are not led to understand that this is the case at B company.
Again link to relevant theory	Unfortunately, a withdrawal will not wipe the slate clean; the CEO will have more difficulty than might have been anticipated, because of the suspicion he has aroused about his aims and methods. Lewin's **force field** idea might usefully be considered here. Lewin suggests that during any programme of change there are likely to be forces both promoting and opposing the new ways of doing things. It is a common management reaction to attempt to strengthen the forces promoting change so that opposition is overcome. A more sensible approach might be to attempt to **reduce the forces opposed to change**, thus avoiding damaging conflict. Several methods could be employed to this end.

BPP
LEARNING MEDIA

The first thing the CEO should do is to include senior executives in the change management process. The process by which this might be undertaken could then be repeated with the rest of the staff. The general approach should be one of **consultation** and **communication**, combined with a willingness on the part of the CEO to respect the concerns of his staff and to deal with them as positively as possible. Any programme of major change will cause apprehension about job security in particular; it is particularly important to deal with people's fear on this topic early in the process. If major cuts are envisaged, they should be announced as soon as possible and made with as much sensitivity as possible.

> The key elements of the approach required

A good starting point might be to hold a **meeting of senior management** at which the perceived need for change could be **explained in detail** and immediate reactions invited. These should then be addressed through a process of joint **consultation** and planning: a more robust and acceptable plan is likely to emerge if the CEO encourages his senior managers to contribute to it. In particular, their specialist expertise is highly likely to enable them to point out potential future problems and ways of dealing with them. Only if there is truly irrational obstruction on any manager's part should it be necessary to impose a solution.

> Good development of the consultation point raised earlier

This process of **communication** and **consultation** could then be extended to the rest of the staff, with the senior managers acting as change leaders in their own departments.

There will be a requirement for **extensive planning** and **preparation** and the **commitment** of significant resources. The communication programme will take time and could involve the use of communications media such as meetings, and (for general points), newsletters. **Training** and **development** of staff at all levels will almost certainly require important enhancements and it may become appropriate to make use of improved technology.

> Develops to look at wider aspects of the change

49 Question with helping hand: Implementing change: types of change – original

Text references. Change management is covered in Chapter 14.

Top tips. Lewin's theory has three main stages – it makes sense to use these stages to provide a structure for your answer to part (a).

Easy marks. Within part (a) you will score some marks for reproducing knowledge of an accepted theory of change. You need to apply this theory to score well, but ensure you first pick up the marks on offer for reproducing book knowledge.

(a)   **Lewin** devised a three stage theory of change that may be used to describe how any major new organisational initiative can be successfully implemented.

Unfreeze

The first stage in implementing change is to loosen up or 'un-freeze' the current situation. If people are satisfied with the current state, they are unlikely to be motivated to change. Lewin's theory recognises the need to 'unfreeze' the status-quo.

This stage involves making people receptive to new ideas, pointing out how a different way of doing something would benefit them. Communication plays an important part here – if people aren't informed about the benefits change would offer they are unlikely to see any need for change – and the status-quo will remain frozen in place.

Move or change

The second stage of Lewin's three stage theory is to actually make the change – to move from the old situation to the new one.

Resources for the transition such as any consultancy skills required and time for staff training must be made available. For change to be implemented successfully, people (individuals and groups) that may instinctively oppose the change must be convinced of its merits. These people, together with others who are positive towards the change, should be included in the planning and implementation of the change.

Participation in the change process can help to reduce resistance and build ownership – therefore motivating people to want the process to succeed. Participation also facilitates communication of what the change entails and why it is being introduced.

Refreeze

After the change has been made, it needs to become entrenched or frozen into place to ensure people don't slip back into the old ways of working. This may involve the use of a range of rewards to reinforce behaviour consistent with the changed state. In order to measure and control performance of the new system or way of working, appropriate monitoring and control action is required.

Part of the re-freeze process could include the use of feedback mechanisms to ensure any on-going concerns are listened to and acted upon. The key to 're-freezing' therefore is to ensure people can see the benefits of working in the new way.

Top tips. The first part of Part (b) should be relatively straightforward as it can be answered through reproducing text book definitions. For the second part, think about the vested interests each of the two people involved – and relate these to the two different types of change.

(b)   **Incremental change** may be defined as 'those changes that can be accommodated within the organisation's current structure and culture'. Incremental change is used to describe relatively small, step-by-step changes. Over time, the combined effect of these small changes may be significant, but the change has evolved over time rather than being introduced suddenly.

On the other hand, **transformational change** is defined as 'a change that cannot be accommodated by the existing structure and culture of the organisation'. These changes require restructuring of the organisation and significant cultural change to be implemented successfully.

The **Zed Bank's spokesperson** describes the change as 'incremental' as she believes that the change does **not** involve a **radical change** of direction. The bank will still be doing the same things, it will just be doing them in a different way (using Internet and telecommunications technology to deliver improved customer service).

The spokesperson believes the change proposed by the Bank can be **accommodated** within the Bank's existing **organisation structure** and **culture**. She is playing down the impact of the change and hoping to reassure staff and customers that the changes will be beneficial for both the bank and customers.

The **trade union representative** sees the proposed changes as transformational, as completely different worker skills (and a different organisational culture) are required to run an Internet and telephone banking operation than to staff a bank branch.

Furthermore, although the change initially involves the closure of **rural** and **smaller branches**, he believes this is just the 'thin end of the wedge' which may eventually lead to the disappearance of traditional bank branches and their **replacement** by Internet banking services. This would alarm union members as it would most likely involve significant redundancies.

The union leader hopes to protect his members position by alerting customers to the possibility of the loss of their local branches, hopefully mobilising opinion against such a change.

50 Question with helping hand: Implementing change: types of change – amended

(a)   **Lewin** devised a three stage theory of change that may be used to describe how any major new organisational initiative can be successfully implemented.

Unfreeze

The first stage in implementing change is to loosen up or 'un-freeze' the current situation. If people are satisfied with the current state, they are unlikely to be motivated to change. Lewin's theory recognises the need to 'unfreeze' the status-quo.

This stage involves making people receptive to new ideas, pointing out how a different way of doing something would benefit them. Communication plays an important part here – if people aren't informed about the benefits change would offer they are unlikely to see any need for change – and the status-quo will remain frozen in place.

Move or change

The second stage of Lewin's three stage theory is to actually make the change – to move from the old situation to the new one.

Resources for the transition such as any consultancy skills required and time for staff training must be made available. For change to be implemented successfully, people (individuals and groups) that may instinctively oppose the change must be convinced of its merits. These people, together with others who are positive towards the change, should be included in the planning and implementation of the change.

Participation in the change process can help to reduce resistance and build ownership – therefore motivating people to want the process to succeed. Participation also facilitates communication of what the change entails and why it is being introduced.

Refreeze

After the change has been made, it needs to become entrenched or frozen into place to ensure people don't slip back into the old ways of working. This may involve the use of a range of rewards to reinforce behaviour consistent with the changed state. In order to measure and control performance of the new system or way of working, appropriate monitoring and control action is required.

Part of the re-freeze process could include the use of feedback mechanisms to ensure any on-going concerns are listened to and acted upon. The key to 're-freezing' therefore is to ensure people can see the benefits of working in the new way.

(b)   **Incremental change** may be defined as 'those changes that can be accommodated within the organisation's current structure and culture'. Incremental change is used to describe relatively small, step-by-step changes. Over time, the combined effect of these small changes may be significant, but the change has evolved over time rather than being introduced suddenly.

On the other hand, **transformational change** is defined as 'a change that cannot be accommodated by the existing structure and culture of the organisation'. These changes require restructuring of the organisation and significant cultural change to be implemented successfully.

The **Zed Bank's spokesperson** describes the change as 'incremental' as she believes that the change does **not** involve a **radical change** of direction. The bank will still be doing the same things, it will just be doing them in a different way (using Internet and telecommunications technology to deliver improved customer service).

The spokesperson believes the change proposed by the Bank can be **accommodated** within the Bank's existing **organisation structure** and **culture**. She is playing down the impact of the change and hoping to reassure staff and customers that the changes will be beneficial for both the bank and customers.

The **trade union representative** sees the proposed changes as transformational, as completely different worker skills (and a different organisational culture) are required to run an Internet and telephone banking operation than to staff a bank branch.

Furthermore, although the change initially involves the closure of **rural** and **smaller branches**, he believes this is just the 'thin end of the wedge' which may eventually lead to the disappearance of traditional bank branches and their **replacement** by Internet banking services. This would alarm union members as it would most likely involve significant redundancies.

The union leader hopes to protect his members position by alerting customers to the possibility of the loss of their local branches, hopefully mobilising opinion against such a change.

> **Top tips.** Ensure your answer to part (c) deals with financial incentive schemes as motivators, rather than simply describing financial incentive schemes. Think about what can be done to help employees enjoy their jobs and enhance job satisfaction.

(c)   **Financial incentive schemes as motivators**

All theories of **motivation** are based to some extent on the idea that human beings have **needs** that they must satisfy; pay can motivate since it permits the satisfaction of many needs. However, the extent to which pay motivates varies from individual to individual and there are some needs which pay cannot satisfy.

Pay (usually in the form of money) is the **fundamental incentive** to work for most people; and in its most basic form it is issued at a flat rate and at regular intervals. In banking, a variety of bonus schemes have been used. Most incorporate a flat lump sum or an individual bonus paid when results exceed a target figure. Sometimes a group bonus is paid when work-group co-operation is critical. Such schemes can incorporate bonuses for wider groups; these are often based upon corporate success and include profit sharing schemes.

It is now common for many employees to receive some form of an **annual bonus**. These are usually **performance related** and **discretionary**. They may be based on individual performance or a wider measure of success such as profitability, or a combination of such factors. In all cases, however, an important reason for paying bonuses is to encourage motivation.

Although pay plays a part in motivation, it is not the **perfect motivator**. Content theories of motivation, such as *Maslow's* hierarchy, indicate the importance of needs such as those for satisfactory **social relationships** and the **fulfilment** of personal potential. *Herzberg* found that pay is a hygiene factor; that is, it is incapable of producing satisfaction and whatever its rate will only ever be capable of avoiding the creation of dissatisfaction.

Expectancy theories such as that of *Vroom* suggest that the power of pay to motivate depends on the **value** to the individual of what can be done with it. This idea is borne out in the study by *Goldthorpe, Lockwood et al* of workers in the British car industry. Their motivation to work was instrumental: they worked for money with which to obtain satisfactions elsewhere, since little or none was available from their boring and alienating work.

Non monetary motivation

The limitations of pay as a motivating force were briefly discussed above. Human beings have other needs, not involving money, that can be satisfied through work. *Herzberg* gives the simplest explanation with his idea of **motivator factors**. He tried to establish what made people feel good about their work. He found a number of factors had this effect.

- Status
- Advancement
- Recognition
- Responsibility

- Challenging work
- Achievement
- Growth in the job

51 Job reductions; resistance to change – original

Text references. Methods to reduce jobs can be found in Chapter 7 and strategies for dealing with resistance to change are covered in Chapter 14.

Top tips. Use the requirement to provide a structure to your answer. So, part (a) should include initiatives and support – and part (b) potential strategies and suitable strategies.

Easy marks. As with many scenario questions the 'easier marks' are those available for reproducing book knowledge. In part (a) this could include items such as the need for communication and consultation. In part (b), Kotter and Schlesinger could be quoted. To score well though, you should go further and relate this knowledge to the situation at R&L.

Examiner's comments. This was a popular question and most candidates answered part (a) in particular well. Some candidates drew purposeful examples from similar organisations including the recent MG/Rover experience.

(a)   The directors of R&L have agreed to act as 'honestly and fairly as possible' in implementing the job reductions.

Redundancy has a massive impact upon many individuals and therefore need to be **handled sensitively**. Redundancies should be treated as a final resort – after other ways of achieving the reduction have been exhausted.

The reductions should be achieved following a **number of steps** over the next year.

- Employees that leave or retire should **not be replaced**. R&L should be able to make a reasonable estimate of how big a dent in the 50% reduction required can be achieved through 'natural wastage'.

- Encouraging employees approaching retirement age to take **early retirement**. Some financial incentive may be required for this.

- Headcount reduction may be helped through **outsourcing** non-core functions (for example IT). It may even be possible to negotiate a transfer of staff to the outsourcing company.

- To reduce the impact on individuals, **job-sharing** schemes could be proposed so that the individuals involved at least keep 'half a job'.

- A **shorter working week** could also be introduced for some staff allowing greater numbers of people to remain employed – but still cutting the 'full-time equivalent' headcount.

- Then, as a final resort if redundancies are imposed **agreed processes** must be followed.

Appropriate **support** for those employees facing redundancy could include the following:

- **Counselling** and support groups for those retiring early (eg pension advice).

- Counselling, **financial advice** and other support for those made redundant.

- Offering **meetings/discussion** with **employment agents** and staging job fairs to help redundant workers find new positions.

- **Training** to make individuals more attractive on the open job market.

The plan to reduce numbers and the support offered must be discussed and agreed with employee groups (for example trade unions).

(b) *Kotter* and *Schlesinger* (1979) identified **six strategies** for dealing with **resistance to change**. We look at each of these below in the context of R&L. The six approaches are not intended to be used separately in isolation – a combination will be required as explained below.

Education and communication. This approach emphasises the need to provide information about the need for, or the nature of, the planned change. This can be time-consuming.

As a good employer R&L should provide information justifying the cuts – but more will need to be done than simply providing information for those made redundant.

Participation and involvement is an approach intended to involve and therefore gain the support of those affected by the change. This method is used most often when the people affected by the change have considerable power to resist it.

It is important that those involved at R&G participate in the ideas for cutting jobs in the lest disruptive way. However, it is likely that those being made redundant will still feel some resentment unless something more is done.

Facilitation and support. This means helping those affected, for example by providing training and counselling. This approach helps reduce resistance to change based on expected/perceived difficulties adjusting to the new situation (perhaps due to insecurity).

This strategy should play an important role at R&L as job reduction is a highly stressful situation.

Negotiation and agreement. This involves agreeing compensation and/or the change process with those affected. This may help draw a line under an event, but it can be expensive in terms of for example redundancy packages.

R&L is a good employer and there appears to be trust between management and staff/unions. Those made redundant are likely to require some compensation (above statutory requirements) if R&L is to maintain its reputation and preserve the morale of remaining employees.

Manipulation and co-optation. This means not being completely honest – presenting a slanted view to gain support. This is a quick and relatively inexpensive approach, but normally results in future problems if the people involved realise they have been manipulated.

This approach would be inconsistent with R&L's wish to be open and honest so is not suitable.

Explicit and implicit coercion. This means forcing the change through.

This would raise ethical and possibly legal problems in a redundancy situation. It would also antagonise unions and remaining staff, and is inconsistent with R&L's 'good employer' philosophy.

52 Job reductions; resistance to change – amended

Text references. Appraisal systems ad employee empowerment are covered in Chapter 8. Methods to reduce jobs can be found in Chapter 7 and strategies for dealing with resistance to change are detailed in Chapter 14.

Top tips. Use the requirement to provide a structure to your answer. So, part (c) should include initiatives and support – and part (d) potential strategies and suitable strategies.

Easy marks. Parts (a) and (b) give you an opportunity to gain easy marks by reproducing book knowledge. This applies to Parts (c) and (d) also but to score well, you should go further and relate this knowledge to the situation at R&L.

Examiner's comments. This was a popular question and most candidates answered part (c) in particular well. Some candidates drew purposeful examples from similar organisations including the recent MG/Rover experience.

(a) **The purpose of an appraisal system**

Performance appraisal is 'the regular and systematic review of performance and the assessment of potential with the aim of producing action programmes to develop both work and individuals.'

The general purpose of any assessment or appraisal system is to improve the efficiency of the organisation by ensuring that the individual employees are performing to the best of their ability and developing their potential for improvement.

Common objectives of a formal performance appraisal system include the following:

- To establish what the individual has to do in a job in order that the objectives for the section or department are realised.

- To assess an individual's current level of job performance. This can be used both as a base line against which performance can be measured in future, as a means of deciding how the individual has improved since the last performance appraisal and to identify weaknesses and training needs.

- To assess the level of reward payable for an individual's efforts, eg, in merit payment systems.

- To assess potential. At the organisational level this permits career and succession planning. At the individual level it permits appraiser and appraisee to assess the most effective development plans for the appraisee.

> **Top tips.** When a question asks you for a definition, it is not necessary to provide a quote from a textbook. You should provide you own definition which is both **precise** and **concise**.

(b) The concept of **empowerment** means allowing employees to take the decisions required to do their jobs. Empowerment reflects the view that those performing a task are best placed to decide how it is performed.

This ideal contrasts markedly with traditional ideas of **top-down management**, in which management is seen as being best qualified to make almost all decisions. The traditional model inhibits decision making at lower levels in an organisation's hierarchy.

Empowerment reflects the need for **flexibility** to react to changing conditions. This is achieved by empowering employees at all levels to take **decisions** on aspects of work that relate to themselves, cutting out the red tape of hierarchical command structures. This has been an important theme in developments such as **quality circles**, **just in time production** and **continuous improvement** programmes. Empowerment therefore plays an important role in devising and spreading best practice.

To be effective, empowerment must be **embraced** by management and staff at all levels of the organisation.

(c)   The directors of R&L have agreed to act as 'honestly and fairly as possible' in implementing the job reductions.

Redundancy has a massive impact upon many individuals and therefore need to be **handled sensitively**. Redundancies should be treated as a final resort – after other ways of achieving the reduction have been exhausted.

The reductions should be achieved following a **number of steps** over the next year.

- Employees that leave or retire should **not be replaced**. R&L should be able to make a reasonable estimate of how big a dent in the 50% reduction required can be achieved through 'natural wastage'.

- Encouraging employees approaching retirement age to take **early retirement**. Some financial incentive may be required for this.

- Headcount reduction may be helped through **outsourcing** non-core functions (for example IT). It may even be possible to negotiate a transfer of staff to the outsourcing company.

- To reduce the impact on individuals, **job-sharing** schemes could be proposed so that the individuals involved at least keep 'half a job'.

- A **shorter working week** could also be introduced for some staff allowing greater numbers of people to remain employed – but still cutting the 'full-time equivalent' headcount.

- Then, as a final resort if redundancies are imposed **agreed processes** must be followed.

Appropriate **support** for those employees facing redundancy could include the following:

- **Counselling** and support groups for those retiring early (eg pension advice).

- Counselling, **financial advice** and other support for those made redundant.

- Offering **meetings/discussion** with **employment agents** and staging job fairs to help redundant workers find new positions.

- **Training** to make individuals more attractive on the open job market.

The plan to reduce numbers and the support offered must be discussed and agreed with employee groups (for example trade unions).

(d)   *Kotter* and *Schlesinger* (1979) identified **six strategies** for dealing with **resistance to change**. We look at each of these below in the context of R&L. The six approaches are not intended to be used separately in isolation – a combination will be required as explained below.

Education and communication. This approach emphasises the need to provide information about the need for, or the nature of, the planned change. This can be time-consuming.

As a good employer R&L should provide information justifying the cuts – but more will need to be done than simply providing information for those made redundant.

Participation and involvement is an approach intended to involve and therefore gain the support of those affected by the change. This method is used most often when the people affected by the change have considerable power to resist it.

It is important that those involved at R&G participate in the ideas for cutting jobs in the least disruptive way. However, it is likely that those being made redundant will still feel some resentment unless something more is done.

Facilitation and support. This means helping those affected, for example by providing training and counselling. This approach helps reduce resistance to change based on expected/perceived difficulties adjusting to the new situation (perhaps due to insecurity).

This strategy should play an important role at R&L as job reduction is a highly stressful situation.

Negotiation and agreement. This involves agreeing compensation and/or the change process with those affected. This may help draw a line under an event, but it can be expensive in terms of for example redundancy packages.

R&L is a good employer and there appears to be trust between management and staff/unions. Those made redundant are likely to require some compensation (above statutory requirements) if R&L is to maintain its reputation and preserve the morale of remaining employees.

Manipulation and co-optation. This means not being completely honest – presenting a slanted view to gain support. This is a quick and relatively inexpensive approach, but normally results in future problems if the people involved realise they have been manipulated.

This approach would be inconsistent with R&L's wish to be open and honest so is not suitable.

Explicit and implicit coercion. This means forcing the change through.

This would raise ethical and possibly legal problems in a redundancy situation. It would also antagonise unions and remaining staff, and is inconsistent with R&L's 'good employer' philosophy.

53 Total learning experience

Top tips. This question tests your ability to critically evaluate an existing information system and to recommend improvements. This is probably as 'techie' a question as would appear in this exam. The examiner expects you to have an understanding of IT in common use but does not expect you to be an IT expert.

MEMORANDUM

To: Finance Manager
From: Accountant
Date: 21 May 20XX
Subject: **TLE's information systems**

This memo summarises my recent analysis of the information system used at TLE.

(a)   **A. Current hardware facilities**

- The hardware facilities provided are inadequate. For example, tutors often have to wait before being able to access a PC to prepare course material – wasting time and resulting in rushed preparation.

- PCs within TLE are not linked together. This lack of a network prevents the easy sharing of information and has led to data duplication and errors.

- The fact that even the administration PCs can be accessed without the use of a user-name and password means information held on administration PCs could easily be accessed, changed or deleted by unauthorised personnel.

- There is also an absence of mobile phones and laptop computers for tutors.

(b)   **B. Current software facilities**

- The individual software packages used at TLE are treated as separate entities, causing a lack of integration. TLE has a database package that may be able to help resolve this problem but staff have not been trained on this software.

- The operating system software does not require user-names and passwords. This places information held on TLE PCs at risk.

- There are no timetabling or diary management systems. The current method of timetabling and management of tutor diaries is inefficient and likely to result in errors.

- TLE tutors don't have access to e-mail to enable efficient, quick 'written' communication.

(c)   **C. Course booking system**

- The current course booking system is inefficient, time-consuming and unnecessarily expensive (eg external printer costs).

- Customers may book a course using a range of methods but there is no consistent format, which increases the work involved processing bookings.

- The system involves too much paperwork, which is costly and time consuming to process. Errors could easily be made, for example tear off slips could be lost.

- The lack of integration between course booking and invoicing means accurate invoicing is dependant upon 100% accurate data entry – which is unlikely to be achieved.

- The current diary management process requires significant effort from tutors and the administration assistant. Time pressures mean the task is often neglected, which has led to a number of booking errors.

(d)   **D. Timetable management system**

- The use of a whiteboard for the complex course planning task is likely to lead to errors, as shown by the recent booking mix-up that resulted in a potential client deciding to look elsewhere.

- TLE operates two timetabling systems – one computerised and one manual. This is inefficient and increases the likelihood of confusion.

- To check timetables and course lists, tutors have to pick them up from the office or have them posted. This is slow and inefficient.

- The timetabling software package is being ignored. Could training be provided that would enable this to be used?

- Time shortages mean that the system that is in place is not being adhered to – for example the administration assistant is not calling tutors once a week.

(e)   **2. New hardware**

The hardware described below would allow a system to be implemented that addressed many of the difficulties being encountered at TLE.

- Replace the existing minicomputer with a powerful new PC able to act as a file server for the PCs in the office network.

- Purchase three more PCs for the use of tutors based in the office. All PCs must be capable of running the latest operating system and the database software. Purchase laptop computers for all home based tutors.

- All PCs and laptops should have network cards. A communications link should be established linking all PCs/laptops.

- Portable projectors that link to PCs should be purchased for use in training rooms and mobile phones should be purchased for use by tutors working off site.

- A colour printer and a scanner should be obtained. The scanner could enable some of the archived paper based examinations to be converted into computer files.

(f)   **3. New software**

Some updating/upgrading of TLE software be required. The measures described below would allow a system to be implemented that addressed many of the difficulties being encountered at TLE.

- The current operating system is designed for standalone PCs – a network version with multi-user licence and unique user-names and passwords is required.

- TLE already has recent versions of spreadsheet, word-processing and database software. However, TLE should ensure that this application software is compatible with the new operating system and hardware.

- Internet browser software, anti-virus software and firewall software

- A multi-user accounting package to allow different users to access different parts of the system simultaneously.

- An integrated database system which allows the integration and management of the accounting information, course bookings and diary management.

- E-mail software for both office-based and home-based computers.

Conclusion

TLE's current information system is inadequate. The new system outlined above would ensure information is stored and managed more effectively, and improve operating efficiency.

54 S&C software project

> **Top tips.** Do not be tempted to write to much in Section B questions – ensure you cover the points clearly then move on.
>
> **Easy marks.** Stating who the users are in Part (c) and why they are important would gain easy marks. Use this list of users in Part (e) and state how (realistically) they would become involved in the project.
>
> **Examiner's comments.** Most candidates handled these sub-questions reasonably well. Some candidates gave only a few points per sub-question or did not develop the single phrase responses.

(a)   An organisation such as S & C has two choices if the software it uses does not fit its **business processes**.

1.   **Customise** the **software** to the match the process.
2.   **Change** the **processes** to match the software.

Both options have advantages and disadvantages discussed below.

Customise the software

The benefit of this option is that there will be **no upheaval** within the firm as the business processes remain unchanged.

However, there could be a large **financial cost** if external experts have to be brought in or if the changes are complex. There is also a risk of introducing glitches into the system from the new programming.

Change the processes

This option **saves** the **cost** of additional programming and the risk of introducing glitches.

However, changing business processes could have a **negative impact** on the **morale** and **efficiency** of the staff as it would represent a major change in the way they work.

This change may have a **positive** long-term impact if the software requires more **efficient** work processes than are currently in operation.

It is recommended that the choice between the options is made on a **suitability**, **acceptability** and **feasibility** basis.

(b)   A **phased approach** is more suitable than a 'Big Bang' approach as it **controls the risk** involved when switching over to a new system.

Under a **'Big Bang' approach**, on one particular day the old system is switched off and the new one switched on. There is **no overlap** or period of **dual running** of both systems and therefore management must have complete confidence in it.

As an established **industry standard package**, management should have a degree of **confidence** in it. However, confidence is reduced due to the mis-match between the system and established business processes.

A **phased approach** would implement the new system in **discrete stages** – corresponding to the current system they replace. This would have the following advantages:

- **Risk is reduced** as glitches will be limited to the new subsystem only.

- **Staff will adapt** to change more easily as it occurs over a longer period in small chunks.

- It allows **time for feedback** from staff involved in earlier phases to be considered when rolling out later ones. For example, small glitches or user-friendliness.

- There is **less disruption** so the benefits of the changes can be felt more quickly.

(c)   The following roles within S & C are important for the implementation to succeed.

- **Partners** – Their support in terms of visible behaviour and making sufficient resources available is crucial.

- **Project manager** – It is their organisation and drive that will keep the project on track and focussed. This will ensure business performance is not affected by the change. A regular presence is required to ensure this, if the current manager cannot keep regular attendance they should be replaced.

- **Steering group** – The group should be available to support staff in the weeks immediately prior and subsequent to the implementation. They also have a key role to play in winning over staff who resist it.

- **HR department** – Should ensure staff receive suitable training and support during the implementation. Where system success depends on targets being met a reward system should be put in place. They should also develop policies to deal with staff who resist the change.

- **Staff** – It is their acceptance of the system that will decide if it is a success. It is important that they communicate ideas and suggestions as this will help them feel that the system is theirs.

- **Managers** – They have a key role to ensure information regarding the change is communicated in a clear, timely manner to the staff. This will help minimise any disruption to the business

(d)   **User involvement** in the implementation phase usually relates to activities designed to obtain user acceptance of the new system, or to user testing. Some specific examples include:

- **Testing**. Developers would ask a group of users to test the system to check that it works as it should and actually meet their needs.

- **Training**. The implementation phase is usually towards the end of the development. Users should start their training on the new system so they are prepared for the changeover.

- **File conversion and transfer**. Data within the old system will need to be transferred into the new system. Users should be involved in the transfer as their knowledge will help sort any errors that may occur.

- **Quality circles and discussions**. Forums that include users should be set up to discuss the overall quality of the system and how it could be improved.

- **Championing Change**. Users who can see the benefits of the new system should become involved in winning over other users who may resist the change.

(e)   There are three distinct groups within S & C who have different training needs.

Partners

Partners will not be using the system on a day-to-day basis, however, they should have a good basic understanding of it so they understand how the work they review was assembled.

Such training could be provided by an executive presentation.

Managers

Managers should receive training to enable them to understand the software involved in areas they are responsible for. In particular, security features that prevent unauthorised access or loss or damage to data.

Users

Users need to be trained in the day-to-day features and processes that the system provides. This would include data-entry and report writing amongst others.

Training can be provided by:

- The consultants/developers
- The in-house IT team
- A combination of the two

Methods of training can include:

- In-house demonstrations
- On-line learning
- Computer based training using dummy data
- Provision of user manuals
- Helplines to the software developer
- 'Buddy training' where competent users train others
- Classroom courses

(f)   **The aims of a post-implementation review include:**

- To **report** as to whether the **objectives** and **performance** targets of a new system have been met.

- To **review** the **actual costs** and **benefits** of the new system, including a comparison to the forecasted costs and benefits in the feasibility study.

- To **learn** from any **mistakes** made so they can be avoided in the future.

- To **recommend improvements** or future updates.

- To **assess** the **overall change process** and project management quality.

The review should be conducted soon after **implementation** is complete so it is still fresh in the memory. However, it should not be too close to implementation as the findings may be distorted by 'teething problems'. A good period to conduct the review is between **one month** and **one year** following implementation.

55 Tracey plc

> **Top tips.** The answer format specified is 'briefing notes'. This implies focussed, concise and clear. Bullet points are acceptable but ensure you provide explanation.

(a)   A set of procedures is necessary to control the change from the old to the new database. The **Systems Development Life Cycle** provides an appropriate model.

The key stages are:

- **Feasibility study** – ensure that the proposed database can be used.
- **Systems investigation** and **analysis** – obtain details of current system to ensure no functionality is missed in the new system
- **Systems design** – design of the new system
- **Systems implementation** – changeover from old to new database
- **Review** – check that the new database is working correctly.

(b)   **Benefits of the database**

- **Promotion** – including advertising, public relations and building a brand image. The database will show how each potential customer heard of Tracey plc showing which promotional activity is most effective.
- **Product** – marketing will assist product design by identifying features customers would like. The database will contain customer 'wish lists' assisting this function.
- **Price** – product pricing. External links to the Internet will enable the marketing department to find prices of similar products to assist with the target price for Tracey plc.
- **Place** (distribution) – or how the product will reach the customer.

Unfortunately, no additional detail will be kept – but as Tracey distributes via mail order only this won't cause any operational problems.

(c)   **Use of the new technology** in marketing will enable the company's marketing efforts to be targeted more effectively. For example:

- The type of marketing that was previously effective in making the customer contact will be recorded. Future marketing expenditure will be directed into the more effective forms of advertising.
- Links can be determined between geographical location and products purchased. Special offers can be directed at specific groups of people to encourage overall increases in sales eg. patio tubs for small inner city gardens or summer houses for larger country gardens.
- Customers who have not purchased from Tracey plc for a while may be identified and targeted.
- The product(s) bought by a customer will be recorded and the information used for 'linked' offers (eg purchase of a greenhouse followed by an offer on greenhouse shelves).
- Feedback can be held and reviewed to ensure that products meet customer requirements. Where appropriate, production specifications can be changed.

(d)   **Marketing information** can be used to **determine production strategy** – as long as the company accepts the necessary operations strategy. Tracey plc could use the **marketing requirements perspective** approach to operations strategy – based on the following principles.

- Tracey plc needs to satisfy customer needs.
- Needs can be satisfied using an appropriate marketing mix, which the marketing department can provide.
- The operational department will set performance indicators to check appropriate goods are being produced.
- Production and product features will be based on customer requirements.

(e) **Organisation structure**

- The new database enables any person in the marketing department to enter and access data, previously only the marketing manager was able to use the database.

- The organisational structure of the department will be 'flatter' – that is the manager will now control 20 sales and marketing staff rather than 5 assistant managers controlling 4 staff each.

- The span of control of the marketing manager is therefore wider – the manager will be in charge of more people.

Organisational culture

Sales and marketing staff will have access to the new database. Changes to culture include:

- Learning new technology and data access/retrieval skills – support for learning needed.
- Staff will work with less supervision – support needed to encourage own decision making.

(f) A **job competence** refers to a capacity that leads to behaviour that meets the requirements of a specific job. Specific skills for the new data controller will include:

- Personal – ability to relate to other people – specifically managers in different departments
- Personal – ability to influence managers to conform to Tracey plc data standards
- Intellectual – understanding of data requirements
- Intellectual – understanding of the functionality of hardware and software
- Work-based – experience with data control issues in other companies
- Intellectual – ability to see strategic data requirements for the company – not just one department
- Intellectual – ability to plan for change and implement new systems

56 Question with answer plan: Zircon company

> **Top tips.** This question format (Section B, six 5 mark questions based on a scenario) requires you to be concise in your answers – or you risk spending too much time on this question.
>
> Practise these type of questions and ensure you remain within the 54 minute limit justified by the 30 marks on offer.

Answer plan

Quickly note down points that could be used in your answer. Use this as a starting point when writing your answer – making changes to what you include if appropriate.

(a) Change triggers

    PEST?

(b) Advantages vertical integration

    Cost, service levels, dependability

> Apply to Zircon through all parts of answer

(c) TQM and six sigma (appropriate?)

    Customer focus, quality, service operation

(d) Pricing enhanced package

    Costs, competitors, quality level

(e) Marketing strategies

    Mass, concentrated, differentiated

(f) Staff independence/motivation

    Should improve motivation, training, pay?

(a)   **Change triggers** relevant to the Zircon Company include:

- **Environmental**. Competitors are providing other channels to market which Zircon currently does not have eg Internet and sending out catalogues.

- **Technological**. Internet technology means that holidays can be booked over the Internet providing significant cost savings for companies.

- **Culture**. Many people like taking more control of their lives – including booking their own holidays rather than relying on a shop to recommend a standard package holiday.

- **Management style**. Zircon management have recognised the need to allow staff more freedom of choice – this has not been reflected in the way Zircon sells holidays causing some demotivation in staff.

- **Social**. People have more leisure time – but want to book holidays with less planning. They may not have time to visit a travel agent to book their holiday.

(b)   The **benefits of purchasing aircraft** and **hotels** to Zircon will include:

- **Dependability of supply**. Because aircraft and hotels will be for use of Zircon customers only, Zircon will be able to guarantee seats and hotel rooms overcoming the problem of overcapacity experienced by some tour operators.

- **Cost**. It is not clear whether costs will fall as Zircon is now taking the risk of finding sufficient customers to make the aircraft and hotels economic. However, commission will not be paid to other companies providing some cost savings.

- **Product quality**. Zircon will be able to respond quickly to issues of quality rather than have to rely on a third party to make changes.

- **Customer service**. After training, Zircon staff will be more familiar with the entire operations of the company, providing more knowledge to answer customer queries.

- **Customer perception**. The ability to offer bespoke packages in terms of flexible flight times, different activities at the hotel etc. should meet changing customer requirements.

(c)   **Total Quality Management** (TQM) is a management philosophy, aimed at **providing continuous improvement** in quality standards.

The **main features** of TQM include:

- Getting things right first time – that is preventing defecting production or provision of poor service.

- Meeting or exceeding the needs of customers.

- Involving the whole organisation in providing high quality goods and services by implementing a 'quality culture'.

Six sigma is one method of implementing quality – it relates to six standard deviations from the mean, or an error rate of no more than 3.4 per million. It is most easily applied to production activities rather than service activities, and so may not be applicable to Zircon. Six sigma may be able to be applied in a service context, but guidelines would have to be devised (eg is an aircraft being delayed 10 minutes an error?).

(d) **Factors to take into account when setting the price of the holiday package** including flights and accommodation include:

- **Cost of providing the service**. Although cost savings may accrue (no commission) the actual cost in terms of aircraft lease costs, staff, fuel, hotel running costs etc. must be determined and apportioned over the number of customers at a realistic utilisation rate.

- **Competitor's actions**. Where competitors are offering similar a similar holiday service, prices may be amended to match or undercut Zircons. Undercutting Zircon's price is a normal strategy to try and prevent new competition from entering the market.

- **Perceived quality**. If customers see Zircon as providing a quality product (which they may given that Zircon can tailor the holiday package to the individual customer) then they may be willing to pay a premium for Zircon's holidays.

- **Income**. If incomes are rising, then pricing becomes less important. Zircon must check how incomes are changing.

- **Staff**. Sales staff may request a wages increase due to the additional responsibilities and skills of selling the enhanced holiday package.

(e) **Marketing strategies** include:

- **Mass or undifferentiated marketing**. A single product is introduced with the hope that as many customers as possible will buy it. Market segmentation is ignored completely. This strategy is not appropriate for Zircon as the holiday product is (hopefully) being directed at a specific market segment.

- **Concentrated marketing**. The company attempts to produce the ideal product for a specific market segment. Zircon is attempting to do this with the new holiday product – although existing standard holidays will still be sold. Focusing on one market segment is therefore not appropriate.

- **Differentiated marketing**. The company markets several product versions aimed at different market segments. Taking the assumption that Zircon is selling two products, then this strategy is appropriate. While any promotional material will have many points in common, the bespoke service will appeal to some people and the standard service to others. However, care must be taken to ensure that there are two markets and Zircon has not over differentiated the product.

- **Micro–marketing**. The requirement for bespoke holidays may allow Zircon to advertise the concept to a relatively small number of people. The problem will be obtaining details on which customers are included in the niche.

(f) Initially, providing more independence in a job will normally enhance **motivation**. The employee will appreciate the additional trust and responsibility being given to them. These points equate to the use of motivational factors suggested by *Herzberg*. However, the change in job may not always be motivating because:

- Staff will have **more responsibility** and in the case of the new holiday initiative may need more knowledge to provide customers with full details of the options available. However, no additional training has been offered.

- Similarly, additional responsibility will normally mean some **increase in remuneration** to take account of this – although there is no mention or additional remuneration in the scenario.

- As noted by *Herzberg*, staff may expect an increase in pay resulting from the additional responsibility. If this is not provided then overall they will become **demotivated**.

It is likely that the management of Zircon need to meet staff expectations by providing an **increase** in wages.

57 Zodiac plc

> **Top tips.** MRP is not an overly large part of the syllabus – but this question shows how even a small topic can be used for this type of question. Ensure you read all of the BPP Text just in case an 'unexpected' topic crops up in the exam.

(a)   The feasibility of the new Material Requirements Planning system can be determined under the following headings:

Technical feasibility. The requirements must be technically feasible. The use of a computer system to run MRP, as well as EDI and an extranet is feasible – the technology exists and is widely used. Links will also be required to the production and customer ordering systems, although again there does not appear to be any technical reason that these cannot be achieved, both use standard software.

Operational feasibility. The MRP system must fit in with the current operations in Zodiac. The system may require a change in responsibilities, with the production controller losing authority to order stock.

Social feasibility. The new MRP system has to be acceptable to the staff in Zodiac or changes made to ensure it is accepted eg training and the possible redrawing of job specifications.

Ecological feasibility. **The new system should** be as environmentally friendly as possible. EDI will reduce paper usage, and hopefully stock wastage will be reduced as only the required amount of stock will be purchased.

Financial feasibility. A **cost benefit analysis** will be needed to ensure that benefits outweigh the costs. This will have to be carried out carefully as many benefits will be intangible..

(b)   Benefits of a Materials Requirements Planning system include:

- **Reduced stock holding**. Stock will only be re-ordered when necessary and then taking into account past usage. This should ensure a more appropriate amount of stock is ordered compared to the current 'guess' by the production controller.

- **Better customer service**. There will be fewer production delays due to stockouts of materials stock will be re-ordered on a timelier basis.

- **Improved information on delivery times**. Linking the MRP system direct to suppliers means that details on delivery times can be sent electronically back to Zodiac plc.

- **Better time management**. The production controller will spend less time having to produce 'emergency' orders allowing more time to control the production activity itself.

- **Improved facilities utilisation**. The amount of warehouse space required to store stock will be reduced allowing for alternative use of this space.

(c)   **Questions to assist the board regarding outsourcing.**

- **Is the system of strategic importance?** Strategic IS are not normally outsourced because they can require a high degree of specific business knowledge which the outsourcing company may not possess. However, a *standard* MRP system could be outsourced, even though it is important to the running of the business; the outsourcing company should have knowledge of this system.

- **Can the system be relatively isolated?** Systems that have limited interfaces with other IS are more easily outsourced. The MRP will have links to production and ordering potentially limiting the ability to outsource it.

- **Can the outsourcing agreement be managed effectively?** In other words, does Zodiac know enough about MRP to be able to monitor the outsourcing company? The answer is probably 'no' so Zodiac will need to hire at least one specialist to understand MRP and manage the relationship.

- **Are requirements likely to change?** If the MRP will be replaced in the near future then a long term outsourcing agreement would be inappropriate.

(d) **Customer**

- New customers acquired – increase in long run with better customer service
- Customer complaints – fall with better fulfilment
- Delivery speeds – overall increase due to fewer stockouts

Internal operations

- Quality control rejects – may not change because production unaltered
- Productivity – should increase with fewer production stoppages resulting from fewer stockouts

Innovation and learning

- Training days – more needed to understand the MRP system

- Average time taken to develop new clothing fashions – probably unchanged because no change to CAD / CAM

Financial

- Return on capital employed – should increase with fewer production stoppages
- Revenue growth – should increase with better customer service
- EPS – increase with better ROCE and profits reported and better image/brand name

(e) **Market segmentation** means subdividing a market into distinct and homogenous subgroups or customers where any subgroup can be selected as a target market with a distinct marketing mix. Market segmentation is likely to be beneficial to Zodiac for the following reasons:

- Clothes for male and female customers tend to be different. Segmenting the market in this way will also for specific marketing activities to attract each segment.

- The marketing budget can be allocated to each market segment and the return from each segment analysed to assist future investment.

- The product range can be designed to meet customer needs. For example, segmenting the market by age as well as gender will allow Zodiac to target specific fashions at different age groups.

- Zodiac may decide to try and dominate one market segment eg clothes for females aged 25 to 40 and attempt to gain specific competitive advantage in that segment.

(f) The steps in an **appraisal system** are described below.

Step 1   Identification of criteria for assessment. The main criterion appears to be quality of the production system, although other criteria such as ability to manage junior staff can also be used.

Step 2   Preparation of an appraisal report, either by the management accountant, the production controller or both individually for comparison.

Step 3   Appraisal interview. Exchange of views concerning work, setting targets for the next appraisal etc.

Step 4   Review of assessment by assessor's superior. To ensure that there is no prejudice in the report. The CEO may be the appropriate person for this job being senior to the management accountant and in charge of running the company.

Step 5   Prepare and implement action plan to achieve improvements and actions agreed.

Step 6   Follow up and monitor the plan.

58 Services marketing

Top tips. Your answer should be placed in context using references to financial services throughout. You must **apply** your knowledge to do well in a question like this.

(a)   **Perishability**. A service cannot be stored or saved. It has an immediacy that cannot be held over until sometime in the future. For example, with a loan the repayments start immediately after it has been set up. If there is a delay with the loan the lost revenue cannot be recovered. Marketers have to give incentives for customers to purchase at off-peak times to counter this potential problem. An investment fund provides another example – the value changes constantly so cannot be held for purchase later.

(b)   **Intangibility**. You cannot touch or feel the service offering as it has an abstract delivery. Unlike a product which you can touch (and smell and see) a service has no physical presence. It is only the paperwork that accompanies the service which has a tangible element. This can give problems since customers cannot see what they are getting for their money and they can only make a judgement based on experience of the service.

(c)   **Inseparability**. A key distinguishing feature of a service is that the provider and receiver of the service are inseparable from consumption and the consumer. The customer has to be present for the service to take place which presents a problem for the marketer as they cannot always ensure that the process is enjoyable for the customer. Many customers have one financial advisor who they prefer to deal with on a range of financial issues.

(d)   **Heterogeneity**. The delivery of the service will vary each time to the customer. This is because a service is dependant on the unique interaction of the provider and the customer which will vary depending on the interaction between the two individuals. The variability created by the influence of human behaviour in the transaction and consistency can become a difficult problem to manage. A financial service transaction such as selling a pension plan will often involve a presentation – the delivery of which will vary each time.

(e)   **People**. There should be a strong emphasis on staff training to ensure a consistently high quality of provision. Poor customer service is the most commonly quoted reason for a change in sourcing services and recovering lost custom is a difficult problem to overcome. The high level of people involvement in management consultancy demands that their customers are treated in a very professional manner throughout the delivery process. As their customers will judge the quality of the service by the conduct of the staff, close proximity of the staff working in a small business magnifies the need to adequately train all employees. This can include such areas as personal presentation, dealing with enquiries, providing quotations and maintaining technical competencies in line with current developments.

(f)   **Process** As part of customer service, efficient administrative processes underpin a high quality of provision. For instance if a client has spent an unnecessary amount of time trying to contact a management consultant they would become very frustrated and annoyed at the waste of their valuable time. It sends all the wrong messages concerning the offering and will become a source of friction between the two parties that will have to be recovered. The small business will need to consider putting procedures and resources into place to ensure these problems are carefully managed and that the client's expectations are at least achieved, if not surpassed.

59 Question with helping hand: Hubbles

Top tips. The question requirement asks for 'a slide outline and brief accompanying notes of two to three sentences'. A slide outline is in effect a list of headings, usually one or two main headings and a number of sub-headings. Keep your notes brief – this will help your time allocation and help keep your answer focussed.

Easy marks. Ensure you answer the question using the correct format – in this case slides and notes. Keep your answer neat – there are often a couple of marks available for format and clarity.

(a)

> **Sales orientation v marketing orientation**
>
> Companies with a **sales orientation**
>
> - 'Let's sell what we've made'
> - A focus on advertising, selling and sales promotion
>
> Companies with a **marketing orientation**
>
> - 'Let's make what the customer wants'
> - All employees, and the organisation as a whole, have a 'customer focus'

Notes. Hubbles' emphasis on 'selling' implies that not enough effort has been made to establish what customers want. If Hubbles produces items that 'strike a cord' with customers, the products should 'sell themselves'.

(b)

> **A marketing orientation for Hubbles**
>
> - Find out what customers want – **market research**
> - What (and how) are **competitors** supplying?
> - Compare customer wants with all items currently on the market – **any gap** is an opportunity
> - Establishing **a true marketing orientation** will require new ways of working, commitment from staff at all levels and a change of culture
> - Some staff may not be suited to the new way of working and may have to leave; others will require information and **training**

Notes. Adopting a marketing orientation will require Hubbles to change how and why decisions are taken. The driving force behind Hubbles' products, markets, prices, and communication must be customer needs. All staff at all levels must see their roles in the context of how Hubbles satisfies or delights customers.

(c)

> **The traditional components of the marketing mix**
>
> - **Product** – the totality of what the customer purchases including product characteristics
> - **Place** (distribution) – how the customer accesses or purchases the product
> - **Promotion** – customers must be aware of the product and what it offers
> - **Price** – linked to perceptions of quality and value for money
>
> Recent thinking recognises the importance of a fifth component
>
> - **People** – the people involved in producing and bringing the offering to customers are crucial

Notes. The marketing mix is a framework that enables organisations to structure their thinking in a way that focuses on the customer. After Hubbles has devised a customer-focussed strategy it will be in a position to develop an appropriate marketing mix to achieve the strategy. This will require Hubbles to meet or exceed customer needs and expectations in all areas of the marketing mix.

(d)

> **Hubbles and the marketing mix**
>
> - **Product**. Identify what products customers want and focus production on these.
>
> - **Place**. Make it as easy as possible for customers to purchase Hubbles products. Ensure widespread distribution; offer on-line sales with next day delivery.
>
> - **Promotion**. Get the message out that Hubbles has listened and has changed. Likely to require advertising campaigns using different media to target groups.
>
> - **Price**. Revise pricing strategy to match the new products. Decide the balance between competing on style and quality or on price.
>
> - **People**. Reorganise along customer-focussed lines. Encourage customer-focussed culture through training programmes, incentives and staff empowerment.

Notes. Must develop a marketing mix that precisely matches the needs of potential customers in the target market. Research the market for data relating to the age, income, sex and educational level of target market, preferences for product features and attitudes to competitors' products.

(e)

> **Human resources helping purchasing**
>
> - **Recruiting** – ensuring people employed are suited to the role
>
> - **Job design** – establishing clear responsibilities
>
> - **Development and motivation** – developing training, appraisal and reward/incentive programmes that result in capable, motivated staff
>
> - **Discipline and conflict resolution** – providing a framework to limit the possible adverse effects of misconduct and conflict

Notes. HR issues are important in all departments, including purchasing. The purchasing department plays a crucial role at Hubble in the procurement of materials and finished goods for sale, supplier selection and relationships, and price negotiation. HR must ensure the purchasing department has people with the right attitude and skills to perform these tasks.

(f)

> **The purchasing department and organisational performance**
>
> - **Supplier selection, links and relationships**. Establishing supplier selection criteria, quality standards, extranet links, Electronic data interchange (EDI)
>
> - **Supplier contract negotiation**. Guaranteed delivery times and quality enables Just in Time (JIT) production methods to be used
>
> - **Co-ordinating purchasing activities** to maximise discounts
>
> - **Relationship management** to encourage mutual co-operation and benefits with suppliers – possible development of a supply network

Notes. The purchasing function is now recognised as being crucial to organisational success, particularly in relation to the creation of value and in supply chain management. Purchasing policies that build close relationships with trusted suppliers should result in higher quality – which customers demand. Effective purchasing policies therefore help meet customer needs which is key to achieving organisational goals.

60 Round the table

PRESENTER'S GUIDANCE NOTES FOR 'ROUND THE TABLE'

Episode: Managing supply to achieve quality and customer satisfaction (30/11/20X5)

(a)   A level capacity strategy involves building up an **inventory buffer** to enable orders to be met from held inventory when demand exceeds capacity.

A Just in Time (JIT) approach involves producing goods (eg cars) when they are needed – **eliminating the need to hold inventory**.

The build up of inventory required under a level capacity strategy contradicts the no inventory approach required under JIT. Therefore, the two approaches are **incompatible**.

Under JIT, production is driven by immediate demand. The capacity management approach consistent with JIT is a chase strategy – which involves adjusting production levels to match demand. This would allow nil (or minimal) inventory, as required under JIT.

(b)   Demand management strategies attempt to **influence demand** to reduce fluctuations to levels above or below capacity. One of the ways demand may be managed is through marketing. Therefore demand strategies influence marketing practices.

If demand is **below capacity**, marketing initiatives such as price incentives and advertising campaigns may be used to **increase demand** (eg free 'extras' and extended warranties on cars).

If demand **exceeds capacity**, it may be decided to **reduce** some marketing activity (eg advertising) and/or to promote orders in a future period rather than those requiring delivery in the short term (eg order next year's new model now).

Marketing may also be used to try and **distribute demand evenly** throughout the year, for example though seasonal offers and other incentives to increase demand in less busy periods (eg interest free finance to purchase a vehicle).

(c)   Chase strategies involve adjusting activity levels in response to fluctuations in demand. To be able to significantly **change production levels quickly and efficiently** (while maintaining quality levels) requires a high level of organisational **flexibility**.

The need to react quickly to an ever changing environment has led to organisations adopting **flexible structures** such as matrix structure, project based teams and virtual or networked firms.

In the automobile industry, **world class manufacturing techniques** are used to provide flexibility. Computes Aided Design, Computer Aided Manufacturing and JIT can all be used to achieve this.

Concepts such as **'economies of scope'** are important in this context, as they provide the flexibility required to change what is being produced in relation to relative changes in demand.

(d) Service organisations differ from manufacturing organisations when considering capacity management in the following ways.

- **Production** and **consumption** occur at the same time. Inventories of services can't be built up in quieter times, which makes the balancing of capacity and demand more difficult.

- Greater **interaction** – the customer plays an active role in the delivery process. Customer service quality is integral to the customer experience.

- Output is **different each time**. Each customer service interaction is different in some way eg different conversation, attitude etc. Achieving a consistently high level of output is more challenging.

- Generally **greater reliance on staff**. Service delivery depends on the people delivering the service. The 'mood' of staff on the front line shouldn't adversely impact upon the customer experience.

- **Intangible output** makes **measuring** the **quality level** of output more difficult as there is no physical product to inspect. Obtaining feedback of customer satisfaction is important.

(e) Inbound logistics refers to the receipt, storage and internal distribution of goods (including material handling and inventory control). A manufacturing organisation could utilise the following types of software relevant to inbound logistics.

- The organisation should have an **inventory software module**, as part of an overall management and accounting system (ideally an **ERM package**). The system should enable accurate inventory records to be held.

- Ideally the inventory software would be linked to **bar code reading hardware and software** used in when goods are received – enabling goods received to be scanned and inventory records updated.

- **Electronic Data Interchange** (EDI) could be used to replace paper documentation such as Invoices. This would help ensure an accurate record of the value of inventory held.

- **E-mail** could be used to advise staff of expected delivery dates of items they are waiting for – particularly if goods are required to fulfil existing orders.

- **Satellite navigation tracking** of delivery vehicles, perhaps viewed via the suppliers **extranet**, would help track inward deliveries.

(f) The following types of computerised assistance could be used by people/organisations trying to improve demand for cars.

- **Advertising on websites** could be used. For example, the car manufacturer could use pop ups on sites used by their target market eg the Automobile Association.

- Individual car dealers may offer a **'buy-now' facility on their website** – although the value of the transaction and need to sign contracts/purchase agreements means some face to face contact will still be required.

- The use of **user registration and cookies** on websites could be used to help identify and track potential customers. The website could also include promotional material and virtual vehicle tours and virtual test drives to encourage purchase.

- A **database** and **Customer Relationship Management (CRM)** software could be used to manage relationships with potential customers and existing customers (repeat purchase is very important – particularly with fleet sales).

- **'M' marketing** may be used to target young, IT literate potential customers (eg if mobile telephone numbers were collected during website registration). 'Text back now to arrange a test drive of the NEW Series 3' or similar messages may be appropriate.

- **E-mail** could be used in a similar way to the text message approach described above.

61 V

(a) The traditional marketing mix includes Product, Price, Promotion and Place. Each of these factors play an important part in the overall offering to customers . V's proposed approach can be understood in this context.

- **Product**. V's products are good quality, fun products with a strong brand. It is important the cosmetics offered are consistent with the established reputation of the brand.

- **Price**. Pricing is competitive, but not the cheapest (ie affordable to most). An important decision is whether the 'list price' will include padding to enable agents to offer discounting. Website sales may be offered at a lower price – although this may make party purchases less attractive to customers.

- **Promotion**. V will rely on word of mouth, Public Relations (such as the radio interview mentioned in the scenario) and the strength of the brand.

- **Place**. V's distribution strategy is to use one level marketing (the cosmetic associates) and some web sales. This relies upon the skill of associates and user acceptance of e-commerce. V also needs efficient transportation options (eg partner a courier business) to ensure order fulfilment.

The 'fifth P', people, is relevant to the distribution strategy explained above. Further 'people issues' are covered in part (b).

(b) V has built a strong brand. The reputation of V must be protected. Allowing cosmetic associates (who aren't employees) to use the V name/reputation carries considerable risk of damaging the brand.

The human resource implications of this include:

- **Agent selection**. Ensuring cosmetic associates (ie agents) have the skills and attitude required is essential. Selection criteria should include a sense of fun, honesty, business awareness and trustworthiness. Formal selection procedures including an interview and reference checking by V HR staff are an important control.

- **Training of cosmetic associates** must be thorough and comprehensive. It should include how to arrange parties, how to ensure they provide a fun customer experience, sales techniques and product knowledge. Specific training will also be required for those dealing with orders/queries submitted via the website or SMS (text).

- **Cosmetic agents remuneration** must be structured in a way that provides motivation/incentive, but without resulting in strong-arm sales techniques. Commission may also be linked to pricing – for example associates may be given the flexibility to sell at a lower price by reducing their commission.

- **On-going monitoring and control** of associates is important to enable any potential problems to be identified before too much damage is done. Customer satisfaction surveys/questionnaires could be useful – as could the use of employed 'area supervisors' who visit or speak to associates and customers.

(c)   **Direct marketing** is a concept that involves the producer of a product interacting directly with the end customer or consumer. The approach can be summed up as 'cutting out the middle-man'.

- This is sometimes referred to as a **'zero level channel'**, as there are zero levels between supplier and the end customer.

- **The Internet** has enabled more businesses to utilise direct marketing. For example, an airline such as British Airways may sell tickets direct to the public via its own website (selling flights via a general travel website isn't 'pure' direct marketing as this involves an intermediary – even if that intermediary happens to be based on the web).

- Using direct marketing has **implications for the marketing mix** – for example promotion can target web users. Order fulfilment (ie actually delivering the product) is key.

(d)   **Advantages** of the **Internet** as a marketing channel include the following:

- Communication is quick allowing rapid response to customer orders/queries
- The range of tasks able to be performed eg promotion, answer queries, display products, e-commerce
- Enables quick price and feature comparison for customers
- Can lower costs through reduced need for physical outlets
- Provides an opportunity for global reach even for very small organisations
- Facilitates the gathering of information and the development of customer databases for future promotions
- Customer convenience as it may be accessed from home or work and any time

(e)   *Note: For study purposes, we have provided more points than would be required to earn the five marks on offer in this part of the question.*

V could use **Internet** and **mobile phone technology** in the following ways.

Internet

- A website with an e-commerce capability would enable orders to be submitted and paid for on-line (using credit and debit cards). Efficient order fulfilment is vital.

- The website could also be used to provide detailed product information to customers, for example the ingredients of different cosmetic products (particularly relevant to those with allergies).

- General information about V as a group and about V cosmetics could also be communicated in this way – helping to cultivate the idea of a 'fun' organisation.

- The site could be used for promotion using web banners and could include links to 'partners' sites and a search facility (eg access to Google from within V's site).

- The website could also be utilised to help attract/recruit cosmetics associates eg 'apply on-line'.

Mobile phones ('M-marketing')

To utilise M marketing V will need access to the mobile phone numbers of those it wishes to reach (possibly through a registration process on the website – or colleted and forwarded from cosmetics associates).

- Reorder requests could submitted by text message

- Associates may wish to text invitations to new parties to the mobiles of past attendees

- V could have an automated text reminder service to remind guests of party time/location

- Details of new products and/or 'special offers' could be texted – eg 'reply with code EYE LINER to take up this offer'

(f)   Ethics is concerned with **right and wrong** – acting **responsibly** and with a sense of **fairness**. The main ethical issues associated with Vs proposal are:

- Will the cosmetics be tested on animals – and if so will associates and customers be informed?

- Where and how will the products be produced? Will this involve factories in developing countries – what about employment conditions, worker remuneration, waste disposal?

- Are associates treated fairly? What mark-up is V making?

- Is it acceptable to target customers through mobile phones? This could be seen as intrusive and an abuse personal information (implications for data protection legislation).

- Is party selling – with the blurring of business and pleasure and often the use of alcohol – ethical? Are people pressured into attending and then made to feel they should 'join in' and buy?

Mock Exams

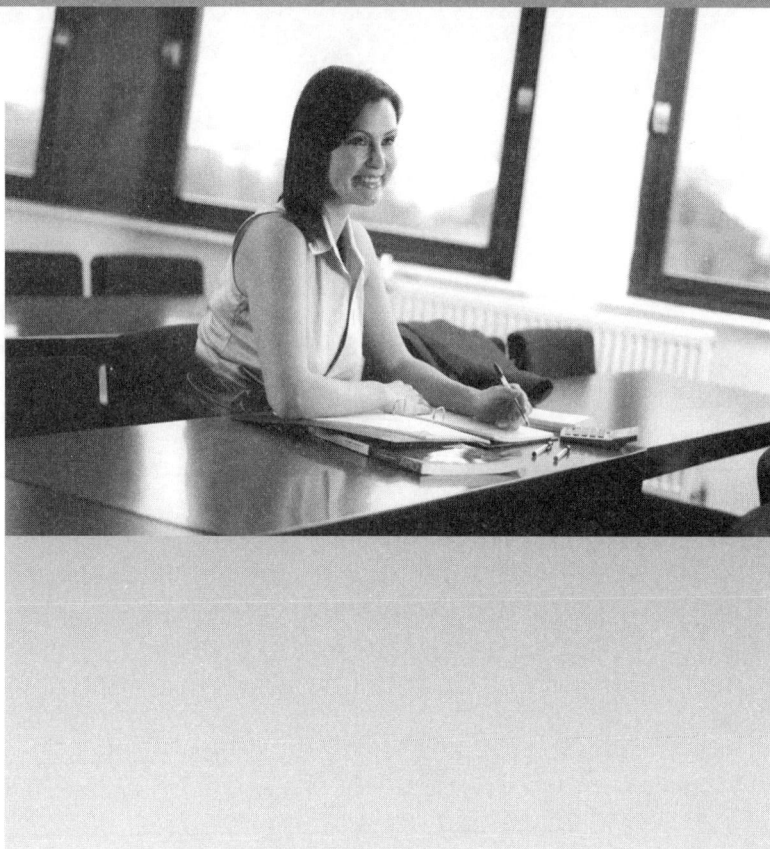

CIMA
Paper P4
Organisational Management and Information Systems

Mock Exam 1

Question Paper	
Time allowed	**3 hours**
You are allowed **20 minutes reading time before the examination begins** during which you should read the question paper, and if you wish, make annotations on the question paper. However, you will not be allowed, under any circumstances, to open the answer book and start writing or use your calculator during this reading time.	
This paper is divided into three sections	
Section A	Answer the ONE compulsory question in Section A. This is comprised of 15 sub-questions
Section B	Answer ALL SIX compulsory sub-questions
Section C	Answer ONE question ONLY (from the two available)

SECTION A – 50 marks

Instructions for answering Section A

The answers to the fifteen sub-questions in Section A should ALL be written in your answer book.

Each of the sub-questions numbered from 1.1 to 1.10 inclusive, given below, has only ONE correct answer, worth two marks.

Question 1

1.1 The operating system is normally responsible for

    A   spreadsheet production
    B   virus checking documents
    C   assisting the user in writing programs
    D   controlling the CPU   **(2 marks)**

1.2 Electronic Data Interchange (EDI) is commonly used in conjunction with

    A   e-mail
    B   an intranet
    C   an internal client/server network
    D   an extranet   **(2 marks)**

1.3 A Data Flow Diagram is used to

    A   show the relationship between items of data in a database
    B   explain the flow of data between entities
    C   define the system boundary and explain how data moves across that boundary
    D   show the links between the different components of a system   **(2 marks)**

1.4 'Push' promotion polices involve

    A   high levels of promotional expenditure to encourage consumers to purchase products
    B   transferring finished goods to intermediaries who then have the task of selling those goods to consumers
    C   using different promotional techniques to influence customer demand in different market segments
    D   using just in time supply policies to meet customer demand   **(2 marks)**

1.5 In terms of market positioning, concentrated positioning means to

    A   target a single market segment with a specific product
    B   target the whole market with a single product
    C   target each market segment with a distinct marketing mix
    D   target a single market with a range of products   **(2 marks)**

1.6 An organisation may show ethical responsibility by

    A   obeying the 'letter of the law'
    B   ensuring that advertising is fair and truthful
    C   suggesting dissatisfied customers purchase products from other companies
    D   selling to any potential purchaser   **(2 marks)**

1.7 The main weakness of performance related pay is

    A   there is no attempt to link profits with the pay structure of individuals

    B   if targets are not met then employees may become demotivated

    C   employees rarely work harder for additional remuneration

    D   it is almost impossible to set appropriate performance targets for manual workers   **(2 marks)**

1.8 Which of the following are valid outcomes of a Human Resource Management strategy?

    A   financial outcomes

    B   behavioural outcomes

    C   performance outcomes

    D   all of the above   **(2 marks)**

1.9 A job description will **not** normally include

    A   the job title of the person to whom the jobholder is responsible

    B   details of any technical procedures, tools, machinery or equipment used by the jobholder

    C   any special requirements to liase or deal with contacts of high significance inside and outside the organisation

    D   the name of the current post holder   **(2 marks)**

1.10 The main advantage of in-house learning is

    A   participants are not exposed to outside influences

    B   participants are available to deal with work problems as they arise

    C   participants can withdraw at short notice without incurring expensive third party cancellation costs

    D   participants can use the organisation's own procedures as examples on the course   **(2 marks)**

(Total for these sub-questions = 20 marks)

Required

Each of the sub-questions numbered **1.11** to **1.15** below require a brief written response. Each sub-question is worth 4 marks.

Each response should be in note form and should not exceed 50 words.

1.11 Explain the goals of a post-implementation review.   **(4 marks)**

1.12 Explain the difference between push and pull marketing.   **(4 marks)**

1.13 Explain the difference between a job description and a person specification.   **(4 marks)**

1.14 In terms of quality management, explain Theory Z.   **(4 marks)**

1.15 In the context of change management, what is meant by 'IT is an enabler'?   **(4 marks)**

(Total for these sub-questions = 20 marks)

Total for Section A = 40 marks

SECTION B – 30 marks

Answer ALL parts of this question

Question 2

The PTR Company designs and manufactures a wide range of ladies' and men's clothes from a large factory. Overall, about 650 different clothes are produced ranging from shirts and blouses to skirts and trousers. The range produced depends on the time of year; the country PTR operates in has particularly cold winters but warm and humid summers meaning that the style and variety of clothes sold vary over the year. Because of the different fabrics required for different weather and changes in fashion from year to year, the fabrics used to manufacture the clothes are rarely used for more than 6 to 8 months.

The Chief Executive Officer has recently learnt that it is cheaper to produce clothes in another country. However, he is reluctant to suggest this to the other directors as PTR has been owned by the same family for the last 60 years, and has a good reputation as a caring employer within the community.

Stock is ordered by the PTR computerised production system automatically placing an order with PTR's suppliers when stock reaches the re-order level. The production system monitors usage for the last six months and automatically raises an order via EDI at the economic order quantity for that particular stock line.

Details of production of each line of clothing are is entered into the company's EIS on a daily basis. The EIS then produces comparison reports of production of each line for the last 12 months, including recommendations for amendments to production according to the time of year. The directors monitor production in terms of ensuring that appropriate cloths are being produced for the time of year. The EIS contains no other data.

Clothes are sold to a variety of different customers from teenagers to business people and a few senior citizens. Fashions vary greatly, and PTR sometimes has difficulty identifying target markets. However, the PTR maintains a good brand name, and consequently the Company is able to charge premium prices in most markets.

Required

Use a separate page of your answer for each key point (meaning that your responses are contained on no more than six pages in total).

(a)   Explain the concepts of open and closed systems and consider to what extent the EIS in the PTR Company is an open system. **(5 marks)**

(b)   Explain the terms coupling and decoupling in the context of the stock ordering system. **(5 marks)**

(c)   Recommend changes to the EIS, clearly showing how the changes will benefit the directors of the company. **(5 marks)**

(d)   Explain the benefits of market segmentation to the PTR company and suggest three ways of segmenting the market for PTR Company. **(5 marks)**

(e)   Explain how societal, economic, technological, and legal factors could affect a clothes manufacturing company such as PTR. **(5 marks)**

(f)   Suggest reasons why the PTR Company may not want to move production facilities to another country. **(5 marks)**

(Total = 30 marks)

SECTION C – 20 marks

Answer ONE question ONLY

Question 3

A company which services all its customers (dealers) from one central warehouse has decided to computerise the stock control, order processing and sales accounting procedures. It has also been decided to close the central warehouse and establish five regional warehouses, each of which will be based on a central mainframe computer with on-line links to regional warehouses where data entry of customer orders and stock replenishment will take place. You are responsible planning the implementation of this system.

Required

(a) Briefly explain the expected benefits of purchasing an off-the-shelf accounting package rather than having bespoke software written.   **(5 marks)**

(b) Describe four possible changeover strategies and recommend one for this situation.   **(14 marks)**

(c) List five general issues that should be considered in the implementation of this system.   **(5 marks)**

(d) Explain the three main types of software maintenance encountered in computer systems.   **(6 marks)**

(Total for Question 3 = 30 marks)

Question 4

The discovery of heavily overstated profits in some of the largest US corporations in 2002 undermined investor confidence in company accounts and called into question the integrity of senior managers, their professional staff and the presumed independence of external auditors.

Required

(a) Describe the key influences on the ethical conduct of senior management of business corporations, their professional staff and those involved with auditing their accounts.   **(10 marks)**

(b) Explain what both businesses and professional bodies can do to influence the ethical behaviour of their organisational members.   **(10 marks)**

(c) Recommend the steps that both professional accountancy bodies and organisations in general can take to ensure that their members take seriously the ethical principles included in their organisations' codes of conduct.   **(10 marks)**

(Total for Question 4 = 30 marks)

(Total for Section C = 30 marks)

Answers

DO NOT TURN THIS PAGE UNTIL YOU HAVE
COMPLETED MOCK EXAM 1

A plan of attack

Before the three hours exam time starts, you are allowed 20 minutes to read through the paper. Use this time wisely – in effect it gives you an extra 20 minutes to gain the marks you need to pass.

What should you do in this 20 minutes? You could read through the two questions in Section C – and decide which **one** of these you will answer. However, this could remove your focus from the Section A questions and clutter your mind with extra information.

We recommend you use the 20 minutes to simply **start working through the Section A questions** – by **writing your answers on the question paper**. These answers can then be transferred **very carefully** to your answer booklet when the exam starts. Remember though, you **must not write in your answer booklet during the reading time**.

Using the time in this way should mean that later in the exam, when you reach Section C, you have sufficient time to read both questions carefully and make the best decision as to which one you will attempt.

Turn back to the question paper now, and we'll sort out a **plan of attack** for Mock exam 1.

First things first

It's usually best to **start with the multiple choice** and **objective test** questions (ie do Section A first). You should always be able to do a fair proportion of these, even if you really haven't done as much preparation as you should have done. And answering even a couple of them will give you the confidence to attack the rest of the paper.

Refer to 'Tackling multiple choice questions' in the front pages of this book for general advice. When answering the objective test questions in this paper, remember your answers must be **concise**, **to the point** and must **answer the question asked**. Don't waste words with waffle!

Allow yourself 36 minutes to do the 10 multiple choice questions, and 36 minutes for the 5 objective test questions – **a total of 72 minutes for Section A**. No more. You can always come back to these questions at the end of the exam if you have some spare time.

The next step – Section B

Question 2 in Section B is compulsory. Attempt this question immediately after you've completed Section A. You've got to do this question so there's no point delaying it. The question is split into sub-parts, all based on a single scenario.

Read the scenario carefully, then take a look at the question requirements.

- Part (a) requires you to use your knowledge of open and closed systems – and to apply this knowledge to the EIS at The PTR Company.

- Part (b) also covers systems theory, this time relating to coupling and decoupling. Again you are asked to apply what you know.

- Part (c) requires suggestions that relate specifically to the EIS at The PTR Company. Don't just make general points – your answer must be realistic in the context of the scenario.

- Part (d) draws upon the marketing area of the syllabus. Suggest three reasonable points.

- Part (e) covers PEST factors – with legal specified rather than political. Your answer must be relevant to the situation faced by The PTR Company.

- Read part (f) carefully. The key word in the question is '**not**'.

Section C

Once you've done the compulsory questions, you are required to choose **one** of the two questions available in Section C. Your choice between questions 3 and 4 should be made on the basis of your knowledge of the topics involved.

Unless you have an excellent understanding of ethics, codes of conduct and their influence on business and individuals it is recommended that you attempt question 3.

- **Question 3**. Parts (a, c and d) offer a chance to pick up relatively easy marks simply by reproducing text book theory. Part (b) requires slightly more thought – you must be able to recommend a suitable strategy for the company.

- **Question 4**. There is a wide range of scope to play with when answering questions such as these as valid, reasonable comments should earn you marks. It is always a good idea to try to structure your answer even if one is not given to you. For example, the answer to part (a) was split into positive and negative influences.

General advice

Don't forget that you have to **answer question 2** and **ONE** question **from questions 3 and 4**. Once you've decided on question 3, for example, it might be worth putting a line through question 4 so that you are not tempted to answer it!

No matter how many times we remind you....

Always, always **allocate your time** according to the marks for the question in total and for the parts of the question. And always, **always follow the requirements** exactly.

You've got spare time at the end of the exam.....?

If you have allocated your time properly then you **shouldn't have time on your hands** at the end of the exam. If you find yourself with five or ten minutes spare, however, **go back to any parts of questions that you didn't finish** because you ran out of ideas or time. A fresh look may spark new thoughts.

Forget about it!

And don't worry if you found the paper difficult. More than likely other candidates would too. If this were the real thing you would need to **forget** the exam the minute you leave the exam hall and **think about the next one**. Or, if it's the last one, **celebrate**!

SECTION A

Question 1

1.1   D   The other options relate to utility programs (B and C) and application software (A).

1.2   D   An extranet links computers in different organisations allowing EDI communication to take place.

1.3   B   The DFD shows the flow of data within the system. Data is only shown moving across the boundary where necessary; it is not the main aim of the DFD to define the boundary or show all of the data moving across the boundary. C is therefore not correct.

1.4   B   'Push' refers to the transfer of goods to third parties – the term is used because the manufacturer 'pushes' goods onto wholesalers or similar intermediaries.

1.5   A   B and C are examples of undifferentiated positioning and differentiated targeting, while D is incorrect as it refers to a range of products.

1.6   B   Obeying the letter of the law is a legal responsibility, so really doesn't qualify (although breaking the law is unethical). C and D are examples of poor ethics – C because dissatisfied customers should be supported, while indiscriminate selling (D) may involve selling to inappropriate market segments (eg targeting young children).

1.7   B   The main risk of performance related pay is demotivation. The other problems can either be overcome or are simply not relevant to PRP.

1.8   D   All of the outcomes are valid as the HRM strategy should impact upon all of these areas.

1.9   D   The name of the current post holder is not normally included in a job description.

1.10   D   Options A, B and C are normally considered to be disadvantages of in-house learning.

1.11   Goals of a post-implementation review:
            • Establish whether the system meets user requirements.
            • Ensure that the performance of the system meets or exceeds the specification/expected performance.
            • Identify and recommend changes to the systems analysis and design process.
            • Compare actual costs against budget; account for any significant variances.

1.12   Push marketing involves transferring goods to wholesalers and retailers – who then sell the goods. 'Push' requires wholesalers and retailers to accept these goods. Pull marketing involves influencing consumer attitudes to create demand for a product – wholesalers and retailers then seek supplies to satisfy this demand.

1.13   Job description: explains the overall purpose of a job and the main tasks carried out within that job.
            Person specification: defines the personal characteristics, qualifications and experience required by person carrying out job.
            The description therefore defines the job, while the specification explains the qualities required to carry out that job.

1.14   Theory Z applies Japanese management philosophy to western management. Key characteristics are:

- Good interpersonal skills to ensure consensus decision making.

- Building relationships on trust while retaining hierarchical authority, rules and control.

- A participative management style facilitating the free flow of information.

1.15   IT may be the driving force behind organisational change. IT can produce dramatic changes in businesses and industries, eg airline industry booking systems that allow easy fare comparison and booking. Even when IT is not a significant factor in the actual change, it can play an important part in change management.

SECTION B

Question 2

> **Top tips.** This is a 'typical' scenario question with a mixture of knowledge reproduction and knowledge application required.
>
> **Easy marks.** Some marks are available for demonstrating your knowledge of systems theory, your understanding of market segmentation, and a grasp of PEST factors.
>
> To score well though you must apply this knowledge to the situation of PTR.

(a)   An **open system** is one which is connected to and **interacts with its environment**. It therefore takes in influences from the environment as well as influencing the environment by its own behaviour.

A **closed system** is **isolated** from and **independent** of its environment. This means that the system is not influenced by, and cannot influence, the external environment.

In the case of the EIS, is open – but not as open as it should be. With respect to the company itself, the system is open because it receives data from the production systems and then occasionally amends those systems by changing output requirements in terms of overall company strategy.

However, the EIS appears to **lack inputs from outside of the company**. No account appears to be taken of customer demand or the product range produced by competitors. This means that actual sale of output happens more by 'accident' than design.

(b)   Systems are said to be **coupled** when the **output from one** system **forms the input for another** system. In the context of the stock ordering system, the output from the ordering system in the PTR Company forms the input to the production systems at PTR's suppliers. As soon as the re-order quantity is reached for an individual stock line, then the economic order quantity is placed with that supplier; no human intervention is required.

Systems are **decoupled** when some systems are allowed to work at their own speed rather than having to wait for inputs from another system. For example, most companies keep stocks of raw materials to allow the procurement and production systems to work at their own pace, rather than having them linked, or coupled, together. Given that the stock ordering system at PTR and the production systems at the suppliers are able to cope with the transfer of information, decoupling appears to be inappropriate.

(c)   The main problem with the EIS at present is it appears to be focused on the analysis of **operational data**, which is more of a Management Information System role. To be useful to the directors, the EIS needs to be **focused at the strategic level** of the company, providing summary information for decision making at this level.

Specific changes that could take place include:

- The initial summarisation of data can take place within some MIS. Only summaries of clothes being produced along with unusual variances for management attention actually need to be transferred to the EIS. A drill down feature can produce additional detail.

- Over time, the EIS can accumulate data on the sales potential of different types of clothes, and different fashions. This information can be used to forecast potential demand helping the PTR Company to provide an appropriate product range.

- As the current EIS is inward looking only, details of customer demands and fashion requirements are not known. Information from customer surveys, fashion trends from magazines and appropriate web sites could be input into the EIS.

- Competitor information is also not available from the EIS. Links can be provided to competitors' websites to show the types of product they are marketing.

(d)   A **market segment** is a group of customers with **common needs**, **preferences or characteristics** who will respond in similar ways to a given set of market stimuli.

The benefits of segmenting the market for PTR include it would enable PTR to identify those groups of customers who are most likely to purchase its products. Marketing activities can then be directed at those groups (eg under 21's are likely to wear different clothes to older people) saving time and effort of attempting to market all clothes types to all people.

Methods of segmenting the market for PTR include:

- By **age** – as noted above, younger customers are likely to prefer different clothes to older customers.

- By **income** – people with more disposable income are likely to purchase more expensive clothes – although this may also be linked to age to some extent.

- By **sex** – some clothes are nearly always worn by one sex eg skirts for ladies and ties for gentlemen.

- By **occupation** – some people require specific cloths for a job eg accountants are normally required to wear suits.

(e)   **Societal factors.** For any product to be sold, it must be socially accepted within the market place. In designing and manufacturing clothes, the PTR Company undertake market research to determine what types of clothes are acceptable, bearing in mind that acceptability will vary between countries as well as within one country. For example, wearing shorts to work in an office some countries such as Australia may be acceptable, but not in the UK.

Economic factors affecting clothes sales may relate to the amount of income available within society to purchase clothes, interest rates affecting the cost of borrowing for PTR and business and personal taxes affecting both price (eg VAT or similar sales tax) and disposable income. Most of these factors the PTR company will have little or no control over.

There are many different **technological factors**. Improvements in production machinery including Computer Aided Design and Computer Assisted Manufacture will change the cost of production of clothes. The use of Internet technology may provide PTR with a new sales channel and ability to reach more customers, both in its home country and foreign countries.

Legal factors relate to legislation regarding the **supply of goods**. PTR will have to ensure that the quality of clothes is acceptable to limit the amount of legal returns and any consequent bad publicity.

(f)   Reasons why PTR may not want to move production facilities include the following.

Social concerns. PTR has the image of being a responsible employer, implying that it treats its' staff well and possibly assists the local community in some way. Moving the production facility would result in making many workers redundant and therefore result in adverse publicity, damaging the responsible employer image.

Family members. The company appears to have been run by the same people for a significant length of time. This implies that the directors and/or shareholders will feel some social ties or responsibility to their workers. Moving production may therefore go against their individual mores.

Distances involved. No information is provided regarding the location of the suppliers for the PTR company. However, moving the production facility may result in an increase in the distance that supplies have to be transported, as well as the finished goods back to the home country. These costs may exceed the savings in labour.

Integration of other sections of supply chain. It is also not clear whether the R&D, admin and other departments would be required to move. Having R&D and production in two different locations may make it difficult to monitor production and ensure that clothes are manufactured as expected by R&D staff.

SECTION C

Question 3

Text reference. Chapters 2 and 3 cover the material in this question.

Top tip. You need to make five points in part (a) to earn the marks, be careful not to write too much on each.

Easy marks. The five 'general issues' in part (c).

(a) The benefits of purchasing an off-the-shelf accounting package should include:

- **Fewer errors**. Off-the-shelf packages are usually widely used so are more likely to have had bugs identified (in previous versions) and rectified. Off-the-shelf packages are extensively tested before being released.

- **Updates readily available**. An off-the-shelf package would have updates issued periodically to ensure the software remains technically up-to-date.

- **Telephone support when necessary**. An off-the-shelf package will normally provide telephone support so queries about the software can be quickly and easily resolved.

- **Similar look and feel to other software**. Off-the-shelf software is likely to be produced by a relatively large software house that produces software with a user interface similar to other widely used packages. This should make it easier for users to learn how to use the software.

- **Documentation and Training**. Off-the-shelf software usually includes appropriate documentation (sometimes provided on CD to be printed) to support the use of the software, and may even provide training courses in the use of that software for staff.

Top tip. There are three marks available for describing the possible strategies.

(b) The following changeover strategies are possible.

(i) **Direct changeover** involves the total replacement of the old system by the new at one point in time. The main advantage are that it is probably cheaper to implement than those implementation strategies which run both systems in parallel, on either all or part of the system. Confusion caused by the concurrent operation of two systems is therefore minimised. However, a crucial disadvantage is that it places too much reliance on system testing, as there may be unforeseen problems which only emerge after implementation. Additionally, all staff must be trained at the same time, which may cause a certain amount of disruption.

(ii) A **parallel running** strategy would mean that both systems are run at the same time for a period. This has the advantage that the results of the new system can be checked against the results of the old, and that should the new system break down, then the old can be run until the problem is sorted out, without any impairment of the organisation's data processing. A disadvantage is that the extra time involved is considerable. This method may not be suitable for situations where not only has the system changed, but also the organisational structure in which it operates.

(iii) Another alternative is a **pilot operation** in which the entire system is run in one location, or part of the system is run in all locations, so that any bugs can come to light before wholesale implementation. Once these difficulties have been ironed out, then each of the other locations can be changed over to the new system immediately.

(iv) **Phased** or **staged** implementation is a strategy which sets out a detailed timetable, so that each location is changed over separately. This has the advantage that the short term disruption is minimised, in comparison to a direct changeover. Also, the change over is easier to manage, by those systems professionals, if any, and management, required to supervise it. Within phased implementation, individual locations may be switched over by parallel running or direct changeover as appropriate.

The **appropriateness** of any particular strategy depends on the **context**. In this case a crucial factor is that both the computer systems and the company's entire method of distribution are changing. **Parallel running** is not really possible, given that the two situations are so different. The same could be said both for a pilot operation and a strategy based on a phased implementation. **Direct changeover** is the only viable option.

(c) Whatever **implementation strategy** is adopted, the following issues will be crucial to its success:

- **System testing** before changeover.
- **File conversion**, with old files reconciled to new.
- Full staff **training**.
- Organisation of **backup** and **standby facilities**.
- Effective **project management**, to ensure smooth implementation.

(d) There are **three** main reasons for software maintenance.

- To **correct** errors or 'bugs' (corrective maintenance)

- To **meet changes** in internal operating procedures or external regulations (adaptive maintenance)

- To keep up with new **technical developments** (perfective maintenance)

Corrective maintenance

Testing procedures should identify most potential faults prior to installation. However, faults may not become apparent until certain combinations of conditions occur. Correction of these more obscure faults may be time-consuming and expensive.

Faults may also become apparent when consistently higher than expected volumes of data are processed. Volume limits are a key part of any transaction processing software and it is important that these are reviewed regularly to maintain efficiency. Increases in volume may require software and hardware upgrades (such as additional RAM).

Hardware failures can require changes to the operating system software. Additional warnings or error messages may be introduced. Procedures to back up files automatically when a system fails may be written into the software.

Some 'bugs' may only become apparent under certain hardware environments.

Adaptive maintenance

Software houses may regularly upgrade standard applications or general-purpose packages to provide additional features or make them user-friendlier. Customers need to decide whether to accept the upgrade, which is rarely supplied free of charge and will involve staff commitment to the new software. Non-acceptance of upgrades may lead to less effective support from the software supplier whose expertise is focused on the latest version of the package.

The operating procedures and needs of the user may change. This is very common with outputs such as reports and screen layouts, which are often changed to suit user requirements. Data processing operations are less often changed because they are more likely to reflect standard procedures whereas computer outputs evolve to meet the needs of the business. Many applications packages now allow users to customise the software (to a certain extent) themselves. For example, one person's 'standard' Excel spreadsheet screen may look different to another's – toolbars, the number of sheets, gridlines, the formula bar are all subject to user settings. Customised user generated reports are a common feature of accounting packages.

Hardware upgrades are common in larger systems and this often results in operating software being changed or entirely rewritten. Hardware changes range from a simple memory upgrade to changing from multi-user to networked systems.

External regulation often leads to mandatory changes in software, which can be quite extensive. A typical example is the change to various tax rates after the annual budget statement in the UK. These are normally straightforward and are often planned for in financial applications packages. However, the consequences of, for example, introducing multiple VAT rates would generally be complex and expensive for most businesses.

Perfective maintenance

Users may request enhancements to software which is not producing errors, but which could be made more user-friendly or improved in some other way. This may involve, for example, redesigning menu screens or switching to graphical user interfaces.

It may be possible to rewrite sections of programs to improve efficiency and response times. As noted above, output may be redesigned to provide better quality information. Off-the-shelf software products may undertake perfective maintenance in response to advances made in a competitor's product.

Question 4

Text references. Ethics and Codes of Conduct are covered in Chapter 7.

Top tips. All the professional accounting bodies are concerned about cases displaying a lack of ethical standards in commercial organisations. These cases undermine public confidence in both the profession and the wider world of business. As this is a topical area, it is likely to feature regularly in the exam.

Easy marks. There are few easy marks if you do not know this topic. You would gain credit for reasonable comments.

(a)   Influences on ethical conduct can be divided into **two groups**: positive and negative.

1. Positive ethical influences

It is possible to discern an **ethical climate** in a society, Notions of right and wrong form part of its culture. It has been reported, for example, that there is concern in Western Europe at the less rigorous attitudes to corrupt practices in business that Eastern European countries may bring with them when they join the EU.

Organisations tend to have ethical climates too, just as they have their own cultures, and like its culture, an **organisation's ethical climate** is heavily influenced by its external environment. Thus we may discern an important difference between employers in the USA and those in Europe in relation to ideas of **corporate social responsibility**. It is inappropriate to overemphasise extremes of behaviour, but we might consider the different attitudes that prevail concerning job security on opposite sides of the Atlantic, for example.

Within an organisation one ethical influence is the **behaviour** of **senior managers**. The conduct of people at the top of the organisation is likely to have a greater impact upon ethical conduct within the organisation than documents and policies (such as a corporate code of conduct). This was a major problem within *Enron*, which paid lip service to ethical behaviour.

Professional institutions have their own codes of professional ethics, such as CIMA's own code and the ethical demands on auditors. These codes can put members under considerable strain when they demand behaviour that is at variance with what is accepted in an organisation. As CIMA's code says, sometimes a professional may have no alternative but to resign.

2. Negative ethical influences

Personal amorality is likely to exist in any organisation to a greater or lesser extent, quite apart from actively immoral or illegal behaviour. Such amorality, or lack of care about right and wrong is likely to lead to unethical conduct.

Financial pressures can be a major problem. These may take the form of personal financial problems resulting from, for instance, gambling, drug use or simple over-spending. Such problems drive individuals to a range of unethical behaviour such as fraud.

Financial pressures leading to **fraud** also exist at the corporate level. **External pressure** from shareholders or markets to improve profitability can lead to bribery to win contracts and to 'creative accounting'. It is also a specific threat to auditors, since efforts may be made to undermine their impartiality and objectivity. The methods employed may range from simple friendliness and the provision of agreeable lunches for the auditors on site, to threats to take more lucrative consulting business elsewhere if the audit is qualified.

Under such circumstances, **unprincipled** demands for **improved performance** are likely to filter down through the organisation as each level of the hierarchy comes under pressure from the one above. CIMA's own code specifically identifies pressure from a superior as a potential cause of ethical conflict.

(b) If organisations and professions want their people to behave in accordance with a particular set of rules, they must be prepared to **enforce** them. Professional bodies, such as CIMA have a set of law-based procedures for doing just that. Organisations, too, are capable of enforcing their ideas about ethics. An allegation of unethical behaviour at *Boeing* in late 2003 led to the dismissal of the head of finance and subsequently to the resignation of the Chairman and Chief Executive.

If a willingness to enforce them exists, **codes of ethics** can have an effect, both in organisations and in professions. If breaches of such codes are ignored or condoned, they will be treated with contempt and demonstrate that senior officers are not concerned by unethical behaviour.

Ethics management has several tasks.

* To define and give life to an organisation's defining values.
* To create an environment that supports ethically sound behaviour
* To instil a sense of shared accountability amongst employees.

There are two approaches to the management of ethics, according to *Paine*, the **compliance-based** and the **integrity-based**.

A **compliance-based** approach is primarily designed to ensure that the company acts within the **letter of the law**, and that violations are prevented, detected and punished. Some organisations, faced with the legal consequences of unethical behaviour take legal precautions such as those below.

* Compliance procedures to detect misconduct
* Audits of contracts
* Systems to protect and encourage 'whistleblowers'
* Disciplinary procedures to deal with transgressions

Corporate compliance is limited in that it relates only to the law, but legal compliance is 'not an adequate means for addressing the full range of ethical issues that arise every day'.

The compliance approach also overemphasises the threat of detection and punishment in order to channel appropriate behaviour. Furthermore, mere compliance with the law is no guide to **exemplary** behaviour.

An **integrity-based** approach treats ethics as an issue of organisation culture. It combines a concern for the law with an emphasis on **managerial responsibility** for ethical behaviour. When integrated into the day-to-day operations of an organisation, such attitudes can help prevent damaging ethical lapses. Such approaches assume that people are social beings with values that can be supported and refined. They attempt to integrate ethical values into the organisation (or profession) by providing guidance and consultation and by identifying and resolving problems.

(c) **Codes of conduct** have become very popular in recent years in organisations concerned about ethical conduct. Where these contain specific **clear rules** they at least have the value of establishing what correct conduct is in the defined cases. This is both of benefit to the individual and useful at any subsequent disciplinary process.

However, such codes have been criticised as tending to be **too legalistic** and encouraging a **compliance-based** rather than **principle-based** approach. Ethics is to some extent a matter of opinion and highly specific codes tend to offer poor guidance in complex situations.

If **professional bodies** or other organisations have codes of conduct, their first requirement is that they are carefully thought out, with a **minimum of loopholes** and adequate coverage of the problems they are meant to address.

The second requirement is that they should be **enforced** by a proper system of **discipline**. Among other characteristics, such a system must conform with over-riding legal requirements, such as, in common law jurisdictions, the rules of natural justice.

Such a system of **discipline** must be **credible**. Among other things, that means that it must be administered **impartially**. For a professional body, this may mean qualified legal input, possibly from a legally qualified president of the disciplinary forum. For a commercial organisation, it may be that non-executive directors can play a part.

The system should also be capable of **detecting abuses**. One method is a complaint system, to be impartially administered. Another feature would be a facility for 'whistleblowing' by insiders.

Another method of encouraging **ethical behaviour** would be a means of providing **guidance** when problems arise. The real difficulties with ethics arise when the rules or principles point in different directions. A telephone hotline to experienced advisers is invaluable in such circumstances.

CIMA

Paper P4

Organisational Management and Information Systems

Mock Exam 2

Question Paper	
Time allowed	**3 hours**
You are allowed **20 minutes reading time before the examination begins** during which you should read the question paper, and if you wish, make annotations on the question paper. However, you will not be allowed, under any circumstances, to open the answer book and start writing or use your calculator during this reading time.	
This paper is divided into three sections	
Section A	Answer the ONE compulsory question in Section A. This is comprised of 15 sub-questions
Section B	Answer ALL SIX compulsory sub-questions
Section C	Answer ONE question ONLY (from the two available)

SECTION A – 50 marks

Instructions for answering Section A

The answers to the fifteen sub-questions in Section A should ALL be written in your answer book.

Each of the sub-questions numbered from 1.1 to 1.10 inclusive, given below, has only ONE correct answer, worth two marks.

Question 1

1.1 In selection interviewing, what does the judgemental error 'contagious bias' refer to?

A Inconsistent marking of candidates on numerical rating scales
B Basing a general judgement on a single attribute
C Influencing the candidate's response by the wording of questions or non-verbal cues
D Incorrect assessment of qualitative attributes **(2 marks)**

1.2 To be of use for marketing research purposes a segmentation variable must define a market segment that has three characteristics. What are they?

A Measurability, stability, accessibility
B Stability, substantiality, measurability
C Substantiality, measurability, accessibility
D Stability, accessibility, substantiality **(2 marks)**

1.3 What is the sourcing strategy where one buyer chooses between several sources of supply known as?

A Single
B Multiple
C Delegated
D Parallel **(2 marks)**

1.4 Where there is a price leader in a market, a cut in price will normally prompt:

A A cut in price by competitors
B An increase in price by competitors
C Maintenance of the original price by competitors
D Competitors moving into other product areas **(2 marks)**

1.5 Market segmentation is normally inappropriate where:

A The market can be subdivided into groups of consumers
B Different marketing approaches are required for different market segments
C The market can only be segmented by age
D The market is large but homogenous **(2 marks)**

1.6 Which one of the following best describes 'benchmarking'?

A Setting and monitoring internal performance standards
B Comparison of actual production against budgeted production
C Comparison of a service, practice or process against one or more similar activities
D Setting a mission statement and ensuring that statement is met over time **(2 marks)**

1.7 What aspect of total quality management (TQM) provides for the participation by selected employees in quality improvement, through meetings to discuss quality-related issues?

    A   Work cells
    B   Continuous improvement
    C   Quality circles
    D   Empowerment   **(2 marks)**

1.8 Which of one the following is true?

    A   Human resource management has a *narrower* focus than personnel management
    B   Human resource management has a *wider* focus than personnel management
    C   Human resource management and personnel management are exactly the same
    D   The term personnel management is becoming more popular   **(2 marks)**

1.9 What category of quality cost is a cost arising from inadequate quality, where the problem is identified before a finished product or service is delivered to the external customer?

    A   Internal failure cost
    B   External failure cost
    C   Appraisal cost
    D   Inspection cost   **(2 marks)**

1.10 Which one of the equations below represents *Victor Vroom's* model of motivation (*Force* may sometimes be replaced by *Motivation* in this equation)?

    A   Force $\times$ Valence = Expectation
    B   Force $\times$ Expectation = Subjective probability
    C   Subjective probability $\times$ Expectation = Force
    D   Force = Valence $\times$ Expectation   **(2 marks)**

(Total for these sub-questions = 20 marks)

Required

Each of the sub-questions numbered **1.11** to **1.15** below require a brief written response. Each sub-question is worth 4 marks.

Each response should be in note form and should not exceed 50 words.

1.11 Describe the 'marketing mix'.   **(4 marks)**

1.12 Explain 'sales orientation'.   **(4 marks)**

1.13 Explain business automation, business rationalisation and business process re-engineering.   **(4 marks)**

1.14 Distinguish recruitment and selection.   **(4 marks)**

1.15 Describe concentrated, differentiated and undifferentiated marketing.   **(4 marks)**

(Total for these sub-questions = 20 marks)

Total for Section A = 40 marks

SECTION B – 30 marks

Answer ALL parts of this question

Question 2

The Kyrano Company manufactures and sells electronic games. Customer data is currently held on four different computer systems, representing the four main areas of business of hand held game consoles, radio controlled cars, train sets and a new division selling electronically operated lights. Almost all sales are made by mail order, direct to individual customers.

Product development is rapid, with individual products progressing through the whole product life cycle in a minimum of 6 months and a maximum of 18 months.

The new management accountant has recommended that a new centralised database is established to maintain all customer data. However, there is also the recognition that existing systems have been in place for more than 12 years, so there is likely to be some resistance to change within the company. There is also the issue that there is no formal IT department and so a database programmer will have to be hired to write the new database.

The new database will provide a significant amount of statistical information on customers including sales history, average customer spend etc. with the option to obtain additional reports based on geographical area, demographic breakdowns such as purchases for different age groups and demand for each product.

Required

To assist in selling the new database to the Board of Kyrano, prepare a slide outline along with brief accompanying notes or two to three sentences, for each of the management accountant's points identified below.

Use a separate page of your answer for each key point (meaning that your responses are contained on no more than six pages in total).

(a)   State the benefits of using a database to manage the customer data in the Kyrano Company.   **(5 marks)**

(b)   Outline methods of reducing employee resistance to change.   **(5 marks)**

(c)   With reference to the product life cycle, explain how recording demand in the new database assists with product pricing.   **(5 marks)**

(d)   List the contents of a job description for the database programmer.   **(5 marks)**

(e)   Explain how a quality plan can be used to monitor development of the database.   **(5 marks)**

(f)   Explain how the new database can be used to provide data for marketing activities.   **(5 marks)**

(Total = 30 marks)

SECTION C – 20 marks

Answer ONE question ONLY

Question 3

Titan plc provides insurance services to individuals including car, house and personal accident insurance. Potential customers telephone Titan's call centre to ask for insurance quotes. The quotes are provided by call centre staff using a computer system to record quotes provided.

The computer system is relatively slow and will be replaced with upgraded hardware and software using a new expert system to assist call centre staff in providing quotes. Staff will enter information such as address, telephone number and driving licence details into the expert system which will then provide a quote based on those details. Call centre staff have no knowledge of the new system and additional assistance will be needed in using the system while talking to potential customers.

Required

(a)   Explain the steps in a training plan, relating your answer to Titan plc where possible.   **(15 marks)**

(b)   Evaluate the effectiveness of on-the-job training.   **(5 marks)**

(c)   Describe the meaning and purpose of a post-implementation review and briefly describe three measures the directors of Titan plc could use to quantify the success of the upgraded hardware and software.   **(10 marks)**

(Total = 30 marks)

Question 4

The Zarni Company produces computer games for the PC market. It is based in the USA and its employees include 60 programmers, 20 strategic games advisors and 10 marketing managers. The company has been trading for 5 years, with turnover growing at the rate of 400% per annum in the last two years due to the success of its two games 'black shift' and 'Z force'. However, none of the company's games have reached the number one position in the games league tables. The company currently has a 12% market share in its target markets.

The company is considering producing a series of games based on black shift, with each game being given a different colour name (eg yellow shift, blue shift…). The average cost of producing one game has increased by 300% in the last two years as a result of the additional details and features now expected by customers. The standard customer of Zarni is aged between 18 and 35, and predominantly male.

There are at least six other similar games companies in the USA, with significant, if declining, competition from the Japanese market. The latter tends to rely on older platform style games featuring characters such as 'chain' and 'mule chimp'.

The games market in the USA is relatively stagnant, although other markets such as South America and on-line gaming are growing rapidly. Zarni has little experience in these segments.

Required

(a)   Explain how you would evaluate the commercial attractiveness of market segments.   **(10 marks)**

(b)   Produce a strategic marketing plan for the Zarni Company.   **(20 marks)**

(Total = 30 marks)

BPP
LEARNING MEDIA

Answers

DO NOT TURN THIS PAGE UNTIL YOU HAVE
COMPLETED MOCK EXAM 2

A plan of attack

Before the three hours exam time starts, you are allowed 20 minutes to read through the paper. Use this time wisely – in effect it gives you an extra 20 minutes to gain the marks you need to pass.

What should you do in this 20 minutes? You could read through the two questions in Section C – and decide which **one** of these you will answer. However, this could remove your focus from the Section A questions and clutter your mind with extra information.

We recommend you use the 20 minutes to simply **start working through the Section A questions** – by **writing your answers on the question paper**. These answers can then be transferred **very carefully** to your answer booklet when the exam starts. Remember though, you **must not write in your answer booklet during the reading time**.

Using the time in this way should mean that later in the exam, when you reach Section C, you have sufficient time to read both questions carefully and make the best decision as to which one you will attempt.

Turn back to the question paper now, and we'll sort out a **plan of attack** for Mock exam 2.

First things first

It's usually best to **start with the multiple choice** and **objective test** questions (ie do Section A first). You should always be able to do a fair proportion of these, even if you really haven't done as much preparation as you should have done. And answering even a couple of them will give you the confidence to attack the rest of the paper.

Refer to 'Tackling multiple choice questions' in the front pages of this book for general advice. When answering the objective test questions in this paper, remember your answers must be **concise**, **to the point** and must **answer the question asked**. Don't waste words with waffle!

Allow yourself 36 minutes to do the 10 multiple choice questions, and 36 minutes for the 5 objective test questions – **a total of 72 minutes for Section A**. No more. You can always come back to these questions at the end of the exam if you have some spare time.

The next step – Section B

Question 2 in Section B is compulsory. Attempt this question immediately after you've completed Section A. You've got to do this question so there's no point delaying it. The question is split into sub-parts, all based on a single scenario.

Read the scenario carefully, then take a look at the question requirements.

- Part (a) requires to state the advantages of databases – and to apply this knowledge to the Kyrano Company.

- Part (b) covers resistance to change – you have studied some theories in this area, this will test if you can remember them.

- Part (c) requires application of the product life cycle. Don't just make general points – your answer must be realistic in the context of the scenario.

- Part (d) the opportunity to be creative. Just make sure the job description is realistic.

- Part (e) requires application of quality plan knowledge.

- Think about part (f) carefully, you should be able to think of enough uses for customer data and opportunities to exploit them.

Section C

Once you've done the compulsory questions, you are required to choose **one** of the two questions available in Section C.

Your choice between questions 3 and 4 should be made on the basis of your knowledge of the topics involved. Both questions have one very large part so you must be certain that you have excellent knowledge in the area concerned to do justice to them.

If you are particularly comfortable with marketing then choose question 4.

- **Question 3**. The big marks on offer in part (a) require you to outline a training plan. Be careful to avoid making it too general as you are required to related it to Titan plc.

  Part (b) requires a few well reasoned comments to earn the marks. Part (c) changes topic but do not let this throw you, well made suggestions will earn you most of the marks.

- **Question 4**. Part (a) requires you to take a commercial point of view, ensure you understand what this means as it is easy to lose marks by looking at attractiveness of segments from the wrong view point.

  Use the structure of a strategic marketing plan to organise your answer to part (c), ensure you write under all headings to maximise your marks.

General advice

Don't forget that you have to **answer question 2** and **ONE** question **from questions 3 and 4**. Once you've decided on question 3, for example, it might be worth putting a line through question 4 so that you are not tempted to answer it!

No matter how many times we remind you....

Always, always **allocate your time** according to the marks for the question in total and for the parts of the question. And always, **always follow the requirements** exactly.

You've got spare time at the end of the exam.....?

If you have allocated your time properly then you **shouldn't have time on your hands** at the end of the exam. If you find yourself with five or ten minutes spare, however, **go back to any parts of questions that you didn't finish** because you ran out of ideas or time. A fresh look may spark new thoughts.

Forget about it!

And don't worry if you found the paper difficult. More than likely other candidates would too. If this were the real thing you would need to **forget** the exam the minute you leave the exam hall and **think about the next one**. Or, if it's the last one, **celebrate**!

SECTION A

Question 1

1.1   C   Don't confuse this with option B – the halo effect.

1.2   C   Stability might seem like a desirable feature in its own right, but it is covered by substantiality.

1.3   B   The definition refers to the use of multiple suppliers.

1.4   A   Price leadership normally involves all prices in a marketing moving in the same direction.

1.5   D   If the market is made up of buyers with the same characteristics, then segmentation is inappropriate.

1.6   C   Although the other options involve some form of comparison, they do not imply comparison against similar activities.

1.7   C   Quality circles were advocated initially by the Japanese management theorist *Ishikawa*. Quality circles are meetings of invited employees from different sections of an organisation, to discuss quality issues and hopefully agree on ideas for improvements. Empowerment is another aspect of employee participation and involvement, but is concerned with giving decision-making powers to employees.

1.8   B   Human resource management has a *wider* focus than personnel management.

1.9   A   Internal failure costs include the cost of materials or components lost or scrapped in the production process, re-working costs, and losses from selling faulty output at reduced prices. The other categories of quality costs are appraisal costs (or inspection costs), prevention costs and external failure costs. Inspection costs are the costs of checking finished goods. Prevention costs are costs incurred prior to making a product or delivering a service, to prevent substandard production. External failure costs are costs arising from inadequate quality, where the problem is identified after the finished product or service has been delivered to the customer.

1.10   D   Force = Valence × Expectation represents *Victor Vroom's* model of motivation.

1.11   The 'marketing mix' is the range of decisions and elements of marketing that achieve the maximum impact for a product or service.

This mix of elements usually include price, place, people and promotion.

1.12   'Sales orientation' usually occurs where a company produces a product without first establishing what the customer needs. This requires the company to focus on selling the product and often sees the launch of a sales drive.

1.13   Automation – involves assisting employees to do the same task more efficiently.

Rationalisation – Involves the automation of a process and amending the process design to improve efficiency.

Re-engineering – fundamentally changes the way an organisation functions.

1.14 Recruitment has the goal of employing people from outside the organisation. It includes:

- Sourcing applicants
- Communicating opportunities and information
- Generating interest

Selection is the process of deciding which of the applicants that responded to the recruitment drive is offered the job.

1.15 Concentrated marketing – is the targeting of one market segment with the 'ideal' product for that segment.

Differentiated marketing – is the application of a different marketing mix to each segment the product is marketed at.

Undifferentiated marketing – is the application of a single marketing mix to all segments.

SECTION B

Question 2

> **Top tips.** In an exam situation, if you are asked to produce slides keep them simple. Each slide is essentially a list of headings – with the main heading the slide title.
>
> **Easy marks.** The job specification is a simple proforma that you should memorise.

(a)   **Slide 1**

Benefits of database
Reduction in data redundancy – customer data held once only
Reduced storage costs – only one system to maintain
Data integrity – no inconsistencies between databases
Privacy – Data kept secure in one location

Notes to slide one.

Existing databases amalgamated into one reducing duplication of data and computer hardware. Inconsistencies (eg different delivery addresses) removed using only one database. Security enhanced by applying good controls in one location only.

(b)   **Slide 2**

Overcoming resistance to change
Provide forum for discussing weaknesses old system
Education – focus on benefits of new system
Participation in system design
Negotiation and agreement on system functionality

Notes to slide two

Employees need to be involved in change, hence providing an initial forum and then inviting user participation in design. Where appropriate, the benefits of the system will have to be 'sold', particularly if employees do not want or resist change. Some form of negotiation may be necessary to provide employees with other benefits if they accept change.

(c)   **Slide 3**

Product pricing – database benefits
Introduction – High price to cover development costs
Growth – Fall in price reflecting increased competition
Maturity – Further fall in price – niche marketing
Decline – Sell below cost

Notes to slide three

Product life cycle information available from demand for discontinued products. The stage of each product in the life cycle can be determined, and from this an estimate made of the most appropriate price. Given rapid product development, it will be important to identify when a product is in decline so as to sell off stocks and concentrate production on newer products.

(d)   **Slide 4**

Job specification

Job title – database programmer

Reporting to – management accountant

Job description – write customer database

Technical procedures – knowledge of database programming needed

---

Notes to slide four

The job specification sets out the purpose of the job – in this case the need to hire a database programmer. The lack of any formal IT department or hierarchy means that the programmer will report to the management accountant. Assistance will be needed preparing the specification for the customer database, but then we must ensure the appointee has the necessary technical knowledge to write the database.

(e)   **Slide 5**

Quality plan

1. Establish standards for the database and method of writing

2. Agree methods of monitoring quality

3. Compare database production against specification

4. Control actions – test database – where below standard implement remedial work

5. Amend plan where necessary

Notes to slide five

A quality plan is necessary because Kyrano Company has no experience in database writing; the programmer must therefore be monitored in some way. The idea of setting standards and then monitoring development against those standards is not unusual. Comparing actual outputs to agreed outputs helps us monitor development without having to understand database design in detail.

(f)   **Slide 6**

Use of new database – marketing

Segmentation analysis – identify target markets by age or geographical area

Purchasing history – send details of new products; repeat purchases

Sales history – identify popular products for new investment

Marketing effectives – type and amount of spend against product type

---

Notes to slide six

The database will provide additional detail on individual products sold. Data will be analysed to identify types of purchase allowing marketing to be directed at specific market segments. Sales of different product types can also be tracked over time to ensure that new products are developed to meet customer requirements.

SECTION C

Question 3

(a)   **Training plan for Titan plc**

1. Determine training needs

Training needs may be satisfied either by training existing employees or by recruiting new employees with specific training skills. In the case of Titan, the change is incremental indicating that in-house training will be appropriate.

2. Identify training objectives

In other words, Titan must specify the knowledge, skills and competences that have to be acquired. This is easier for technical training where skills match a specific computer system, as in Titan. Identifying objectives is more difficult where 'soft' skills, that is personnel skills, are involved as they are more difficult to define. For example, telephone skills can be taught, but these will have to be refined over time as experience is gained of working with people.

3. Develop criteria against which to measure performance

Training will normally be checked to determine that it has met the training needs. This means identifying criteria to measure the training against. In terms of Titan, criteria such as number of customer queries handled or average waiting time can be used.

4. Determine current levels of proficiency

This information is required to target training to meet specific skills gaps in the organisation. In Titan, for example, staff are already familiar with computer systems but not with the specific credit scoring software. Training on general use of computers therefore is not required – but training on the credit scoring software is.

5. Arrange training

This step simply involves production of training material, booking training rooms and communicating the time and purpose of training to participants.

6. Implement training

Carry out the training. The content and delivery must be clear and appropriate for trainees.

7. Evaluate the training

Performance criteria have already been set in step 3. Improvements in skills will be checked at the end of training, using questionnaires or skills based testing. Evaluation should be repeated after a few weeks to check that skills have been retained.

(b) There are various forms of on-the-job training, but all relate to training being provided as the trainee is carrying out specific tasks that form part of their role.

Advantages of on the job training include:

- Training is provided that is relevant to the job being undertaken.
- Training is 'just-in-time' – that is specific queries are identified.

Disadvantages include:

- Training is difficult when real customers are being talked to – they may not take kindly to a person being trained when they are attempting to arrange insurance.
- Where training is being carried out by a manager, they may not have the appropriate training skills.

It may be possible to train some staff away from their desks, and then have these trained staff pass on their knowledge to others (depending on the complexity of the software).

> **Top tips.** Part (c) provides an opportunity to pick up easy marks for simply reproducing 'book knowledge'. If questions of this type appear in the exam, ensure you explain yourself sufficiently to pick up all of the marks on offer.

(c) A **post-implementation review** usually takes place a few months after system implementation is complete. The purpose of the review is to receive feedback from users on how well the system is working and to check that the objectives of the project have been met. The review normally takes the form of a meeting between the management and users.

The review will investigate both the **procedures** used throughout the project and the **systems** that have been produced. The purpose of doing this is to **identify** what features of the project went **well**, and what went wrong or **badly**, so that future projects will avoid these problems.

In reviewing the objectives of the project, the review will also check whether or not the **business benefits** expected from the project have been **achieved**. Where benefits have not been achieved, or other objectives of the project have not been met, the review may also recommend remedial action to ensure that the required benefits are obtained.

Measures of success for hardware or software

(i) **Number of errors reported**

A log can be maintained, either by individual users or the management, of the **number** and **type** or **errors** found in the system. The actual error rate provides an indication of the quality of programming and the effectiveness of the different stages of testing (user acceptance, system and module).

(ii) **Number of quotations processed**

The original **software specification** will indicate how many quotes should be processed. Comparing the specification with the **actual** number processed will provide information on the **usefulness** of the system (if the system is not useful then presumably it will be used less than expected). A small number of quotes being processed could also be indicative of poor programming or inadequate hardware specifications, so further analysis may be needed to determine which of these is relevant.

(iii) **Number of change requests**

Users may request changes to the system, either where that system did not meet their **original requirements**, or where the system as implemented does not meet their **expectations** in some way. Changes requested due to initial specifications not being met provides some measure on the quality of the design and testing processes. Changes requested because the software is not meeting expectations may indicate weaknesses in this method of obtaining data for initial specification.

Question 4

(a)   There are a number of methods to evaluate the **commercial attractiveness** of market segments. We need to understand the performance within each segment and how effective the targeting and positioning has been from our efforts. To be useful, market segments must have the following characteristics:

Measurable. How easy is it to ascertain the actual attribute within each segment? The size, buying power and profiles of the segments need measuring.

Accessibility. The market segment needs to be reached effectively and properly served.

Substantiality. The market segments need to be large enough and have sufficient profit potential to be attractive propositions. A segment should be the largest possible homogenous group worth pursuing with a tailored marketing programme.

Actionability. Effective programmes need to attract and serve segments.

There is a need to understand the **potential** for each segment to **grow**, to assess current **competitor activity** and the likelihood of future targeting by other businesses of particular segments. There may also be change in **tastes**, **lifestyles** and **aspirations** that need to be considered.

Strategic marketing plan

(b)   **1. Executive summary**

This document sets out the marketing plan for the Zarni Company for the year end 20X7. The main goals for this period are:

- Produce a top selling game
- Increase market share

The main recommendations for this report are:

- Authorise increased marketing budget
- Investigate other markets

2. Situation analysis

The current situation is presented below, in SWOT format.

Strengths	Weaknesses
High growth	Lack of Number One game
Good reputation	
Opportunities	**Threats**
Expansion into South America	Lack of experience with new markets
Expansion into online gaming	USA based companies
Produce brand of games	Declining threat from Japan

3. Objectives and goals

The company needs to continue to grow to support increased expenditure on games manufacture. Growth targets are set at:

- Market share of 15%
- Sales growth of 450%
- Net profit of 10%

4. Marketing strategy

The company's main target market of 18 to 35 year old males will be maintained. However, additional information is be obtained on the South American games market. This will be easier to access than online gaming using the assumption that the company's existing products can be sold there.

5. Strategic marketing plan aims

The marketing plan for the next 3 years is:

- Produce a 'shift' game every year.
- Focus marketing activities on building the brand name of 'shift'.
- Investigate, and where appropriate, enter new markets.

6. Tactical marketing plan aims

In the next year the company will:

- Investigate the South American market.
- Produce the next 'shift' game – research needed on the most appropriate colour.

7. Action plan

Marketing mix strategy

- Product – produce the shift required
- Price – target $49
- Place – distributed via wholesalers as previous games
- Promotion – continue existing promotion in gaming magazines
- People – employ five new programmers
- Processes – investigate South America

8. Budget

An initial budget of $550,000 to be set for marketing activities including advertising.

9. Controls

Any expenditure over $40,000 to be authorised in advance by the Financial Accountant.

CIMA

Paper P4

Organisational Management and Information Systems

Mock Exam 3 (November 2006)

Question Paper	
Time allowed	**3 hours**
You are allowed **20 minutes reading time before the examination begins** during which you should read the question paper, and if you wish, make annotations on the question paper. However, you will not be allowed, under any circumstances, to open the answer book and start writing or use your calculator during this reading time.	
This paper is divided into three sections	
Section A	Answer the ONE compulsory question in Section A. This is comprised of 15 sub-questions
Section B	Answer ALL SIX compulsory sub-questions
Section C	Answer ONE question ONLY (from the two available)

SECTION A – 50 marks

Instructions for answering Section A

The answers to the twenty sub-questions in Section A should ALL be written in your answer book.

Each of the sub-questions numbered from 1.1 to 1.10 inclusive, given below, has only ONE correct answer. Each is worth two marks.

Question 1

1.1   Data redundancy arises as a result of

    A   Viruses and computer misuse
    B   Downsizing the organisation.
    C   A lack of password controls
    D   Duplication of data held   **(2 marks)**

1.2   A network topology refers to

    A   The physical arrangement of a computer network.
    B   The type of hardware used.
    C   The hierarchy of access.
    D   The range of software operated.   **(2 marks)**

1.3   Kurt Lewin's ideas on change are based on the view that change is

    A   Capable of being planned.
    B   Emergent.
    C   Inevitable and uncontrollable.
    D   Transformational.   **(2 marks)**

1.4   Entity relationship modelling is a technique used within

    A   An assessment centre test used in staff selection.
    B   Market research and product testing.
    C   Database analysis and design.
    D   Business process re-engineering.   **(2 marks)**

1.5   The intervention of a consultant or change agent is a common feature of

    A   Co-operation and negotiation strategies for change.
    B   An inclusive culture.
    C   High levels of management visibility.
    D   A programme of Organisational Development (OD)   **(2 marks)**

1.6   Remuneration is an example of

    A   Self-actualisation reward
    B   An intrinsic reward
    C   An extrinsic reward
    D   An individual's work/life balance   **(2 marks)**

1.7 A local area network (LAN) normally contains

   A   File, print and communications server(s)
   B   Distributed processing and local solutions
   C   E-trading and e-marketing
   D   Internet access and firewall protection   **(2 marks)**

1.8 Charging a very low price on one item in order to generate customer loyalty and increased sales of other items is called

   A   Market penetration
   B   Loss leader pricing
   C   Product penetration
   D   Skim pricing   **(2 marks)**

1.9 'Corrective', 'perfective' and 'adaptive' are terms associated with

   A   System maintenance
   B   Change management approaches
   C   Quality assurance
   D   HR disciplinary processes   **(2 marks)**

1.10 In the expectancy theory of motivation 'valence' refers to

   A   A belief that an outcome will satisfy organisational tasks
   B   A person's own preference for achieving a particular outcome
   C   A belief that the outcome will be shared by others equally
   D   An understanding of the probability of an event happening   **(2 marks)**

(Total for these sub-questions = 20 marks)

Required

Each of the sub-questions numbered 1.11 to 1.15 below requires a brief written response. Each sub-question is worth 4 marks.

This response should be in note form and should not exceed 50 words per sub-question.

1.11 Explain the concept of physical evidence when applied to the marketing mix   **(4 marks)**

1.12 Identify the potential benefits of a marketing database and the source data from which it might be constructed   **(4 marks)**

1.13 In HR planning how might an organisation match the projected 'supply' of human resources to future demand   **(4 marks)**

1.14 Identify the advantages and disadvantages of a policy of succession planning for a large organisation   **(4 marks)**

1.15 Identify both the advantages and disadvantages of a decentralised Human Resource provision for an organisation that has many business units and sites.   **(4 marks)**

(Total for these sub-questions = 20 marks)

Total for Section A = 40 marks

SECTION B – 30 marks

Answer all parts to this question

Question 2

The country of Chapterland has a principle that healthcare should be free to its citizens at the point of access. Healthcare is funded from national taxation and organised through a series of large health units, one of which is known as 'Q2'. Q2 operates a huge, single site hospital and offers a variety of community services (such as health visiting) that are taken to the local population. Q2 has a management structure consisting of eight clinical and administrative directors who report to Q2's Chief Executive Officer (CEO). The Q2 CEO is directly accountable to the national government through regular returns of information and year-end reporting.

Published 'quality league tables' of hospital performance against government targets suggest that Q2 has one of the worst records in the country. (Targets are for cleanliness of hospital wards, treatment waiting times and staff employed per patient cases dealt with.) In addition, Q2 has in recent years been operating to a budget in excess of its funding, which is against government regulations. The current year budget again exceeds projected funding.

Last year, Q2's previous CEO decided that certain changes were necessary including:

- Better cost control
- Improved performance, measurement
- Benchmarking

He revealed this thinking for the first time in a global email he sent to Q2's staff. Later, when conducting the annual performance appraisal of the Director of Human Resources (HR), he tasked her with implementing 'each and every form of benchmarking' within the next four months so that 'true' performance deficiencies could be addressed. However, the Director of HR left for a new job elsewhere within that period. The CEO then undertook to manage the changes himself but was surprised to find directors unenthusiastic and even uncooperative. Under pressure from the government the CEO resigned 'for personal reasons' and no progress was made with his initiatives.

A new CEO has just been appointed. Her immediate concern is to reduce expenditure and improve performance. On her first day as CEO she spoke of a need to re-establish a culture of 'care through quality' within Q2. She wishes to discuss a number of ideas and issues with her clinical and administrative directors at a special 'away day' meeting to be arranged soon. You work in the CEO's central policy team and she has informed you that some ideas for initiatives include outsourcing, improved supply management and new performance management measures.

Required:

You have been asked to provide the new CEO with briefing notes on a number of issues that will help prepare her for the 'away day' meeting. These notes should:

(a) Explain why the changes attempted by the previous CEO were unsuccessful **(5 marks)**

(b) Explain the role Human Resources could perform in supporting any new initiatives for change **(5 marks)**

(c) Analyse the potential of outsourcing as a means of overcoming some of the problems facing Q2. (The CEO has identified two services initially; IT/IS and cleaning.) **(5 marks)**

(d) Discuss which forms of benchmarking Q2 should use in order to contribute to better performance management **(5 marks)**

(e) Discuss how a culture of 'care through quality' might be established within Q2 **(5 marks)**

(f) Describe the performance measures that will be needed in order to satisfy future management and strategic reporting requirements of Q2 **(5 marks)**

Use a separate page of your answer book for each sub-question. You should limit your answer for each sub-question to no more than one page.

(Total = 30 marks)

SECTION C – 20 marks

Answer ONE question ONLY

Question 3

B3 is a family run personnel agency. It offers a range of services to both individuals and corporate clients (mainly local medium-sized organisations). The son of the managing director (MD) is currently studying for a specialist university business degree. His course includes a 'management consultancy' module where students are required to analyse an organisation and identify a range of development options for the business. The MD's son's investigations of B3 have led to a consultancy report being produced, extracts of which include:

'B3 should maximise the opportunities offered by information technology to a greater extent. In particular:

- Opportunity 1. B3 could develop its recent successful experiment in e-cruitment (the identification of employment opportunities through the world wide web and the emailing of clients). Currently details of vacancies are collected and matched to individual client's search criteria. When a match is identified clients are emailed and, if they are interested, interviews arranged. This service is not offered by any of B3's main competitors. There is a difficulty, however, in that many companies have barred access to personal emails at work and web access to recruitment sites such as B3's site from their offices. Market research suggests that significant opportunities for m-cruitment (jobs by mobile telephones) also exist. Making use of recent software developments, a text message containing a job title and some contact details could be sent out to individual clients instead of an email, so providing a more convenient and speedy service.

- Opportunity 2. Virtually all CVs are currently received in electronic form and a policy decision should be made to develop a paperless operating environment through the development of databases, so upgrading existing office technology.

Analysis of profit indicates that executive searches, corporate 'headhunting' and vacancy identification for individuals (traditional and especially e-cruitment) are all profitable activities.

Involvement in selection processes with corporate clients is unprofitable and should be discontinued. Instead B3 should identify clear guidelines for corporate clients to follow once the short-listing of candidates has occurred'.

Required:

(a) Evaluate the opportunities for B3 identified in the consultancy report. **(12 marks)**

(b) Produce guidelines for the selection process that should be adopted by an organisation presented with a short-list of candidates. **(8 marks)**

(c) Explain the acceptable reasons for dismissing employees **(10 marks)**

(Total = 30 marks)

Question 4

CM's founder first began producing breakfast food from a start-up unit on a small industrial estate. Now CM is the market leader in Europe and Oceania. Once established in Europe, the company made the breakthrough into Oceania thanks to demand from ex-pats and contacts with a family member who happened to be a director of a supermarket chain in Australia. The company's founder is very 'hands on' and has made all the major strategic decisions to date based on intuition.

CM spends heavily on promoting most of its twenty products on television, normally before and after childrens' programmes with high viewing figures. Research conducted ten years ago shows that children love small gifts contained within packs and the association of certain of the products to cartoon characters. CM also manufactures its most popular lines and packages them as 'own brand' alternatives for some large supermarket chains. These sell more cheaply than CM branded products, are less costly to produce (they contain inexpensive packaging and no gifts) but sales remain low.

CM is now facing a more uncertain environment with increasing competition (from a North American firm), sales levels that seem to have peaked and the prospect of the founder retiring very soon. Management consultants advising CM have identified a need to develop a structured marketing strategic plan for the organisation and for greater involvement of other staff in future strategic decisions. As a further complication, CM has recently received some adverse publicity from an international health 'watchdog' body that claims that CM's products contain potentially harmful levels of both sugar and salt.

Required:

(a) Evaluate CM's situation making specific mention of marketing and ethical issues. **(10 marks)**

(b) Explain how CM might develop a marketing strategic plan. **(10 marks)**

(c) Briefly explain five benefits of market segmentation to CM **(10 marks)**

(Total = 30 marks)

Answers

DO NOT TURN THIS PAGE UNTIL YOU HAVE
COMPLETED MOCK EXAM 3

A plan of attack

Before the three hours exam time starts, you are allowed 20 minutes to read through the paper. Use this time wisely – in effect it gives you an extra 20 minutes to gain the marks you need to pass.

What should you do in this 20 minutes? You could read through the two questions in Section C – and decide which **one** of these you will answer. However, this could remove your focus from the Section A questions and clutter your mind with extra information.

We recommend you use the 20 minutes to simply **start working through the Section A questions** – by **writing your answers on the question paper**. These answers can then be transferred **very carefully** to your answer booklet when the exam starts. Remember though, you **must not write in your answer booklet during the reading time**.

Using the time in this way should mean that later in the exam, when you reach Section C, you have sufficient time to read both questions carefully and make the best decision as to which one you will attempt.

Turn back to the question paper now, and we'll sort out a **plan of attack** for Mock exam 3.

First things first

It's usually best to **start with the multiple choice** and **objective test** questions (ie do Section A first). You should always be able to do a fair proportion of these, even if you really haven't done as much preparation as you should have done. And answering even a couple of them will give you the confidence to attack the rest of the paper.

Refer to 'Tackling multiple choice questions' in the front pages of this book for general advice. When answering the objective test questions in this paper, remember your answers must be **concise**, **to the point** and must **answer the question asked**. Don't waste words with waffle!

Allow yourself 36 minutes to do the 10 multiple choice questions, and 36 minutes for the 5 objective test questions – **a total of 72 minutes for Section A**. No more. You can always come back to these questions at the end of the exam if you have some spare time.

The next step – Section B

Question 2 in Section B is compulsory. Attempt this question immediately after you've completed Section A. You've got to do this question so there's no point delaying it. The question is split into sub-parts, all based on a single scenario.

Read the scenario carefully, then take a look at the question requirements.

- Part (a) requires you to explain why the CEO's changes were unsuccessful. Consider what is needed for a successful change and see where he was lacking.

- Part (b) covers how HR can support change. There are a wide range of areas that it can be involved in. Think logically.

- Part (c) requires a general evaluation of outsourcing but you must relate your answer to the scenario.

- Part (d) you should have learnt the types of benchmarking, apply them here.

- Part (e) requires some logical thinking and knowledge of change management with a cultural twist.

- Part (f) may seem tricky as it focuses on performance measurement, but there are plenty of clues in the scenario you can use to answer it.

Section C

Once you've done the compulsory questions, you are required to choose **one** of the two questions available in Section C.

Your choice between questions 3 and 4 should be made on the basis of your knowledge of the topics involved. Both questions represent a change of question styles, focusing on strategic issues – take a deep breath and don't panic.

If you are particularly comfortable with marketing then choose question 4.

- **Question 3**. In Part (a) you are required to evaluate the two opportunities presented. The key is to keep an open mind and try to think of as wide a range of points as possible. Be realistic and think if they would really be possible in the real world. Sensible suggestions earn marks.

  The key to Part (b) is to read the question. Think about the **whole** process.

  Part (c) should be a welcome relief. You should have learnt the acceptable reasons for dismissal.

- **Question 4**. Part (a) requires you to think on your feet and appraise CM's position. There are many strategic and marketing theories you can use. The ethical aspects of children's food and TV advertising is in the news so bring in your wider knowledge.

  Marketing plan development is the source of several exam questions in this text, so you should make a good attempt at Part (b). Remember you are not required to write one, just explain the stages of how it would be developed.

  You can use your 'text book' knowledge in Part (c). The benefits of segmentation should be clear in your head by now.

General advice

Don't forget that you have to **answer question 2** and **ONE** question **from questions 3 and 4**. Once you've decided on question 3, for example, it might be worth putting a line through question 4 so that you are not tempted to answer it!

No matter how many times we remind you....

Always, always **allocate your time** according to the marks for the question in total and for the parts of the question. And always, **always follow the requirements** exactly.

You've got spare time at the end of the exam.....?

If you have allocated your time properly then you **shouldn't have time on your hands** at the end of the exam. If you find yourself with five or ten minutes spare, however, **go back to any parts of questions that you didn't finish** because you ran out of ideas or time. A fresh look may spark new thoughts.

Forget about it!

And don't worry if you found the paper difficult. More than likely other candidates would too. If this were the real thing you would need to **forget** the exam the minute you leave the exam hall and **think about the next one**. Or, if it's the last one, **celebrate**!

SECTION A

Question 1

1.1 D Data redundancy occurs when data is duplicated.

1.2 A Network topology refers to how a company network is physically arranged.

1.3 A Kurt Lewin's ideas are based on the idea that change is capable of being planned.

1.4 C Entity relationship modelling provides an understanding of the logical data requirements of a system and is therefore used in database analysis and design.

1.5 D A key feature of organisational development is the involvement of change agents who are consultants brought in to an organisation to help manage the change process. Their role is to gain support and co-operation of the affected employees and requires some negotiation between the staff and senior management to achieve it.

1.6 C Remuneration is an extrinsic reward as it is a reward that is external to the actual performance of a task or role. For example, a carpenter may gain satisfaction from creating a high quality bookcase (intrinsic reward), and also receive cash (extrinsic reward) from selling it. Self-actualisation is achieved through the achievement of personal goals. Whilst remuneration may in part help achieve a work/life balance, it is more than this since it includes non-monetary elements.

1.7 A A LAN normally contains file, print and communication servers. A LAN is internal, and covers a relatively small area.

1.8 B Loss leaders are products that have a very low price set with the objective of attracting consumers to buy other products in the range with higher profit margins.

1.9 A The three terms are associated with system maintenance.

1.10 B Victor Vroom's Expectancy Theory states that valence is the strength of an individual's preference for a certain outcome.

1.11 Physical evidence is an essential ingredient of the marketing mix especially for service organisations. It is the **tangible items** that a consumer comes into contact with **before**, **during** or **after service provision**, and provides **reassurance** to customers who may perceive the transaction as high risk.

1.12 **Benefits of a marketing database**

- Enables detailed analysis/better targeting
- Reduces data redundancy
- Quick and easy to access and maintain
- Generates increased revenue

Sources of data

- Existing customer records (eg sales ledger)
- Website visitors/registered users
- Purchased from third party marketing organisations
- Generated by employees within the business (eg sales leads)

1.13 Methods to match staffing demand and supply

- Recruitment or redundancies
- Internal transfers
- Introduce technology to increase employee productivity
- Ask employees to work overtime
- Recruitment 'freeze' or restrictions
- Flexible working
- Use contractors and part-timers
- Job sharing

1.14 Advantages

- Retains employees and their knowledge
- Encourages long-term planning
- Saves time and expense of replacing senior management.

Disadvantages

- Large talent pools make it hard to choose the right successor
- Reduces the supply of fresh ideas from outside the business
- May reduce motivation of those not 'chosen'

1.15 Advantages

- A central HR team may lack an understanding of local issues in regional sites.
- Reduces the time taken to resolve local issues, as there is less distance between HR and the individual.

Disadvantages

- May cause inconsistent treatment of employees.
- May duplicate HR work and therefore increases the organisation's overheads.

SECTION B

Question 2

> **Top hints**. Highlight key information in the question and look for opportunities to slot them into your answer.
>
> **Easy marks**. This is a tough question with few easy marks, however the scenario does give strong clues for the content of performance measures if you spot them.

(a)   There are **several** possible reasons why the change was unsuccessful.

Unrealistic aims

The previous CEO attempted to react to the situation by making three **major** changes in a very short space of time. It's unlikely that all types of benchmarking are appropriate – those that are (eg against successful health care units) should be implemented in a systematic manner.

No consultation

It appears that very little **planning** and consultation was done by the CEO who decided on the changes that were required and **dictated** them to his staff. Involving other directors could have generated **alternative** solutions that may have been more successful, and have more support.

Lack of support

The lack of consultation in planning the change resulted in a lack of support for the project. Enthusiasm and **complete support** of the senior management team would have enabled the changes to have implemented more successfully.

Poor communication

The CEO failed to communicate his ideas appropriately. A global e-mail is unlikely to be given the attention this issue deserves. Nor did he set a channel up to allow staff under him to **feedback** any problems or comments they had. If such channels were set up, the project could have evolved new, improved ideas and suggestions that would have supported the project.

Resistance

The lack of involvement and communication identified above caused **resistance** to the project. Had the CEO involved others at an earlier stage he may have been in a position to overcome the resistance by creating an opposing driving force for change, and the use of one or more 'change agents'.

(b)   Q2's HR department could have the following **roles** in supporting the new initiatives:

Develop a scheme to reward behaviour that supports the change

The changes require expenditure to be reduced and performance improved. Employees could be offered **bonuses** or other **rewards** for suggesting ideas that are then implemented or by meeting performance targets. HR would be involved in implementing such a scheme.

Identify staff who may act as champions of change

HR keeps **employee records** and these might be used to identify employees who are likely to be **supportive** of the change. They could be involved at an early stage and be used to communicate ideas and procedures to their fellow workers. Their **enthusiasm** could win over sceptical employees.

Develop an appraisal system

As **performance measurement** is being introduced, it is important that **appraisal systems** are in place to monitor individuals' performance and to feed this back to the individual concerned. HR can **provide** and **implement** such a system, which can be linked to the reward scheme already discussed.

Provide a system to deal with staff who oppose the change

However well organised the change, some employees will **oppose** and **disrupt** the process. HR should be prepared to step in to talk to the individual's concerned privately to **resolve** the situation and if necessary instigate disciplinary action against them.

Ensure training is available for any staff who may require it

The change may require employees to adopt different **working practices** or roles. HR should ensure all staff who require **additional training** and **guidance** receive it in a suitable, timely manner. Without staff performing their roles correctly the change may not be effective.

(c) Outsourcing IS/IT and cleaning services will have several implications for Q2.

Cost

Outsourcing removes **uncertainty** of cost as Q2 would be able to fix the price of the contracts over a number of years. This will help the organisation keep control of its expenditure.

Skills and knowledge

Specialist organisations employ **knowledgeable** and **experienced** staff who may be better qualified than those currently employed by Q2, therefore the quality of service and performance of those departments may improve. Q2 may also lose staff with **thorough understanding** of the organisation and it may take sometime for the outsourced staff to become up to speed.

Flexibility

Outsourcing allows greater flexibility over **staff numbers** in response to demand. Without outsourcing Q2 would find it is over or under staffed at certain times. Outsourcers would ensure **optimum** staffing levels are maintained as they can pull in employees from other projects for assistance when demand increases and release them afterwards.

Confidentiality

Health service information contains **confidential** patient records and senior management may feel it is too risky to allow commercial organisations to have access to it – if it hands over control to a third party there could be a greater risk of leaks occurring. Outsourcing IT/IS for a Health Care unit may not be a feasible option.

Unsatisfactory contracts/service levels

There is a risk of Q2 being **locked-in** to an unsatisfactory contract. Cleaners from outside the health authority may not be familiar with the needs of hospitals – and the absolute need for a clean environment. Removing itself from the contract could be costly to Q2.

(d) The following types of benchmarking are applicable to Q2:

Internal benchmarking; Q2 would identify an internal activity that is showing 'best practice' within its organisation and a compare it to other similar internal activities. Where these other activities fail to meet the benchmark, improvements can be suggested to improve performance. Q2 could only use this method of benchmarking if sufficient 'best practice' departments can be found.

Functional benchmarking: Q2 would compare each of its functions with the best external practitioner of that function regardless of industry. By doing this, deficiencies may become apparent and improvements can be suggested using the practitioner's procedures.

Strategic benchmarking: Q2 would seek to improve its performance by examining the long-term strategies and approaches that have enabled high-performing competitors to succeed. However, this type of benchmarking is unlikely to be of immediate benefit to Q2 as it is difficult to implement and the benefits are likely to take a long time to materialise.

Competitive benchmarking: Q2 would gather information about its industry rivals (for example, private providers and/or a health unit in Chapterland or in a similar country that are performing well). This is likely to be most appropriate for Q2.

(e)   Q2 is a large organisation that employs a large number of people. It is likely to encounter several problems when establishing a **new culture**, most of which are caused by the need to change attitudes from top to bottom.

The main issue that Q2 faces is to change the behaviour of its employees from one of **ineffective working** and **poor practices** to one where **quality** of work is **paramount**. One way this could be achieved is through the use of quality circles. Quality circles would involve small groups of Q2 staff meeting on a regular basis to identify quality related issues and solutions. This should foster commitment to quality throughout Q2, eventually changing the culture. The circles or groups should be comprised of people from different areas and functions of Q2. This provides a fresh perspective and also ensures the 'culture of quality' spreads throughout the organisation.

(f)   In the future, senior management will require performance measures that allow them to monitor the changes that they have implemented.

Expenditure

Performance measures are needed to monitor actual expenditure against budget. Explanations for variances both above and below budget should be provided. Senior management can use this information to prevent future overspends by resolving issues that cause them.

Performance measures are particularly important in the following areas.

(i)   **Waiting times**

Records should be kept of how long patients have had to wait for treatment. Time would start when the patient is first referred to the hospital and would end once treatment is complete.

(ii)   **Cleanliness**

Q2 should test its cleanliness in exactly the same way as the government does, possibly by calculating levels of bacteria, the number of outbreaks of bugs such as MRSA or the frequency of cleaning.

(iii) **Staff per patient case**

This is an efficiency measure and is calculated by dividing the number of medical staff by the number of patients treated. The hospital should seek to reduce the staff employed per case as this means its overall costs per patient will fall.

Outsourcing

If aspects of the organisation are outsourced then targets will be set as part of the service level agreement with the contractor to monitor their performance. Q2 should carefully monitor each target of the SLA with actual performance of the contractor using the same criteria, (for example in IT Q2 may monitor response times to call outs).

SECTION C

Question 3

> **Text references**. The evaluation in Part (a) requires a wide range of knowledge from across the text. Selection and dismissal are covered in Chapter 7.
>
> **Top tips**. Open-ended questions such as Part (a) are best attempted by drawing up a list of reasonable points first. Once you're happy with them you can flesh out your answer.
>
> **Easy marks**. Part (c) offers one mark for each acceptable reason for dismissal, textbook knowledge is enough to score well here.

(a) **Opportunity one: develop e-cruitment and m-cruitment**

The report identified a potential opportunity to expand B3's business by using the internet as a source of employment opportunities and to match them with particular clients who have registered with them. Clients would then be contacted by email or text message and interviews arranged.

The following issues should be considered.

(i) **The matching process**

How will candidate details be matched to appropriate vacancies? This is likely to rely on 'keywords' but the matching criteria must be tested and refined to prevent unsuitable matches being suggested.

(ii) **Speed of service**

Providing the client's requirements and job specifications from the employers are held in a database, the process of matching clients to jobs would be very quick indeed. This speed would increase client satisfaction and could result in more clients being registered due to the good service being spread by word of mouth.

(iii) **Communication cost**

Despite many clients not being able to access personal emails and B3's website at work, they could still access them from home or internet cafes. Email is far cheaper than telephone or post and a large number clients with similar needs can be contacted by a single email. This will help keep B3's costs down.

(iv) **Text content**

Are text messages a suitable format for this type of communication? Can sufficient detail be provided to enable an informed judgement?

(v) **No agreement with employers**

A common reason why employers often post vacancies on their websites is to reduce the cost of recruitment. If this is the case it is likely that many would refuse to interview clients that B3 puts forward as it would mean paying B3 an introduction fee if they are taken on.

(vi) **Database accuracy**

As the database would not be linked to the employers' websites (due to lack of agreement) it is possible that the database could hold out of date information – B3 would only remove jobs from its database when they had been removed from the employer's database and B3 had spotted this. Candidates may fail to inform B3 that they're no longer looking for a new position. Therefore B3 would waste its (and its clients) time applying for interviews for positions that had already been filled.

Opportunity two

This opportunity involves B3 adopting a paperless office through the upgrading of office technology.

The following issues should be considered.

(i) **Data security**

B3 would be storing the personal details of individuals. It is important that steps are taken to protect the security and privacy of data that is held.

(ii) **Data protection**

As the organisation would place very high reliance on the database, system failure and complete data loss could result in its operations ceasing it. This risk can be reduced by B3 regularly backing up its data and storing it in a safe location offsite.

(iii) **Practicalities**

It may not be practical for all tasks to be made paperless, for example client companies may not wish to be invoiced electronically or may not have sufficient systems to process such invoices. Where agreements or contracts are made between employees, employers and B3, paper copies may still be required for signing and to give to the employee for their records.

(iv) **Backup systems**

In the event of a disruption to power supplies or equipment failure, B3 would struggle to continue its operations. Therefore some kind of back up paper based manual system should be available just in case.

(v) **Cost-saving**

The expense of developing new software and investment in systems should create a benefit to B3 that offsets these costs. Paper, printing, filing, storage and general administration are fairly cheap and it may take sometime for B3 to recoup its investment.

(vi) **File conversion**

Care must be taken when converting existing paper and electronic files into the new database. Steps should include:

- Ensuring the source data is complete and accurate.

- Set up control checks in the data entry process for example validating data input into certain fields (eg to prevent entering dates of birth into email address fields).

- Verifying data once input is complete, this may be achieved by checking each entry, or a sample of entries.

(b) **Selection process**

Once a short-list has been created from a number of suitable applicants, the selection of the most suitable can be made using the following.

(i) **Standardise information** in one suitable candidate application form. This allows direct comparison.

(ii) **Interview**

The aim of interviews is to find the best candidate for a position through **direct assessment**.

The potential employer must decide the type of **interview** that is most appropriate. Where the line manager makes the decision of who to select, a one to one interview should suffice.

Where the **input** of more than one person is required, a final or sequential interview can take place.

The interviewer should use a **job description** for the vacancy as well as a person specification. This will enable them to understand what is expected of a suitable candidate.

The interview should be conducted in a **location** that is quiet and comfortable to enable all parties to relax.

Candidates should be given the opportunity to talk and ask **questions** as it is important for them to learn about the organisation as much as the organisation to learn about them.

(iii) **Testing**

Testing candidates is a method of selection that allows the **comparison** of abilities and personality traits that would not be discovered by interviewing alone.

Testing should be set directly in **relation** to the person and job specification. This will ensure the personality and ability traits tested are required by the role.

The type of testing selected should be **relevant** to the position concerned. For example psychometric tests may not be relevant to select between candidates who have applied for a manual job making door knobs, however it would be for a senior management position.

Care must be taken when **interpreting** test results since they do tend to over simplify results – the best score may not indicate the best person for the job. Results should always be considered in relation to other selection methods.

(iv) **Assessment centres**

Particular roles, such as those requiring **leadership**, **problem solving** or **creative abilities** may benefit from the use of assessment centres in the selection process.

The **location** of centres should be easily reached by candidates and assessors. They should provide all the **facilities** that are required by the types of assessment being carried out. Care must be taken to select assessors with the right **skills** to make meaningful judgements.

(v) **Final steps in the process**

Further into the process, reference checks, medical examination and the final decision/selection should be made. The offer should be made in a formal letter.

(vi) All steps in the process should be reliable, valid, fair and cost effective.

(c) Five acceptable reasons for dismissal are:

Conduct

The employee's **behaviour** breaches acceptable limits deemed by the employer. Unacceptable conduct may or may not be laid down in the contract of employment, however most employers have rules concerning **drunkenness**, **immorality** or **misconduct**.

Before conduct becomes an acceptable reason for dismissal, the employee should be given **warnings** and an **opportunity** to change behaviour. However, certain misconduct may be deemed so serious that it warrants summary dismissal.

Capability

The standard of the employee's work is below that what is expected and after appropriate support and guidance it is clear that they are not capable of performing the role.

Before dismissing on the grounds of capability, the employer should give an employee a **reasonable chance** to improve. This can involve consulting with the employee to identify difficulties and providing training to help them.

Breach of statutory duty

It is an acceptable reason for dismissal if by continuing the employment of the employee the employer would breach a statutory duty (for example, a solicitor could not continue to be employed if they are struck off the professional register). The employer would be justified in terminating the employment as soon as the issue comes to light since the employer must not break the law.

Other substantial reasons

Employers are entitled to dismiss an employee where another **substantial reason** affects them adversely. Examples include loss of trust in an employee or even where an employee marries a direct competitor.

Redundancy

Redundancy occurs where the business ceases, is relocating far away (so the employee cannot attend work), or where the role an employee performs is to cease and they cannot be accommodated within the organisation in another role. To be an acceptable reason for dismissal, the employer must select employees for redundancy **fairly**, provide **reasonable notice** and consider offers of **alternative** employment.

Question 4

Text references. Marketing issues and plans are covered in Chapter 10 together with segmentation.

Top tips.

Alternative method

Answers could have also been structured around the following 5 stage approach.

(1)   Situation analysis
(2)   Set corporate objectives
(3)   Devise marketing strategy
(4)   Devise strategic marketing plan (Scope and SMART objectives)
(5)   Monitor and control

Easy marks. You should be able to think of five benefits of segmentation without too much trouble.

(a)   CM has positioned its own brand products as **premium brands**, it is clearly spending considerable sums of money on television advertising, something economy or bargain brands do not do.

The company is **targeting children** as it is they who the television advertising and free gifts are aimed at. It is therefore taking a **concentrated marketing** approach since it is attempting to produce the ideal product for a single segment of the breakfast food market.

The targeting of children is increasingly being seen as unethical. A complete rethink of marketing strategy may be required.

However, for all its efforts, sales have peaked, seemingly caused by **increasing competition** from a North American rival and possibly health concerns over levels of sugar and salt.

CM has adopted a **'pull'** approach to its marketing activities. TV advertising and free gifts are aimed at creating consumer demand for its cereals. However it is clear that this approach is not working. To counter the increased competition CM may need to consider a **'push'** approach. The aim is to persuade retailers to buy more of its goods than its competitors as increased shelf space means greater sales to consumers. This would be achieved by offering bulk discounts or other special offers to retailers just for stocking its products.

The sales problems may worsen if the **bad publicity** surrounding sugar and salt levels continues to grow. CM clearly faces a challenge to ensure its products remain acceptable. It could also be argued that CM has a responsibility to ensure its products are relatively healthy, particularly as they are targeted at children.

The main issue is should CM continue to sell foods high in sugar and salt? There is (currently) nothing **illegal** in what it is doing so why should it change? Children form the majority of CM's customers so by pulling out of the market or stopping the advertising and promotion of such foods to children would cause it to lose most of its business.

The continued sale and promotion of its current products could lead to increased **adverse publicity** and this could (in the long-run) cause it to lose business. Fast food companies such as McDonalds have recently faced such challenges. However it is likely that this would only affect the main CM **branded** range, its generic supermarket 'own brand' product would be unaffected as consumers do not necessarily realise the manufacturer of such products.

Therefore in the near future it is quite possible that CM will have to **research** and **produce** 'healthy' alternatives for its products. However, this will be expensive and could increase the cost of its new products when compared to its competitors.

In conclusion, CM clearly has a strong brand but faces **strong competition** and needs to handle the issue of social responsibility carefully. It may wish to wait to gain agreement between itself, its competitors and the food industry before spending money on developing healthy alternatives.

(b) CM might develop a marketing strategic plan using the steps outlined below.

Step 1 Set its corporate objectives

- CM should decide on a mission statement.
- Using the mission statement, corporate objectives can be set. For example to become the number one selling brand of children's cereal.

Step 2 Carry out a marketing audit analysis

- **PEST** analysis – CM should review the marketing environment for marketing opportunities and trends that may allow it to further meet its customers' needs and perceptions. It should also monitor its competitors' strategies.
- **SWOT** analysis – CM should review its internal position (its strengths and weaknesses) and the general environment (for opportunities and threats).

  By analysing its current internal position and the environment it operates in, CM can start to develop a plan that is relevant and realistic.

Step 3 Set its marketing objectives

- CM should set and prioritise what it wants to achieve based on its business objectives and given its current position.
- Marketing objectives should be SMART – specific, measurable, achievable, real and timed. For example to achieve 10 million unit sales in the UK by the end of the next financial year.

Step 4 Devise an appropriate marketing strategy

CM should identify its broad perspectives and consider the following:

- **Marketing mix** – CM should use the marketing mix to determine the correct strategy for product, place, promotion and price
- **Segmentation** – should CM approach other segments such as adult cereals?
- **Targeting** – should they just target children?
- **Positioning** for the brand, should it remain a premium brand?

BPP
LEARNING MEDIA

Step 5   **Devise the tactics** – plan marketing mix

- **Pricing policy** – will reducing price increase sales?

- **Product policy** and **brand** – should it promote healthy eating or not?

- **Place** or **distribution** – are there any alternative locations to sell the cereal?

- **Promotion** (mix of advertising, sales promotion, public relations) – CM should consider whether it is wise to continue advertising its products on children's TV.

Step 6   **Determine the implementation of the plan**

How should the strategy and tactics be implemented to best effect?

(c)   Five benefits of market segmentation to CM

(1)   **It may identify new marketing opportunities**

Segmentation creates a better understanding of customer needs and this may enable CM to spot new marketing opportunities. For example identifying children's favourite pop groups could result in CM including free gifts associated with them, rather than just TV characters.

(2)   **Allows proportionate allocation of marketing budget**

CM will have a limited marketing budget which it must use wisely to maximise the benefit that it will generate. Segmentation allows the marketing budget to be allocated on the basis of segment size and likely returns from each segment. This will optimise the return on investment CM can achieve from the budget.

(3)   **Promotes effective use of resources**

CM needs to make effective use of all its resources if it is to remain competitive. Even small adjustments to the product or promotion can have great benefits in terms of sales. Greater understanding of the market through segmentation will lead to improved allocation of resources since they can be targeted in a more effective way and better use can be made of them.

(4)   **Domination of segments creates competitive advantage**

Understanding customers within a segment and fulfilling their needs allows companies such as CM to dominate the segment, with very little room for competitors to manoeuvre. Domination allows the business to create economies of scale and other synergistic benefits such as improved competitive ability and ensures the business remains strong.

(5)   **Improved responsiveness to customer needs**

Effective marketing requires being responsive to the consumer. Segmentation increases this responsiveness as the business is far more in touch with its customers. This places companies such as CM in a better position to meet these needs than competitors who do not segment.

Review Form & Free Prize Draw - Paper P4 Organisational Management and Information Systems (1/07)

All original review forms from the entire BPP range, completed with genuine comments, will be entered into one of two draws on 31 July 2007 and 31 January 2008. The names on the first four forms picked out on each occasion will be sent a cheque for £50.

Name: _____   Address: _____
                                              _____
                                              _____

How have you used this Kit?
(Tick one box only)

☐ Home study (book only)
☐ On a course: college _____
☐ With 'correspondence' package
☐ Other _____

Why did you decide to purchase this Kit?
(Tick one box only)

☐ Have used the complementary Study text
☐ Have used other BPP products in the past
☐ Recommendation by friend/colleague
☐ Recommendation by a lecturer at college
☐ Saw advertising
☐ Other _____

During the past six months do you recall seeing/receiving any of the following?
(Tick as many boxes as are relevant)

☐ Our advertisement in *Financial Management*
☐ Our advertisement in *Pass*
☐ Our advertisement in *PQ*
☐ Our brochure with a letter through the post
☐ Our website www.bpp.com

Which (if any) aspects of our advertising do you find useful?
(Tick as many boxes as are relevant)

☐ Prices and publication dates of new editions
☐ Information on product content
☐ Facility to order books off-the-page
☐ None of the above

Which BPP products have you used?

Text	☐	Success CD	☐	Learn Online	☐
Kit	☑	i-Learn	☐	Home Study Package	☐
Passcard	☐	i-Pass	☐	Home Study PLUS	☐

Your ratings, comments and suggestions would be appreciated on the following areas.

	Very useful	Useful	Not useful
Passing CIMA exams	☐	☐	☐
Passing P4	☐	☐	☐
Planning your question practice	☐	☐	☐
Questions	☐	☐	☐
Top Tips etc in answers	☐	☐	☐
Content and structure of answers	☐	☐	☐
'Plan of attack' in mock exams	☐	☐	☐
Mock exam answers	☐	☐	☐

Overall opinion of this Kit	Excellent ☐	Good ☐	Adequate ☐	Poor ☐

Do you intend to continue using BPP products?   Yes ☐   No ☐

The BPP author of this edition can be e-mailed at: stephenosborne@bpp.com

Please return this form to: Nick Weller, CIMA Publishing Manager, BPP Learning Media Ltd, FREEPOST, London, W12 8BR

Review Form & Free Prize Draw (continued)

TELL US WHAT YOU THINK

Please note any further comments and suggestions/errors below.

Free Prize Draw Rules

1   Closing date for 31 July 2007 draw is 30 June 2007. Closing date for 31 January 2008 draw is 31 December 2007.

2   Restricted to entries with UK and Eire addresses only. BPP employees, their families and business associates are excluded.

3   No purchase necessary. Entry forms are available upon request from BPP Learning Media Ltd. No more than one entry per title, per person. Draw restricted to persons aged 16 and over.

4   Winners will be notified by post and receive their cheques not later than 6 weeks after the relevant draw date.

5   The decision of the promoter in all matters is final and binding. No correspondence will be entered into.